BETTER LI
THROUGH ʙAD
MOVIES

BETTER LIVING THROUGH BAD MOVIES

Scott Clevenger and Sheri Zollinger

iUniverse, Inc.

New York Lincoln Shanghai

BETTER LIVING THROUGH BAD MOVIES

iUniverse books may be ordered through booksellers or by contacting:

iUniverse
2021 Pine Lake Road, Suite 100
Lincoln, NE 68512
www.iuniverse.com
1-800-Authors (1-800-288-4677)

ISBN-13: 978-0-595-40023-2 (pbk)
ISBN-13: 978-0-595-84408-1 (ebk)
ISBN-10: 0-595-40023-X (pbk)
ISBN-10: 0-595-84408-1 (ebk)

Printed in the United States of America

Contents

Introduction

President Woodrow Wilson recognized the enormous potential of motion pictures in 1915, when he observed, "It's like writing history with lightning, and my only regret is that it is all so true." Of course, he was talking about *Birth of a Nation*, in which the heroes were Ku Klux Klansmen and the villains were white guys in blackface, so he might more accurately have said, "It's like writing history in the snow with your own pee, and my only regret is that I didn't drink more beer." Still, he makes a good point.

Motion pictures have helped to shape social and moral values since *The Kiss* (1896) first taught women how to successfully maneuver the tongue past a highly waxed handlebar mustache. Movies have taught us how to love with honor (*Casablanca*), how to die with dignity (*Whose Life Is It Anyway?*) and how to sneak our semen into a friend's beer (*American Pie*). And yet, most films emerge so muddled from the design-by-committee development process that no matter what message the filmmakers *think* they're sending, it's almost never the same message we, the audience, actually get, assuming their movie says anything at all besides "Enjoy our cross-promotional merchandising deal with Taco Bell." Because of this tragic miscommunication, legions of filmgoers miss out on the edification to be found in movies like *Coyote Ugly*, *Batman and Robin*, and *Battlefield Earth*.

Anyone who has played Little League baseball is familiar with the dictum, "you learn more from failure than you do from success." Which means that all those hours spent watching crappy movies wasn't a waste of your precious and ever-dwindling life span; it was an education. And since each movie autopsied in this book fails on every conceivable level, it follows that you can learn a lot more from a film like *Star Wars Episode One: The Phantom Menace* than you can from *Citizen Kane*.

Take the Richard Gere/Winona Ryder romance *Autumn in New York*, for instance. On the surface, it appears to be the most cynical piece of emotional manipulation since *The Triumph of the Will* and yet, it contains the secret to forging a love that will last a lifetime (simply put: date the moribund). *Indecent Proposal*, on the other hand, shows how one can ensure a long and happy marriage through prostitution, psychoanalyzing cinder blocks, and sponsoring zoo animals, while troubled lovers will learn how to bridge the gender gap once they realize that—looked at a certain way—*Beaches* and *Armageddon* are exactly the same movie.

But it's not just advice to the lovelorn that Hollywood offers. The films profiled within this volume also offer practical advice for dealing with such day-to-day problems as juvenile delinquents, horny robots, NASCAR, and the devil. Do It Yourself enthusiasts will enjoy the helpful tips on repairing those annoying rips in the space-time continuum, while housewives and heavily armed hermits from Michigan's Upper Peninsula will appreciate the high fashion hints for surviving the apocalypse in style.

So, you have a choice: either spend a lifetime developing character, acquiring skill sets, and mastering complex interpersonal relationships; or shove a movie in the DVD player and sprawl on the La-Z-Boy in your Fruit of the Looms, eating Hot Pockets and Hostess Ding Dongs, and washing them down with 40 oz cans of malt liquor. Using this method, you can achieve enlightenment in about 90 minutes, and complete oblivion in less than two hours. We know which one President Wilson would choose.

Marital Success and Thinner Thighs the Hollywood Way

Today, marriage is enjoying a resurgence of popularity, and yet the institution itself is in serious peril. Weddings on a per capita basis are up, but more than half of all marriages end—either bitterly, in divorce, or embarrassingly, in a "Jerry Springer" booking.

The modern husband and wife face a plethora of perplexing problems. Can I have both a family and a career? Are Razzles candy or gum? And where can one find the secret to an enduring union of souls? Many turn to experts like John Gray, who posits that the opposite sex comes from a different planet than you, and so can't be expected to know the customs of *your* world. Good advice, especially when you consider that, whenever discord arises, your first impulse is to talk, while your husband's initial urge is to bombard you with a deadly proton beam from high geo-synchronous orbit.

But for many people, that guidance just isn't enough, especially people with brain cells. So, we are going to share a formula for wedded bliss that you can't get from any book (except this one). We are ready to reveal the rock-solid precepts that have made the marriages of people such as Julia Roberts, Elizabeth Taylor, and Mickey Rooney so enduring—the powerful marriage secrets contained in Hollywood movies!

Let's go to that mystical font of connubial wisdom known as the video store, and take a look at a trio of movies made by two of Tinsel Town's happiest couples: Demi Moore & Bruce Willis, and Nicole Kidman & Tom Cruise. We're sure that by applying the precepts taught in these films, your marriage can be as happy as theirs.

Indecent Proposal (1993)
Directed by Adrian Lyne
Written by Amy Holden Jones; based on the novel by Jack Engelhard

He pimped his wife to a millionaire. She told her husband the sex was pretty darned good. Can this marriage be saved?

We meet husband Woody Harrelson at the pier, where he is gazing at the water and thinking moody, over-dubbed thoughts about his lost love, Demi Moore. Demi, who is riding a bus in her prom gown, intones, "If you ever want something badly, let it go. If it comes back to you, then it's yours forever. If it doesn't, then it was never yours to begin with." So, we know we are in for a deeply philosophical movie about the nature of love, loss, and Hallmark Cards.

We then flashback to Woody and Demi's life together. She was a realtor. He was an architect. After Woody came up with the unified field theory of architecture, he began building his Santa Monica Dream House (not to be confused with Barbie's Malibu Beach Dream House, since Barbie's had a better designer and higher quality materials). But then the recession hit, the couple got a month behind on the mortgage payments, and they stood to lose everything. (Don't you hate it when bad things happen to vapid people?)

Woody and Demi thought about getting *jobs* in an effort to dig themselves out, but then decided the more sensible course would be to borrow money and head for Vegas. Because when you're attractive and in love, the laws of probability are suspended in your favor.

Once they're installed in a high-class casino, Woody heads for the gambling tables. Demi does her part by sneaking into a boutique and stealing their chocolates. This impresses billionaire Robert Redford, who offers to buy her the tarty Cher gown she was mooning over. She indignantly retorts, "The dress is for sale. I'm not!" Attention everybody: incoming plot point!

Alas, while Demi was setting up the movie's premise, Woody lost all their money. The couple's expressive faces indicate that they are sad. Robert notes their distress and offers Woody a million dollars for a night with his wife. Apparently, Vegas is experiencing a big hooker shortage, and so it's a sellers' market. At first Woody and Demi are outraged—what kind of a girl does Robert think Demi is! But after talking it over, the couple decides to accept Robert's offer: because they could really use the money, and because Demi actually *is* kind of slutty.

The deed done and the couple one million dollars richer, they drive back to L.A. to redeem the Dream House. But then the bottom falls out of their world! It turns out that on the *very day* they were in Vegas, earning money through pimping and prostitution, the bank foreclosed and somebody else bought their property! What kind of God would allow something like this to happen?

And even more tragically tragic for the couple, their relationship starts to deteriorate. Woody becomes jealous and suspicious, and finally demands to know, once and for all, if Robert was good in bed. Demi admits that he was, but avers that she did it all—the moaning, the screaming, the multiple orgasms—for Woody. Woody visibly experiences some sort of emotion, and runs away from home. Demi weeps, because men are just so unappreciative, and because an off-camera stagehand is helpfully waving ammonia crystals under her nose.

However, Demi isn't alone for long, for it seems that Robert's dream woman is a demure, old-fashioned girl who will sell herself for large sums of money. So, he begins courting Demi. He is boyishly charming. She is cold and hostile. It's perfect! She finally agrees to a relationship, apparently giving him the Frequent Buyers' sex rate.

Things don't go as well for Woody. He and the dog live in a tool shed that Woody has plastered, in true psychopathic stalker fashion, with photos of Demi. Eventually he gets a job teaching bitter architecture, and imparts bits o' wisdom such as, "Even a common brick wants to be something better than it is." The students are spellbound by these insights into the secret life of bricks, but Demi still wants a divorce. She informs him that he can keep the million dollars as a lovely parting gift.

It's hard out there for a pimp.

Robert takes Demi to a zoo benefit where the crowd is wowed by a feckless stranger who bids $1,000,000 to sponsor a hippo. Yes, that idiot is Woody, who threw away the million just to impress Demi with how rock stupid he really is. They look at each other longingly, then Woody signs the divorce papers and walks away, probably to spend his million-dollar night with the hippo.

On the ride home, Robert tells Demi that she was the best of the "Million Dollar Club." It seems that he has done this kind of thing a couple dozen times before. This announcement causes Demi to jump out of the car and into a bus that happens along. We realize that Robert mentioned the Club in order to end the affair, because "She never would have looked at me like she looked at Woody." We're impressed by his generosity of spirit, letting her go back to the man she loves. But we're more impressed by the fact that Robert has spent 24 *million dollars* on sex! Jeez, this guy really needs to comparison shop!

The bus Demi boarded just happens to be going to the pier where the movie started; Woody is there being gloomy. Maybe being attractive and in love *is* enough to cause the universe to suspend the laws of probability! Anyway, she confides that she still loves him, and always will. He loves her too. Tremulous smiles. Fade out. The end.

So, what did this movie teach us about making marriage work? First, that open communication is of vital importance. The flame of marriage begins to flicker when not fed by the fuel of conversation, and then the wieners of romance can no longer be roasted at love's fire pit, if you know what we mean. So, let your partner know that he or she is appreciated and loved. Hop on a bus in your prom dress and tell your mate that you still love him. Discuss your work with her—let her know what the bricks told you today about their hopes and fears. And if sex with another man was really good, let your husband know *just* how good, with visual aids like a PowerPoint presentation comparing penis sizes.

Secondly, we learned that working as a team makes a marriage strong. For example, if you lose all your money (through no fault of your own except stupidity), find a project you can do *together* to recoup your fortunes. If you decide to emulate our movie role models and work as a joint pimp/ho team, incorporate togetherness in all aspects of the operation. Let her help you shop for your full-length fur coat, gold chains, and foppish headgear. Have him help you pick your street name, even if he does vote for something classless like "Peaches LaTarte" or "Christina Aguillera." And if you don't feel qualified for work in today's modern prostitution and gambling industry, try drug trafficking, extortion, or contract killing. Remember, experts say that couples who slay together, stay together.

And lastly, we saw how even a couple who truly love each other can drift apart. Perhaps she is too busy to hang out with him, due her demanding career as a courtesan; and he just isn't around much because he's living in a tool shed with the dog. To combat this emotional estrangement, look for little ways to put the romance back in your relationship. Perhaps you could try something new and adventuresome, like quitting your 9-to-5 jobs and developing a trapeze act for Barnum & Bailey—and then you could let her go from the high wire, to see if she is yours forever.

Our next movie provides us with startling information about marriage; i.e., that it's *tough*. In the early days, Hollywood went out of its way to emphasize that while marriage meant sacrifice—working things out, deferring one's dreams, sleeping in twin beds—the secret to a successful marriage was love. Modern Hollywood believes this is still true, but nowadays the actual work is done by personal assistants, the deferred dreams are excuses ("I passed on starring in

Gladiator and instead made *Police Academy XXI* in order to spend more time with my family"), and the sleeping in twin beds is only the case if you are married to Tom Cruise. But the main difference is that current movies teach us that the secret to marital success is access to an AVID Media Composer 1000.

Let's take a look at the ex-Mr. Demi Moore's movie about the agony and ennui of long-term relationships, and see what it can teach us about the age-old connection between love, marriage, and postproduction.

The Story of Us (1999)
Directed by Rob Reiner
Written by Alan Zweibel & Jessie Nelson

He wore a rug on his head; she wore a pith helmet. Can this marriage be saved?

Our story begins with Michelle Pfeiffer telling us that everything she ever needed to know about marriage, she learned from "Harold and the Purple Crayon". See, Bruce is Harold, she is the person who has to wash the walls, and the crayon seems to be a penis metaphor or something.

Then Bruce flashes back to how he and Michelle first met—he threw paper clips at her, and she countered by donning a pith helmet with a flashing light on top. We now comprehend the root of their marriage problems: he's abusive and she's clinically insane.

Now it's time for a montage of highlights from their fifteen years of fighting, which serves to illustrate Tolstoy's saying about all happy families resembling each other, but each movie montage being boring in its own way.

In one key sequence, we see how their differing temperaments lead to a lack of communication. Michelle is trying to cope with a flooding washing machine, two kids who are demanding that she mediate their spat, and her husband's telephone call asking her to get nostalgic with him because the apartment where they first lived—where they "became an *us*"—is being demolished. Michelle hangs up on him. This scene shows us that Bruce is spontaneous, romantic, and an idiot, while Michelle is practical, diligent, and a shrewish moron. (Note: Those of you who look to the movies to learn how to deal with real life should *not* follow Michelle's example. No, this is how you really cope with this situation. First, unplug the washer. Second, order the kids to shut their traps and start mopping. Finally, tell Bruce that you are sorry they are tearing down the apartment, because it was there that you first had an orgasm—with his best friend, Paul Reiser.)

Bruce and Michelle decide to separate while their children are conveniently at Camp Idawannacustody. With the kids away, Bruce can hang out in restaurants with Reiser and Rob Reiner (who must have slept with the director to get the part). Michelle too has her assigned friends, and the loud, ribald banter of both groups teaches us important things about love, marriage, commitment, and the excruciating horror of having loud, ribald friends who think they are funny.

Eventually Bruce drops by the house to pick up his dry cleaning. There are long, lingering shots of Bruce and Michelle's faces. Apparently, we are supposed to think that Michelle is too beautiful to be alone, and that Bruce's toupee is really his own hair. The couple ends up in the bedroom, and they engage in fore-play consisting of flashbacks about their various marriage counselors, including one who said that every time they go to bed there are actually six people there: Bruce, Michelle, his parents, and her parents. And then, in a wacky, Woody Allen moment, both sets of parents *are* in the bed with them! This kind of kills the moment for Michelle. (And understandably so—who could maintain proper lubrication while Red Buttons and Jayne Meadows were watching?) But Bruce is still in the mood, and is annoyed when Michelle won't put out. "What happened to that fun girl in the pith helmet?" he asks. Michelle replies, "That was Groucho Marx—did you sleep with him too, you pervert?" No, she actually says, "You beat her out of me!" which is even funnier.

Bruce finally comes to the realization that love is just an illusion and that life is rough for white, male, rich people. He seeks counsel from Rob Reiner, who tells him that, "We do not possess butts, but merely fleshy parts at the top of our legs."

His head brimming with ass-related wisdom, Bruce goes on a vision quest, and has a montage of Michelle crying, fretting, complaining, and shrieking at him. This is a breakthrough for Bruce, who now understands just how great it was to be married to her. He goes home and tells Michelle "Tonight I saw myself through your eyes!" Having learned what a putz she thinks he is, he wants to get back together. The movie could end right there, but it turns out that Michelle has a date with Tim Matheson. Bruce demands a divorce, because he won't share his wife with the voice of Jonny Quest.

Bruce and Michelle go to pick up their spawn from camp, having agreed to tell the kids that while they are divorcing, they still love each other—"But in a different way." You know, the way where daddy calls mommy a whore, and mommy tells daddy that he isn't the kids' real father. However, Michelle is suddenly hit by the movie's trailer, a mega-flashback of ironically juxtaposed moments from their entire marriage, set to the music of "Classical Gas." She is no match for this overwhelming schmaltz, and it causes her to erupt in a five-minute monologue of incoherent nonsense, all done in a squeakily cute voice and without pause for breath, much like Sylvester Stallone's climactic speech in *First Blood*. The speech conveys key information, like the location of the Bactine, exactly what *did* happen to the fun girl in the pith helmet, and how they can't get divorced because they're an *us*! This is enough to mend the rift, so they each say "I love you" and everything is fine! Another marriage saved!

So, how can this movie help you revitalize *your* marriage to a nagging shrew or a whiny baby? Well, to begin with, if you're meandering along on connubial cruise control and you happen to hit a patch of black ice, don't talk about it with your friends. They'll just respond by being embarrassingly loud and ribald in public, or even worse, will recite Zen koans in an effort to prove that your ass doesn't exist.

Secondly, while "Harold and the Purple Crayon" offered Michelle profound truths about her crummy marriage, we think that Bruce's early exposure to "Curious George" caused his pith helmet fetish, and so led to his misalliance with Michelle. So, search your own childhood reading material and try to determine if you were betrayed by Dick and Jane into forming unrealistic beliefs about gender roles, family duties, and the amount of running done by dogs.

And finally, men, whenever your gross insensitivity brings your marriage to the brink of separation, don't try to make up by bringing her flowers or jewelry. Have a montage! According to our focus groups, women can't resist them.

Now that we've learned valuable lessons from Bruce and Demi about spicing up your marriage with hippos and pith helmets, let's turn to Nicole Kidman and Tom Cruise for a little lesson about orgies, and how they're fun…until somebody dies! And besides, they're never conveniently located, and the other guys all look like Sydney Pollack, and eventually you decide you'd rather just stay home with the wife and watch "The Flying Nun."

Eyes Wide Shut (1999)
Directed by Stanley Kubrick
Written by Stanley Kubrick and Frederic Raphael; inspired by the novella by Arthur Schnitzler

She was completely nude; he was dressed like a pirate. Can this marriage be saved?

Even before the title, Nicole Kidman has slipped out of her clothes. This is so people who just rented the movie to see her naked don't have to waste their time watching the next 158 minutes (but it only seems like 18 months). But for those of you intrepid enough to venture onward, Kubrick will reward you with a meticulously detailed film exploring important themes. Oh, and an orgy.

Nicole Kidman and Tom Cruise are a happily married Manhattan couple who live in a fabulous apartment with a Christmas tree and a daughter. But this is all put to the test when they attend director Sydney Pollack's lavish party at Versailles, and it turns into "Euro Temptation Island." Nicole gets hit on by a lascivious Yugo salesmen, while a Bulgarian supermodel propositions Dr. Tom—he removes a cinder from her eye, and she claims it's like pulling a thorn from a lion's paw, in that the lion must later sleep with you.

But before anything happens, Tom is called to assist Sydney with a medical emergency: a nude woman with large, economy-sized implants has passed out on his bathroom floor. Tom cures her by showing her his dimples, and Sydney Pollack promises him the lead in *The Firm* if he will keep his mouth shut about the whole thing.

Tom and Nicole go home and discuss the party. Nicole gets mad because Tom says the oily guy only wanted to have sex with her, but insists he wasn't jealous because he knows that she would never cheat on *him*. Tom, Tom, Tom—obviously Scientology doesn't increase intelligence as claimed. ("Why am I a clueless lunkhead? Page 213.")

Nicole sweetly retaliates by recounting how last summer she fantasized about a handsome naval officer she'd met. "If he wanted me, even if only for one night, I was ready to give up everything," she murmurs. Oh, and his name was "Iceman" Kazanski! Take *that*, Top Gun!

This confession does not sit well with Tom, who wanders around town having lurid daydreams of Nicole in bed with Iceman, and himself in bed with Viper Metcalf. Tom eventually finds himself in the club where old pal Nick Nightingale plays piano. But Nick can't stay and chat, since he's got a gig at the Trilateral Commission's office Christmas party. Tom wants to go too, but Nick says that everyone will be costumed and masked, and where is Tom going to get a costume at this time of night?

Tom runs to a costume shop, wakes the owner, and informs him that he's a doctor who has a medical emergency requiring a Captain Hook outfit. Now properly attired, Tom enters the party to find that a crowd of scary figures in robes and masks are chanting in Latin. It's the Vatican's production of *The Omega Man*! Then a circle of worshippers drop their gowns to reveal they are beautiful women attired in nothing more than g-strings, high heels, and perky chapeaux. Ah, so it's actually Vegas night at the First Satanist Church.

A nude woman in a feathered headdress (and enough silicone in her chest to meet Intel's production needs for the next fiscal year) warns Tom that he is grave danger. And it *is* true that orgy participants are at high risk for strokes, heart attacks, and jock itch.

But before Tom can learn to orgy sensibly, he is revealed as a trespasser and forced to remove his mask.

"Now get undressed," the head guy demands.

"Undressed?" Tom responds. (He apparently didn't have time to learn his lines, and so throughout the movie repeats everybody else's.)

The woman in the headdress interrupts to say that she will take Tom's place, since she's already undressed and stuff. Tom is free to go—but if he ever tells anybody what he saw, he will suffer the *direst* consequences. Presumably, the same penalties that one incurs for early withdrawal from a money market account. Meanwhile, somebody keeps playing one piano note over and over, very loudly; it's either meant to create tension, or to drum up Excedrin sales.

Tom can't leave the mystery alone and becomes the Joe Friday of the AMA, flashing his doctor's ID and questioning people right and left. Eventually, he reads a newspaper account about a dead ex-beauty queen, and rushes to the hospital morgue, reasoning that since it's the only newspaper story he's ever read, it *has* to be significant. We see that the nude body on the slab has breast implants so large that they had to cut holes in the top of her storage drawer. Yes, it's the woman from Sydney Pollack's party *and* the woman from the orgy, the one who said it could cost her her life! And it did! Tom now regrets his unyielding stand on nudity, and wishes he had at least offered to strip to his briefs and lip-synch "That Old-Time Rock and Roll" for the group.

Sydney calls, and Tom finally realizes he may be more than just the sinister director of *Tootsie*. But Syd tells Tom that he has it all wrong—the secret conspiracy is actually a service organization that runs bake sales and walkathons. Everything that happened at the party—the threats, the warning, the woman's intervention—was all fake.

"Fake?" replies Tom.

"Yes, fake," repeats Sydney impatiently; as a director, he has no sympathy for actors who don't learn their lines. He explains that it was all just to scare Tom. Basically, the whole movie's a "Scooby-Do" episode. And they got away with it too, despite the meddling kid.

Tom goes home to find his Captain Hook mask on his pillow. This causes Tom to break down and sob to Nicole, "I'll tell you everything." Immediately, police departments all over the country start putting Captain Hook masks on the pillows of suspects.

And what did this final movie teach us about marriage maintenance?

The first lesson is obvious to even the most dimwitted of guys: do *not* tell your wife that she would never cheat on you with a sleazy old gigolo she met at Sydney Pollack's house. Because then she will be forced to do it, since it's in the script, which you would have known if you'd bothered to learn your lines.

Next, we learn that while sexual fantasies are fine, and are good for enlivening your regular Saturday night thing (whatever *that* may be), there are some dreams you should never share with your partner because they might hurt him or make him run around town in a pirate costume. In our movie, Nicole told Tom that she had fantasized joining the mile-high club with Iceman. This really got to Tom, and caused him to do stupid things, like reading a newspaper and barging into a rich folks' version of a sci-fi con.

A final lesson we can take from this movie is that if you suspect that your husband may be cheating on you, put the mask from his Captain Hook costume on a pillow, and he will break down and confess all. And then, once you know all about him and Tinkerbell, you can either forgive him and move on, or feed another part of him to the crocodile.

It's the End of the World As We Know It, And I Feel Fine, But You're All Dead

Is Hollywood, as its critics charge, nothing more than a soulless assembly line churning out vacuous, amoral escapism to a cynical and increasingly desensitized public? Well, yes. But there's another facet to Hollywood's output: the clarion call which alerts an unwary populace to perils within its midst. In recent decades, studio films have awakened Americans to the importance of disaster preparedness with *Earthquake*, the dangers of nuclear power with *The China Syndrome*, and the effects of hexavalent chromium and push-up bras with *Erin Brockavich*. Yet there's one potential disaster that Hollywood has warned of in film after film, without apparent success. Take a look around your own home, and you'll see what we mean. Are *you* prepared for the Apocalypse?

For all its pervasiveness, our civilization is really quite fragile. Think of the various technologies we depend upon daily: our computers, our cars, our spleen trusses. Stripped of the instrumentality we take for granted, our existence would be tenuous indeed. Most of us lack the skills necessary to find food and shelter, to build a fire, or to survive persistent harassment from a spear-wielding tribe of radioactive mutants. Hollywood frequently reminds us how easily civilization could be snuffed out—by a plague, an asteroid, a nuclear war, or, in the case of *The Postman*, by the final-cut clause in Kevin Costner's contract.

Older readers may remember a time when we actually prepared for Armageddon. Back then, elementary schools would pause for Duck and Cover drills, while our cartoons were frequently interrupted by tests of the Emergency Broadcast System, and yet, it wasn't the actual atomic blast that scared us—it was the aftermath. For Hollywood has sought to highlight the need for disaster preparedness by imagining a post-apocalyptic world in which John Travoltas and Sylvester Stallones were free to roam the irradiated wastes, overacting at will. With the collapse of civilization, such creatures would be released at last from the punishing constraints of movie reviews and focus groups. Film critics, after all, are a blinking, mole-like species, as pale and doughy as Poppin Fresh, and not the most likely bunch to rise from the ashes of destruction and tame a savage new world. To put it another way, if the world ends tomorrow, we don't expect to see Roger Ebert riding across the burning dunes, clad in nothing but a leather bandoleer and a rabbit-fur G-string. Just savor that image for a moment, and see if you don't agree that the survivors would envy the dead.

Now's let's examine the following examples of *fin de monde* cinema, to learn what *you* can do in the event of an apocalypse.

Judge Dredd (1995)
Directed by Danny Cannon
Written by Michael De Luca (story) William Wisher, Jr., Steven E. De Souza

Our movie starts with the usual sci-fi film crawl, explaining the usual premise, narrated by the usual James Earl Jones. Climate's gone bad. Nation's in chaos. People crowded into a mega-city (called Mega City), ruled by all-powerful Judges who are a combination of Police, Jury, and Executioner. Basically, we're about to be hand-dipped in Antonin Scalia's most lubricious wet dream, so you might want to do what people at a Gallagher concert do, and huddle under a big plastic poncho.

Mega City is a dark, rainy, densely packed metropolis full of gun-toting psychopaths and a huge, riot-prone underclass. The filmmakers have taken great pains to vividly depict a bleak and joyless dystopia, so I think we can all agree that adding Rob Schneider to the scene is just redundant. Nevertheless, up he pops, playing the sort of part that Peter Lorre would have rejected as "too weasely."

Into the midst of this violent unrest strides Sylvester Stallone as Judge Dredd. He cuts an imposing figure with his aluminum shin-guards, but he seems to be under the false impression that he's acting in a Pinter play, since he peppers his dialogue with huge, arbitrary pauses. "I am…the Law. *Drop*…your *weapons*! The [unintelligible]…are under…*arrest*! This is…your final…warning!"

I don't know. It worked for Alan Bates and Donald Pleasance in *The Caretaker*, but it seems less effective coming from a guy in a Teflon codpiece.

As part of his magisterial regalia, Judge Dredd has an extraordinarily high-tech, multi-function handgun (rapid fire, armor-piercing, grenade-launching, etc.) that is voice activated. And perhaps the only part of the filmmaker's carefully designed, fully imagined future world that I don't believe is that the gun understands a frigging word Stallone is saying.

Anyway, he uses it to kill a bunch of people, and then he finds Rob cowering inside a noodle vending machine, and sentences him to five years for destruction of public property and attempted comic relief.

Later, at the Council of Judges meeting, we learn that Mega City is descending into anarchy. Jurgen Prochnow, as Judge George W. Bush XXVII, wants to deal with violence by expanding executions to lesser crimes, like failing a smog check, or tearing the tag off your mattress. But he's thwarted by Chief Justice Max von Sydow, who believes in a kinder, gentler form of fascism.

Meanwhile, in the Aspen Penal Colony, Armand Assante is in solitary confinement. The warden enters the cell to deliver a package and some exposition: Armand was once a Judge, before he started killing even more indiscriminately than Stallone. But he's not only more ruthless, he's actually *harder to understand than Stallone is*, sounding like a combination of Mushmouth from "Fat Albert" and Jodie Foster from *Nell*. Anyway, Jurgen sends Armand a gun hidden in a Rubik's Cube, and he escapes.

Meanwhile, pert, idealistic young summary executioner Diane Lane tries to befriend Judge Dredd, who seems terribly alone. Turns out that Dredd *did* have a friend once, but he had to execute him when he violated alternate side of the street parking regulations.

Armand kills a reporter, and frames Judge Dredd for the crime. It seems he and Stallone are actually brothers, and are both the product of a secret eugenics program called Janus. Twenty years ago, the Council attempted to genetically engineer a breed of super-Judges, but—in a shocking twist for a sci-fi film—it went horribly wrong, and the results were Armand, Stallone, and Judge Judy.

Stallone is convicted of the reporter's murder, and sentenced to life in the Aspen Penal Colony. His mentor, Max von Sydow, is devastated by the verdict. Combined with the presence of Jurgen, Max suffers a mental breakdown, and apparently thinks he's back on the set of *Dune*, since he dons his old Fremen stillsuit and wanders out into the wasteland with a big flashlight to look for night crawlers and giant sandworms.

Meanwhile, Stallone's cruel and unusual punishment begins on the prison shuttle, when he's seated next to Rob Schneider. The pain is cut relatively short when they fly over Texas, and the descendants of the Leatherface family shoot down the shuttle with a surface-to-air missile.

They hang Stallone and Schneider like a couple of honey cured hams, and invite Max over for a Texas-style cannibal barbecue. But Max had a snack earlier, and really just stopped by to drop off some more exposition and get killed. Seems that Jurgen framed Dredd so he could revive the Janus project and make an army of Stallones and rule the Earth! (Or at least Planet Hollywood.) Stallone snaps into action, and immediately infiltrates Mega City to foil Jurgen's plan. Instead, Jurgen kills all the other members of the Council, and promptly frames Dredd for *that*.

Meanwhile, Armand uses the Janus system to reproduce himself, creating an army of psychopathic judges, and exponentially increasing the number of hammy performances he can give in any fiscal year. Dredd and Diane rush to the Janus lab to stop his mad scheme, and promptly fail. This allows Stallone and Armand to stand face-to-face, twist their mouths up, and bellow incomprehensibly at each other in some sort of chest-pounding contest of simian diction. It's like if Jane Goodall directed *The Parent Trap*.

Eventually, Stallone's greater experience as a mush-mouthed homunculus pays off, and he wins. In desperation, Armand pulls the gestating clones from their cryo-chambers to tear Stallone limb from limb. But he hatches them prematurely, and the clones are underdone, and in some cases, still frozen in the middle. So Stallone throws Armand off the Statue of Liberty.

In the end, Jurgen's brutal fascism is discredited, and Stallone's bleeding heart fascism is triumphant.

We leave you now with a heroic shot of Dredd silhouetted against a golden sunset and the monumental, Albert Speer-like architecture of Mega City, as director Leni Reifenstahl is brought in to wrap up the movie.

In many post-apocalyptic films, the key to survival lies in cultivating a positive relationship with the rump authorities, who often wield powers unchecked by civil liberties. There is perhaps no better illustration of this than in *Judge Dredd*, where Stallone's character combines the normally discrete powers of law enforcement and the judiciary, leading the viewer to conclude that the dominant social caste has evolved from the Sheriff in *Macon County Line*. Therefore, to help you prepare for this particular future, we have compiled a few quick tips: Stock up on plugs of Red Man chewing tobacco, pork rinds, and Yvette Mimeaux videos. Also, you might want to buy a gun and practice talking to it with your mouth full of ball bearings, or Malt-O-Meal. Finally, declare your allegiance to the duly established local authorities by displaying an appropriate bumper sticker. We suggest "Support Your Local Police, or They'll Kill You."

We believe that following these few simple steps will help to prepare you for the impending fascist Zeitgeist (or at least the version depicted in this film, which might best be termed Fascism Lite—only one-third the extrajudicial killings of our regular fascism, but with all the leather fetishism you've come to expect).

Of course, no one knows just what form Armegeddon will take, and it's entirely possible that the grim remains of post-apocalyptic Earth will not in fact be administered by inarticulate mesomorphs clad in jodhpurs and pleather jerkins. Instead, we may face a future in which law enforcement is the purview of nomadic vigilantes decked out in rags and skins. This, by the way, is invariably a tip off that they're evil. According to Hollywood, if the authorities in a post-apocalyptic world are poorly dressed, your best bet is to violently revolt, in order to sweep away tyranny, and bring about a rebirth of decent civil service fashions.

In our next film, Kevin Costner proves that no matter how great the odds, there is no resisting a man in uniform; even if it's the famously dowdy duds sported by the U.S. Postal Service.

The Postman (1997)
Directed by Kevin Costner
Written by Eric Roth, based on the novel by David Brin.

Tagline: "The year is 2013. One man walked in off the horizon and hope came with him."

Yes, the movie takes place in 2013, and if you start watching it now you just might be done by then. It may not be the *best* movie ever made about a nameless drifter who restores hope to a post-apocalyptic world by pretending to be a mailman, but it's certainly the longest.

We soon learn that there was a big catastrophe about 15 years previously (which would have been right about when this movie came out—not that we're *implying* anything). This disaster brought plagues and pretentiousness in its wake, and led to the collapse of the United States Postal Service.

In this desperate and desolate future, our mythic hero, Kevin Costner, and his mule Bill go from town to town, performing one-man-and-a-mule versions of Macbeth in order to get free soup. The three branches of the federal government are gone, but somehow the NEA is still managing to fund highly offensive art.

Following one such performance, the town is invaded by the Hardasses, a White Supremacist militia led by General Bethlehem (Will Patton), a former Xerox® salesman who went over to the dark side (Cannon). The Hardasses, a group apparently based on the Amway plan, terrorize the Pacific Northwest with their post-apocalyptic protection racket. The wimpy people of the future don't dare fight back, for they lack regular mail delivery.

Kevin and Bill are forcibly enlisted and taken to Hardass Headquarters, where Kevin is made to play "musical chairs" and exchange shower gifts with the other recruits, and Bill is pureed and served for lunch. As part of freshman orientation, Bethlehem explains "The Law of Eight," which has something to do with Dick Van Patten, then he forces Kevin to recite some Shakespeare for the group, which immediately inspires them to send him on a suicide mission. Kevin escapes, and eventually takes shelter in an old mail van. Mindful of how badly he was upstaged by the mule, Kevin spends the next five minutes acting with a human skeleton, and barely manages to steal the scene. He also steals the skeleton's uniform, hat, and sack of mail, and heads out to live the dream of every boy since time immemorial—impersonating a postal carrier.

Kevin approaches the nearby town of Pineview, and tells the citizens that the U.S. Government has been restored, and as its first act, Congress has reestablished the postal service. The people are rightfully suspicious, since everyone knows that Congress's *first* priority would be giving themselves pay raises. But Kevin demands entrance, citing U.S. Legal Code requiring that everybody give mailmen sanctuary, food, and women.

That night at the You've Got Mail dance, Kevin meets Abby, a comely young woman who asks about his height, IQ, and semen. It turns out she wants a baby, but her husband had "the bad mumps" and so they want Kevin to be the child's "body father." Of course, the one-time bedding is successful and she becomes pregnant—proving that while FedEx may have a better on-time record for package delivery, the U.S. postal service is still your best bet for delivering sperm. (A better title for this movie might have been "The Postman Cometh.")

Kevin visits the town's abandoned post office, where he meets Ford Lincoln Mercury, a teen with one burning desire: to be a mailman! Kevin reveals that only another postman can make you a postman (just like vampirism), and he reluctantly swears Ford into the club. Kevin knows the whole postal service thing is a scam, much like a chain letter, but Ford is intrigued by the new overnight semen delivery service, and his guileless idealism inspires Kevin to press on with his route. As Kevin heads out of town with his sack of Visa bills and Valu-Paks, there are numerous shots of the hopeful faces of the crowd. A little blonde girl (played, in an utterly bizarre coincidence, by Kevin Costner's real-life daughter) sings "America the Beautiful." The whole ceremony makes you proud to get junk mail.

However, shortly after Kevin's departure, General Bethlehem shows up, and spies Abby. "First class piece of ass," he declares, which is crude, but much nicer than calling her a "bulk mail piece of ass." He claims Abby as his concubine, invoking *droit de seigneur*, then hand-delivers the point of his sword to her husband's liver. The little Costner girl is present at the murder; the camera cuts to her face, and we can plainly see she is horrified by the brevity of her close-up.

Meanwhile, Kevin is distributing mail in some town somewhere else. Everyone applauds. Crowds are much easier to please after the apocalypse. One woman wants to know if New York City survived the plague. Kevin tells her Broadway is up and running, and Andrew Lloyd Webber is playing! So, no, the plague is still with them.

About then, Bethlehem and his troops arrive. The town refuses to pay tribute, now that they have mail. But Kevin realizes that while mail is nice and all, the Hardasses have guns, so he sweeps Abby away on his horse, and they gallop off into a blizzard, even though it was July five minutes ago.

They set up housekeeping in a deserted barn and wait for the pass to clear. Like many couples, Abby feels that Kevin doesn't do his share around the place. She's pregnant with his body child, but still has to chop the wood. She has to gather the snow. She has to shoot the horse *and* make it into soup. Kevin responds that he *would* help out more, but he got shot in the stomach during that last battle, and the horse isn't agreeing with him. Now, at last, the disparate threads of this movie are finally pulling together: We've got an axe-wielding woman in the throes of pre-partum depression sharing a snow-bound, isolated cabin with a gut-shot whiner, and we're all set for a highly satisfying homage to Stephen King's "Misery." Unfortunately, Abby just burns the barn down, and then it's spring.

On their way back to Pineview, Kevin discovers that Ford has declared himself Postmaster General, and recruited all the teens to deliver mail in a post-apocalyptic pony express. Kevin is touched by their plucky endeavor, and joins in, taking all the really dangerous routes, for he is…The Postman.

In the scene that encapsulates the whole movie, another of Costner's small, blond spawn writes a letter, but doesn't get it out to the mailbox before The Postman canters past. The kid is crestfallen. This is clearly a turning point in his young life, for he has learned that sometimes, even though you try your hardest, your letter just doesn't make the 5:00 pickup. However, the Postman senses a disturbance in the Force, and turns around to gaze at the lad. For a really long time. The kid holds up the letter. For a really long time. You're thinking Kevin might just decide to trot back the ten yards and get the letter, but instead he thinks awful long and awful hard. Finally, he turns his horse around and gallops towards the boy. He snatches the letter from the boy's hand, then thunders off, a hero who was not too big to ride a horse full speed past a six-year-old kid for no reason whatsoever.

Meanwhile, General Bethlehem hates the Postal Service, because they represent the spirit of resistance to his tyrannical rule, and because they're always late with his monthly copy of *Sassy*. So, Bethlehem starts killing the people of Pineview, and Kevin and Abby flee to a town ruled by Tom Petty. Kevin is ready to give up, but Abby pleads with him to re-don the Postman outfit, for he is Oregon's last, best hope for getting their Publishers Clearinghouse Sweepstakes notifications. She tells him passionately that he "gives out hope like it was candy in your pocket," meaning that it's hope softened by body heat and flecked with lint. So Kevin challenges Bethlehem for leadership of the Hardasses, under "The Law of Eight," which allows for the replacement of Diana Hyland's character with Betty Buckley. Kevin wins, of course, for he is…The Postman. He then institutes a new law: Peace. Everyone nods in appreciation. What a good idea—why didn't anybody think of this sooner? We probably could have avoided that whole apocalypse thing.

It's now 2043 A.D. A new civilization based on Martha's Vineyard has arisen, and, thanks to regular mail delivery, Mankind has rediscovered the ability to order pink Polo shirts from J. Crew. Kevin and Abby's daughter is present for the dedication of a statue to The Postman. It is an exact replica in bronze of the scene where Kevin snatched the letter out of the hand of little Anakin Skywalker. A man in the crowd says, "That was me!" And how nice that a sculptor was there to capture the moment. But hey, let's just replay that "letter grabbing" scene one more time, shall we, and let it tug on your hearts some more. The End.

But wait, who is that singing a duet of "I Didn't Have to Be So Nice (I Would Have Loved Me Anyway)" with Amy Grant over the closing credits? Why, it's The Postman himself! Don't leave your seat or you'll miss that great, heart-swelling moment when The Postman mounts his horse one last time, gallops through the recording studio and snatches the sheet music out of Amy Grant's hand for no reason whatsoever.

To sum up: In *The Postman*'s vision of the future, the survivors live in isolated fortifications, ignorant of the outside world, and regressing to a pre-industrial state of technology. Fortunately, it is still possible for one man to inspire hope by gadding about in clothes filched from a decayed corpse and foisting 15-year old *Lillian Vernon* catalogues on the apathetic masses.

So what lesson can the average viewer draw from this film? Well, if you're planning to rise from the ashes of Armageddon and become a beacon of light to a world swathed in darkness, you should probably start thinking now about what sort of federal, state, or municipal employee you plan to impersonate. Forget being a letter carrier—Kevin's got that sewed up—but perhaps you could be...The Sanitation Worker, bringing new life to a devastated world by restoring regular trash collection. You could impregnate the women on your route, battle evil bands of nomads who indiscriminately kill and litter, and "hand out hope like it's garbage from a can." Or perhaps you could be...The County Department of Weights and Measures Compliance Auditor, shattering the gloom like a bolt of lightning by ensuring the accuracy of commercial weighing and measuring devices, and verifying the quantity of both bulk and packaged commodities. Think how many women would want your sperm then! Of course, these are just suggestions; in fact, there are countless job possibilities for post-apocalyptic saviors. You could be...The Mosquito Abatement Program Coordinator, or...The Fictitious Business Names Registration Clerk, or...that guy at the County Department of Agriculture who issues permits to have disabled livestock euthanized.

The thought of a world-ending cataclysm is certainly terrifying. But as we have seen, virtually any clown can yank Mankind back from the brink of utter extinction, so long as he's willing to wear an ugly polyester uniform, donate sperm, and subsist on a diet of mule soup. But what if Armageddon throws you a curve? Suppose global warming melts the polar icecaps, and all five continents are submerged beneath the turbid sea? Suppose man must find a way to survive while adrift in this hostile environment? And suppose he must put up with Dennis Hopper overacting, and Kevin Costner not acting at all? In that case, public sector employment opportunities are not going to be sufficient to save the world, despite their generally attractive benefits packages.

Our next film will divulge the secrets for surviving a global deluge, so take the hand of the person sitting next to you, and let's proceed two-by-two...

Waterworld (1995)
Directed by Kevin Reynolds and Kevin Costner (uncredited)
Written by Peter Rader and David Twohy

In its day, *Waterworld* was the most expensive movie ever made, reportedly costing almost $200 million. While it's nice to know that they cared enough to spend the very most, you have to wonder if nearly a quarter-billion dollars is a reasonable sum to pay for a routine action yarn about an irritable post-apocalyptic yachtsman who drinks his own pee. But that's all *you* know, since you're not a moviemaker! But then, neither are we. However, we *do* have a copy of *The Mak-*

ing of Waterworld we got at the thrift store, and as we proceed with our summary, we'll point out how each dollar is being spent.

Our movie begins with the Universal logo melting ($100,000). Then God ($150) announces that it's the future and the Earth is covered with water. And then we catch our first glimpse of our hero, Kevin Costner ($25 million), as he pees into a cup. Despite what you might imagine, this isn't a studio-ordered urinalysis to make sure their money didn't go for drugs, as Kevin runs the pee through a primitive cappuccino machine and drinks it. And to show that his effluent has an especially piquant bouquet, he swirls it around his mouth, gargles it, and then spits a few drops onto a papier-mâché lime tree ($2), so it can also taste his goodness.

Kevin is a noble but crabby loner, much like Rambo or the Unabomber, and like them he also goes by only one name: Mariner. (I don't dispute the hero's right to assume the name of a major league ball club, although personally I would have picked one with a better bullpen.) Kevin lives aboard his boat made from scavenged eggbeaters, ice cube trays, and other crap, and ingeniously kept afloat by a large, inflated ego. He ekes out a living from the harsh and unforgiving sea, diving into its inky depths, where no ordinary man dare go, to recover leather mugs from the Renaissance Faire.

But before he has the chance to bring up a soggy pair of pantaloons, who should appear but evil incarnate: the Smokers! Yes, in the future, really strict clean-air legislation has divided the world into two groups: the Smokers and the Non-smokers. The Smokers are a gang of Jet Ski-riding Hell's Angels who kill, rape, plunder, burn fossil fuels, and eat Spam. They are led by a gratuitously villainous Dennis Hopper, who was apparently asked to reprise his performance from *Speed*, but make it a little less restrained.

In contrast to the depraved Smokers, the noble Non-smokers inhabit a man-made atoll composed entirely of recyclables ($50 million); they eat only free-range fish, drink only Evian distilled-urine, and only watch PBS. But one thing both groups share is a fondness for leather clothing, an odd choice for Post-Apocalyptic beachwear because it is hot and becomes really smelly, which you'd think would be a disadvantage in a society lacking Arid Extra Dry. And hey, since there are no animals in this world, one is forced to conclude that Soylent Garments are made from people!

Anyway, before the Smokers can give him emphysema, Kevin heads over to the Non-Smoking section, but they won't let him in until he displays what's in the leather mug: dirt! He takes it to the assay office, where the county agent tastes it and pronounces it pure. It seems that in the future a 5-pound bag of peat moss makes you Donald Trump. This could also explain why the people of this particular future are so dirty—they wear their alluvium as a status symbol, with only the really wealthy being able to afford not to bathe.

Kevin takes his dirt money and buys a tomato plant from Jeanne Tripplehorn, who is apparently the poorest person in town, judging by her cleanliness. As Kevin leaves with his tomato, the Non-Smokers accost him, and attempt to shake him down for his man-seed, just like in *The Postman*. The reoccurrence of this motif suggests that Kevin is a thoughtful futurist with a brave vision of things to come: specifically, a time in which the current model of transnational capitalism has evolved into an entirely jism-based economy.

However, Kevin is apparently a skinflint (or in this case, a skinfluteflint) and denies them his essence. The Non-Smoking leader promptly accuses Kevin of hiding something. Oddly enough, it's not his sexual orientation that he's hiding, but gills and webbed toes! Kevin is arrested for being a mutant, and sentenced to languish in a dangling cage as a warning to Dan Ackroyd.

Meanwhile, let's check in on little Ebola, a girl with a strange tattoo on her back, which is rumored to be a map to Dry World (where the Wet Head is Dead). She is busy doodling cave drawings of horses, trees, and soap, things no one in this society have ever seen. Her foster-mother Jeanne, and foster-uncle Coot (an amalgamation of Leon Russell and the Wizard of Oz), want to escape to the legendary Dryland, but they can't figure out what the tattoo means (Mr. Roark often had the same problem).

Suddenly, the atoll is attacked by the Smokers, who are seeking the fabled Girl With a Map To Dryland Tattooed On Her Back. (Apparently the demise of the Automobile Club has left a real cartographic void.)

Coot's balloon ($2 million) is inadvertently launched, and he has to leave Jeanne and Ebola behind; he can't come back, he doesn't know how it works! So, Jeanne releases Kevin from his birdcage on the condition he takes her and Ebola with him on his boat. But as soon as they are at sea, Kevin threatens to dump his passengers because there's not enough urine for three. Jeanne disrobes and offers to have sex with Kevin if he'll spare them. He stares at her naked form for some time, waiting for her to lay her eggs so he can fertilize them; when she doesn't follow through with her part of the bargain, he clubs her on the head. Kevin hates a tease.

The fish, woman, and child begin to bond during their time at sea. Ebola uses Kevin's crayons without asking, so he throws her overboard. Jeanne breaks a mast fighting off Smokers, so Kevin chops off her hair. In exchange for an old *National*

Geographic, Kevin pimps Jeanne to a crazy Irish Robin Williams-impersonator. So, they are becoming a family.

But this idyllic life comes to an end when the Smokers find them again and grab Ebola. Kevin and Jeanne jump overboard to escape death from secondhand smoke. When Jeanne complains that she can't breathe underwater, Kevin says he'll breathe for both of them; he proceeds to blow carbon dioxide into her mouth while sneakily frenching her. When they surface, Kevin's boat has been burned and the Smokers are nowhere in sight. So, there's nothing they can do but have sex ($3.2 million), as Jeanne learns the origins of the term "cold fish."

Kevin is saved from cuddling by the reappearance of Coot and his balloon. Coot indicates that the survivors of the Non-Smoking Section have started a new atoll made from old egg cartons and beer cans, and invites Jeanne and Kevin to join them. But Kevin declares that he must rescue Ebola, even if it means certain death Not because he's after her map, but because she's his friend. And because she still has one of his crayons.

Over in Smoking Section Headquarters, the ancient oil tanker *Exxon Valdez* ($70 million for rental, plus a $5 million surcharge for Irony), Dennis Hopper tries to get Ebola to tell him what her map means. She doesn't know, since she can't see her own back, but she does know that her Westley...er, Mariner will come for her. And *then* they'll be sorry—because he'll make them watch *Robin Hood, Prince of Thieves*.

Just then, a lone, dark figure walks across the deck. Yes, it's Mad Mackerel, the Roe Warrior! He's a post-apocalyptic laconic hero who's come to eat fish flakes and kick butt, and he's all out of fish flakes! Dennis best sums up the situation: "He's like a turd that won't flush." And since this was before *The Postman, Message in a Bottle, 3000 Miles to Graceland*, and Many More, Dennis is starting to look like Miss Cleo.

Kevin throws a torch into the tanker's fuel hold and rescues Ebola. Uncle Coot arrives in the balloon, saving Kevin's butt yet again (and if you want to see that butt, check out *For Love of the Game*, on DVD!)

Coot looks carefully at Ebola's tattoo and suddenly realizes how to read the map (although he still has trouble refolding it). Armed with this convenient plot twist, he leads the other survivors to a lush, verdant land with pure, clean water—but alas, still no soap. The group spots a grass hut ($3 million), and inside, two skeletons lying next to tattoo needles and a copy of the graphic on Ebola's back. And now it all makes sense! Ebola is actually the child of Gilligan and Mary Ann, the last of the castaways. They sent her to the mainland for help, but the stupid kid spent all her time coloring and forgot to tell the authorities about her parents, leaving them to die of coconut cream pie poisoning.

But everyone is so thrilled to have enough dirt to live like kings that there are no recriminations. However, the gilled-and-webbed Kevin isn't at home on the land, and he must tell the tearful Ebola that she's a fine girl, and what a good wife she would be, but his life, his love, and his lady is the sea. Kevin and Jeanne exchange half-hearted good-byes, then he steals director Kevin Reynolds boat and sails off, taking the remaining $100 million of the studio's money with him. Because even a mutant can see that his back-end participation points are going to be worthless. The End.

Of all the films reviewed for this book, *Waterworld* presents by far the darkest vision of the future: a time in which Man's natural habitat has vanished, leaving him crammed onto rusty, floating hulks, where he is preyed upon by violent locals, forced to inhale noxious fumes, and reduced to eating Spam washed down with pee. In other words, it's a Carnival Cruise, so the people best equipped to survive this harsh new environment are probably elderly Jewish women from Coral Gables.

But how can we use the wisdom imparted by this film to better prepare ourselves for the apocalypse? Well, to begin with, if you finally *do* get that tattoo you've been thinking about (oh, don't deny it) you should forget the rose on your breast, the butterfly on your ankle, or the ying-yang symbol on your ass, and instead have Buzz at Inka-Dinka-Doo on Hollywood Boulevard inscribe the entire Rand McNally World Atlas on your back. (Oh sure, it'll *hurt*, but at least when the apocalypse comes you'll get to have middle-aged potheads and faded matinee idols listlessly tussle over you.) Other than that, there's lots of little things you can do to prepare for the Deluge: load up on leather pants and Sea 'n Ski, Dramamine, Underwood Deviled Ham, and sphagnum moss. Take swimming lessons at the Y. Get your semen appraised. Cancel the newspaper. Oh, and you'll want to start mutating. But don't go crazy with it, or you could wind up like John Travolta in *Battlefield Earth* (alternate title: *When Sweathogs Ruled the Earth*), whose alien digestive tract required him to continually chew, swallow, and regurgitate scenery like cud. Which brings us to our final lesson in apocalypse management.

As we have seen, the end of the world can be triggered by many different factors—fascism, plagues, global climate change—but to a large extent these are human-created problems, and remain susceptible to human solutions. But there is one cause of worldwide catastrophe that lies beyond our control: alien invasion. Granted, this scenario may not seem as likely as global warming or nuclear war, but from H.G. Wells to the present day, writers of speculative fiction have served up a ceaseless parade of genocidal out-of-towners who descend upon our planet like Bud-sodden fratboys on Daytona Beach, and in each case, it hasn't really gone that well for us. So it might behoove humanity to study a recent example of the genre, and see what tips we can find for dealing with unwelcome guests who eat you out of house and home, run up your long distance phone bill, and exterminate you.

Battlefield Earth (2000)
Directed by Roger Christian
Written by L. Ron Hubbard (novel), Corey Mandell and J.D. Shapiro

A crawl informs us that it's the Year 3000, and for the past thousand years, Earth has been ruled by Psychlos. How did such an advanced race of space-faring beings wind up with such a stupid name? Well, they're obviously a nutty bunch, judging by John Travolta's performance, and they seem to have wiped out every trailer park on the planet, so I'm guessing that author and Church of Scientology founder L. Ron Hubbard just combined the words "psycho" and "cyclone," hoping to terrify his readers with a name that conjured images of an emotionally unstable amusement park attraction. Anyway, they're big-assed aliens from a planet where George Clinton is the dominant life form.

The Psychlos have been mining Earth's natural resources for the past millennium (apparently, they get paid by the hour) and teleporting the ore back to the Planet Psychlo. Amazingly, the film predicts that in the future, the most valuable metal will actually be *gold!* (Unlike now, when its use is largely confined to electroplating the fixtures in Ivana Trump's bathroom, or decorating the incisors of rap artists.)

Humans (represented by pasty white people dressed like Vikings) are confined to pockets of wasteland, where they are rapidly becoming extinct—so I guess all those dead 19th century Indians are having a bit of a laugh. Just so we get the point, the director pans the pristine, snow-capped Rocky Mountains (giving us a glimmer of hope that even in the bleak, post-apocalyptic future, there will still be beer commercials) and a subtitle reads: "Man is an endangered species." Despite this, the Bush Administration still wants to drill in the Arctic National Man Refuge.

The survivors of humanity have adopted the usual trappings of barbarism—furs and buckskin clothing, polytheism, and French braids. One courageous lad (Barry Pepper) defies the anger of the gods and boldly ventures forth alone to find his destiny. Within thirty seconds he gets thrown from his horse, and panicked by a miniature golf course. Fortunately, he runs into a pair of hunters, and offers them snacks in exchange for exposition.

They take shelter in the Apocalypse Galleria and huddle around a cook fire. But one of the Psychlos turns out to be a mall walker, and he takes exception to their careless use of an open flame so close to Lane Bryant. The alien stuns the two hunters with its ray gun, but Barry is too fast for it, perhaps because the alien isn't entirely at ease clomping around in Gene Simmons' platform boots from KISS.

Eventually, Barry and the hunters are put in a cage built into the belly of an alien jet. Yes, even though it's a thousand years in the future, and the aliens can instantly teleport across the galaxy, they still use internal combustion engines. Take *that*, Al Gore!

The jet flies to the Psychlo's capital, Biosphere 2. The humans are issued those little anti-snoring patches for their noses, which somehow helps them to survive the extraterrestrial environment inside the dome. But it's not only the air that's different; the entire domed city is perpetually bathed in a dim blue glow, making it clear that the Psychlos can only exist in the atmosphere of a soft-core porn film.

The jet lands at the "Human Processing Center—Denver," and we look forward to watching Barry get rendered into a form of alien Velveeta. Instead, he startles his captors by shooting one of the Psychlos with its own gun, and making a break for it. Almost immediately, he slips and falls, for along with man's loss of art, science, and medicine, he has also forgotten the ancient admonition not to run on linoleum in your socks.

Barry slides to a stop at the platformed feet of Psychlos John Travolta and Forrest Whittaker, who were in the middle of discussing how beeswax will help to keep down the fuzz on your dreadlocks.

Travolta, it seems, has fallen from favor with the Home Office, and has been condemned to serve as security chief of Earth for another 50 years. All the other Psychlos laugh at John, except for his immediate supervisor, who's too busy cultivating the largest dewlap in the galaxy.

Cut to Planet Psychlo. It's a grim, inhospitable world; dark urban landscapes stretch to the horizon, studded with towers belching fire and pollution into the perpetual twilight of a purple sky, and inhabited by cruel beings thirsting for wealth and power. So basically, it's Houston.

Cut right back to Earth, where John is getting drunk and working himself into a thick, creamy lather of overacting, which is later harvested, and dispensed as food to the humans with the help of a sour cream gun from Taco Bell.

John plans to buy his way off the planet by secretly training "man-animals" to mine a newly discovered vein of gold. First, however, he sets the humans to remodeling his office with pickaxes. But Barry, who is evolving faster than the apes in *2001*, turns on John's stereo and boldly messes with his equalizer settings. The outraged Travolta immediately straps Barry into a dentist's chair and has a Portuguese Man O' War teach him Conversational Psychlo. Then they shoot some pollen in his eye, and suddenly, he's The Computer Wore Moccasins.

John, realizing that Reading Is Fundamental, takes Barry on a field trip to the Denver Library, and tells him that "Man is an endangered species," because Barry was ignorant when the film began, and couldn't read the opening titles.

Later, John takes Barry and his friends out to the forest, and proves his technological superiority by shooting the legs off a cow. Just as he's about to win the plush toy, he's jumped by a feral tribe wearing fox pelts on their heads, which menace him with spears. John miraculously escapes, however, when the tribe itself is attacked by PETA.

Suddenly, Forrest arrives with Barry's girlfriend, who they've identified because she was carrying a chamois with a face scratched into it. The image looks remarkably like one of Red Skelton's clown paintings, so the Psychlos immediately deduce that it must be Barry. The Girlfriend is then accessorized with the latest in explosive collars.

Back at Biosphere II, John sexually harasses his new secretary, giving us the opportunity to see that female Psychlos have prehensile tongues and male pattern baldness, which I guess is *somebody's* idea of a fun night in Vegas.

Suddenly, Travolta discovers that governor Dewlap has been skimming profits, and threatens to report him to the Nevada Gaming Commission unless he does something about that Elizabethan ruffle of loose skin hanging from his neck. Then John activates the first phase of his master plan by making Barry play "Asteroids."

Cut to the Rockies, where Travolta forces Barry to fly the human miners up to the gold vein, since the thin atmosphere at high altitudes doesn't supply enough oxygen to support the Psychlo's spittle-flecked, mouth-breathing acting style. Instead, Barry flies to Ft. Hood, where the illiterate, spear-wielding fox-head guys climb into the flight simulator and learn how to pilot F-16s, while Barry watches the How to Assemble an Atomic Bomb slide show that they always used to make us watch on rainy days in junior high. Then they fly to Kentucky and rob Ft. Knox in a scene that's not exactly the climax of *Goldfinger.*

Later, Barry manages to sow doubt and distrust between Forrest and Travolta, with the result that John decapitates a bartender, and shoots off Forrest's hand. Forrest looks confused, and considers reporting John to the EEOC for creating a hostile work environment.

Barry riles up all the human prisoners in the Planet of the Apes Memorial Cellblock, and sparks a revolt, but it doesn't go very well. Just in the nick of time, however, a tribe of primitive hunter-gatherers arrive, flying jet fighters which are in perfect working condition after a thousand years of neglect. But let my car sit for more than a week, and I can just forget about getting it started again without begging one of the neighbors for a jump. Anyway, face-painted, fur-wearing savages suddenly turn into Top Guns, shouting things like "I'm right on his tail!" as they dogfight the Psychlos.

The humans blow up Biosphere 2. Then Barry uses his girlfriend's explosive collar to blow off Travolta's right arm, in a ruthless act of attempted irony. Meanwhile, one of Barry's posse teleports to the Planet Psychlo with an atomic weapon. This is where the aliens really pay for basing their entire economy on the petrochemical industry, since the bomb causes their atmosphere to catch on fire. And even though the film isn't explicit about this, we sense that as every living thing on the surface of the planet is incinerated, certain cashiered whistleblowers from the Psychlo EPA enjoy a moment of smug vindication.

So what new truths have we gleaned from *Battlefield Earth*? First, we have learned that spirituality is a fine thing, but it's probably best to avoid joining denominations that make action movies (see *Omega Code*). And while traditional faiths do not satisfy the soulful yearnings of every pilgrim, it still might be a good idea to shy away from any religion whose prophets write crappy sci-fi novels on the side. Just a suggestion.

Finally, what have we learned about the end of the world? To begin with, each home should maintain an Apocalypse Preparedness Kit, containing bottled water, fresh batteries, leather Viking pants, bandages, a flashlight, and a can of Kevin Costner repellant. Maybe two cans.

Also, we've seen that after the fall of civilization, existence will be bleak and cheerless. The formula for soap will be lost, and everyone will be dirty and smelly, even on Waterworld. The war- or pollution-ravaged landscape will resemble much of Nevada, although happily, without Siegfried and Roy. Even worse, we'll lack basic liberties, such as the right to a jury trial, the right to free assembly, and the right to be secure against unreasonable exposure to Rob Schneider. We suggest that you prepare yourself for this dreary future by spending your vacations in Utah.

Lastly, we've learned that after the apocalypse, Bad Guys (be they genetically engineered traffic court judges, ill-mannered pirates, megalomaniacal copy machine salesmen, or really stupid-looking aliens) will oppress humanity. Fortunately, messianic heroes will rise up to oppose them; and then, after they've restored hope to mankind, ride off into the sunset with an attractive babe. Unfortunately, half of these heroes will be Kevin Costner, and fully one fourth will be Sylvester Stallone. So, the remedy could well be worse than the disease, especially if you're an attractive babe.

Coping with Grief:
The Five Stages of Bad Sequels

As William Goldman memorably observed, nobody in Hollywood knows anything, including how to make successful movies. And when they *do* manage to make a picture people want to see, they don't know when to quit. Instead, they rob the grave of the original movie and try to pass off the moldering corpse as an old familiar friend with whom we're eager to renew our acquaintance. Because they don't know anything, however, including *why* the original was popular, they often steal the wrong body.

Maybe it was the movie's gimmick we responded to, like in *Highlander*. Sure, the idea of immortal headhunting Scotsmen roaming the centuries has a certain intrinsic appeal, but did anybody really enjoy *Christopher Lambert*? No, of course not. So what do they do for an encore in *Highlander 2*? Ditch the whole premise of the original, but bring back *Chris*.

Or maybe it was a character the audience enjoyed, such as *Batman*. So in *Batman and Robin*, let's bury him under a bunch of other, stupider characters that everybody hates, not to mention a barrage of badly-edited action sequences that make the jittery, nauseating camera work in *The Blair Witch Project* look like *My Dinner with Andre*.

When you get right down to it, there's a certain ghoulish quality to sequels, sort of like that *Twilight Zone* episode where the old woman kept a party of mummified dinner guests sitting around her table. It's like you had a really fun friend—we'll call him Bob. Bob was such great company that when he reached the end of his natural lifespan, it left you with an unrequited hunger for additional Bob-specific shenanigans. Ordinarily, you'd have to be content with your memories, but let's say that Bob's an organ donor. Now, his liver may still be capable of filtering toxins and storing glucose, but you're not going to find the remaindered organ as charming and fun to be with as Bob was. And if you did try to recreate the unique chemistry you two had by taking his liver to Fenway Park and sitting in the stands chugging Budweiser and swapping dirty jokes with it,

29

you would likely find the experience fell short of the expectations set by your previous outings with Bob.

This, basically, is the Hollywood Sequel in a nutshell: It's sitting in the bleachers under a hot sun, drinking beer with some organ meat. Looked at from this perspective, it's clear that those who believe that Hollywood's endless production of sequels represents creative bankruptcy, corporate cowardice, and a grim determination to squeeze blood from an already desanguinated turnip are wrong. Far from crass commercial exploitation, we believe that the Hollywood Sequel represents a form of grief counseling.

Dr. Elizabeth Kubler-Ross has identified Five Stages of Grief: Denial, Anger, Bargaining, Depression, and Acceptance. As we will show, every movie sequel represents one of these emotional rest stops along the road to enlightenment or boredom. To quote a time-honored aphorism, "When the traveler is burdened with woe, his journey may begin with a single step, but it will end with *Speed 2: Cruise Control.*"

Let's begin, shall we?

Highlander II: The Quickening (1991)
Directed by Russell Mulcahey
Written by Brian Clemens and William Panzer; based on characters by Gregory Widen

It's August, 1999, and according to a cheery drive-time DJ, the ozone layer is completely gone, and millions are dead. But immortal Scotsman Connor MacLeod (Christopher Lambert) and his chunky sidekick are about to change all that. "They'll remember this day for a thousand years," coos Chunky Sidekick, as he gives Christopher a hug. "The day we protected the Earth from the Sun." Because apparently the Sun has been picking on the Earth at recess, giving it Indian burns, and stealing its lunch money.

Chris shoots a beam of light out of the Transamerica building, which throws up a shield around the planet that sunlight cannot penetrate—a sort of artificial nuclear winter. Neat, huh?

25 Years Later. Christopher has acquired gray hair, jowls, and a tendency to talk in voiceovers. Thanks to his shield, Earth is plunged in perpetual darkness. Agriculture is impossible, madness, starvation and disease are rampant, and humanity is regressing to barbarism, as illustrated by the cast of *Charles in Charge* doing Redi-Whip hits off an oxy-acetylene torch. *Good* one, Chris.

Later, this self-styled savior of the Earth is dozing at the opera when he's suddenly awaked by a competing voiceover. It's Sean Connery, who has apparently decided to play a practical joke on Chris by intoning, "Remember, Highlander. Remember your home. Another galaxy. You were chosen. Remember?" Having seen the previous movie, one expects Christopher to tell Sean to put down the Mr. Microphone and stop talking crap during the opera. Alas, the poor lunkhead falls for it, and abruptly decides that he's actually an alien from the planet Zeiss (known the universe over for its quality line of precision binoculars). Suddenly, we flash back 500 years. It seems the Muumuu Men of Zest are sick of the tyrannical General Katana, and his brutal remarks about their efforts to disguise holiday weight gain with loose-fitting clothes.

Sean Connery appears before the rebel army and declares that at last they have a *leader*. But this announcement turns out to be yet another of Sean's increasingly cruel practical jokes, since the guy he's pointing at is Christopher Lambert. Once again, however, the cow-eyed nitwit falls for it, and Chris promptly leads his army into battle against General Katana (Michael Ironside, sporting Al Sharpton's hair). Naturally, Chris's followers are promptly massacred, while Katana exiles Sean and Chris to Earth, where they face the deadly challenge of reconciling all the continuity errors between this film and the first one.

500 Years Later: Virginia Madsen leads a team of eco-terrorists into the Shield generating station. Not far away, Christopher stops into a bar, where Bella Abzug beats him up and cuts him with a broken bottle.

Cut back to the planet Zeitgeist. Something's been nagging at Katana for the last 500 years. What was it? Dang. It's on the tip of his tongue...

Oh! Right. He meant to have Chris killed, but he's been procrastinating for the past half-millennium. And don't even get his wife started about that bathroom tile he's been promising to re-grout!

Katana orders a couple of fey porcupine men to immediately teleport to Earth and snuff the Highlander. But Christopher proves he's still The One by running around in a tizzy, smashing into things, and surviving the encounter through sheer dumb luck. One attacker even goes so far as to obligingly lie under a train at just the perfect angle to snip off his head. And even though this looks suspiciously like a suicide, the judges award his Quickening to Christopher, who promptly redeems it for a new wig and a jar of Porcelana.

Cut to Scotland. Despite being decapitated and killed in the previous *Highlander*, Sean returns from the dead, thanks to some bad special effects and some even worse advice from his agents.

Meanwhile, Virginia meets the now (relatively) young Christopher who tells her that he's an extraterrestrial Scotsman with a French accent who was banished from the planet Seuss 500 years ago. Oh, and he can never die. Rather than running away or shouting for the cops, Virginia takes this bizarre assertion as a signal to start French kissing.

Virginia is saved from further embarrassment by Sean, who distracts Chris by trying to cut his head off. When that sadly fails, they start to drink. Sensible members of the audience put the DVD on Pause and do likewise.

Realizing the movie is bogging down, they go break into a high-security prison where the government is secretly raising Spanish Moss, but almost instantly blunder into a death trap—a cylindrical chamber with a lawnmower blade descending from the ceiling. Fortunately, Sean summons his life force and uses it to repel the blade (and the audience). Unfortunately, his life force emits the annoying sound of bagpipes. Oh, and it also opens the death trap's sealed doors. And snapples caps off any jug, bottle, or jar.

Finally, Christopher gets into a cutlery-assisted hassle with Katana, and they stumble into the room where the Shield is generated by a huge column of blinding white light. Chris steps inside this unimaginably powerful laser beam, in the mistaken belief that it's a tanning booth, and the whole place blows up.

The Shield instantly evaporates. Virginia gazes into the night sky, a look of wonder in her eyes as she glimpses the stars for the first time in her life. Christopher, on the other hand, gets caught in a freeze-frame with a goofy, gap-mouthed grin that makes him look like he's just popped up out of the cornfield to deliver a punch-line on *Hee Haw*. The End.

Stage of grief: **Denial.** In this stage, the affected person denies that a loss has occurred. As you can see, this is a pretty advanced case, since the filmmakers actually tried to make a sequel to a film they deny ever existed. And even though they lopped off Sean Connery's head in the first one, to director Russell Mulcahy, this simply calls for a Do Over. You can imagine how difficult it might have been to reach the director in the early days of his grief, when he wept inconsolably over the realization that he'd killed off the only appealing actor in his movie, leaving him with a potential franchise headlined by a weird-looking Frenchman with all the heroic gravitas of a Tickle Me Elmo. The conversation might have gone something like this:

"You can't bring Sean Connery back for the sequel—his character is dead."

"No he's not! (sob)"

"Your own movie says the only way to kill an immortal is to cut his head off, and he got his head cut off!"

"No, but...he's not just an immortal. He's...an *alien*! From another *galaxy*! And he gets brought back to life in the present day by an...inter-dimensional time...portal...thingy."

"You really expect the audience to believe in an alien from a distant galaxy named Ramirez?"

"I didn't expect them to believe in a Spaniard with a Scottish burr slightly thicker than Jackie Stewart's, but they swallowed *that* like a bad clam."

Of course, denial can only be sustained for so long, before one's inability to cope with an unbearable, yet persistent truth turns to frustration and anger. At this point, the affected individual begins to lash out at those around him, giving voice to irrational suspicions and recriminations, making friends the target of misplaced rage, and depressing the tourist industry by unleashing the vengeful specter of Spanky McFarland.

Blair Witch 2: Book of Shadows (2000)
Directed by Joe Berlinger
Written by Dick Beebe, Joe Berlinger, based on characters by Daniel Myrick and Eduardo Sanchez

1999's *The Blair Witch Project* was proof that people will pay to see anything if you hype it enough, even a movie filmed in shaky "Lose-Your-Lunch-O-Vision" and made for less money than what the average moviegoer spends on popcorn and Pepsi. BWP was a big hit, so little time was lost coming up with a sequel about another group of stupid, annoying young people who go into the woods with video cameras, get scared, and swear a lot.

Titles declare that it's Summer 1999 (right after BWP came out).

Then it's one year earlier, and a guy in a mental institution is getting force-fed lemonade.

Now it's November 1999, and the mental patient is undergoing police interrogation about a murdered tour group.

Then it's long ago, in a galaxy far, far away, and our mental patient is the tour guide for the "Blair Witch Hunt," a venture designed to exploit fans of the first movie. Everybody with us so far?

Besides Mental Patient/Tour Guide, the Witchmobile contains Preppy, a pompous jerk; Girlfriend, his sweet, mousy helpmate; Wiccan Chick, who came along to nag us about picking on witches; and Goth Girl, who claims to be clairvoyant and who thought *The Blair Witch Project* was "cool." (So, while she may possess eerie mental powers, she is clearly lacking some of the regular ones.)

Tour Guide passes out video cameras so the group can record the upcoming paranormal events, and so he can give us the moral of the movie: "Video never lies; film does." Well, maybe it's not a moral so much as a Sony slogan, but remember it—it'll be on the test.

The group is camping by the haunted house from the first movie when a rival tour group shows up. There is an angry confrontation, but our group gets rid of the interlopers by sending them to hunt snipe at Coffin Rock, the location of a notorious made-up historical massacre from the first movie. Then our dedicated team of truth seekers proceeds to smoke joints and guzzle several cases of cheap beer. Maybe the tour should have been called the "The Share Schlitz Project."

The Teen Gang wakes up the next morning to a gentle snowfall of shredded paper. Yes, the director has torn up the script in frustration. Well, actually Preppie's witch research has been shredded—and nobody can remember what they did last night! The group watches the tapes to discover what occurred during those missing hours (presumably, they're looking for more than the giggling, puking, and inane remarks like "I really, really love you, man" that one would expect to see on such a tape.) And then the weird stuff starts to happen. Girlfriend has a scary dream about the Little Rascals looking up her skirt. Everybody else gets heat rash in the form of ancient pagan symbols. The owl from "Twin Peaks" makes a cameo appearance. Every few minutes we see flash cuts of somebody's appendectomy. It's enough to keep you from ever going into the woods, lest you encounter the teddy bears having a picnic.

Careful review of the videotapes shows a woman doing the Hokey Pokey in the nude. Digital enhancement reveals her to be Wiccan Chick. She denies it, claiming her contract provides for a body double. After watching this footage ten or twenty times we are chilled to realize that Wiccan's breasts are big, yet also perky; this is probably the most unexplainable thing we've seen yet.

The next day Wiccan Chick has vanished, leaving her clothes and jewelry lying neatly on the floor. Having seen *Left Behind*, we suspect that she was raptured. The group blames the absent Wiccan for the eerie visions of Alfalfa and Buckwheat they've been experiencing, and for all the calligraphic eczema.

Just then the sheriff, a Southern redneck who can only aspire to a performance as understated and nuanced as Jackie Gleason's in *Smokey and the Bandit*, announces that the other tour group was murdered and disemboweled, their entrails arranged in a festive holiday pattern.

Tour Guide opens a closet to change his shirt, and it now contains the body of Wiccan Chick, clad only in her panties. (Amazingly, even in death her breasts are perky.)

The remaining witchbusters are certain that the answer will be found on the videotape of their night in the woods. Eventually they play it backward and learn that Paul is dead, miss him, miss him. It also shows our Scooby Gang having an orgy, flogging each other, and then engaging in a community sing-a-thon. We also see Girlfriend give each of them a knife, which they use to kill the rival sight-seers. Preppie tries to make Girlfriend confess to being a witch, but she just laughs and calls him a "pathetic, no-balls bitch." He then pushes her off a balcony completely by accident.

Back at Redneck HQ, we next see videotape evidence of Tour Guide killing Wiccan Chick. Although we were with him the whole time and swear he is innocent, the sheriff refuses to believe us, because if we're so smart, why are we still watching this movie? He has a good point, and we agree to turn State's Evidence.

So, which are we to believe: the 32mm portions of the movie, or the videotape sequences? Well, Tour Guide told us that while film lies, video never does. But then, he's a mental patient, so why are we listening to him? Having been forced to watch many, many hours of videotaped birthday parties, summer vacations, and dance recitals, it seems to us that while video may tell the truth, it is not the kind of truth that sets one free, but rather the kind that offers no time off for good behavior.

Stage of Grief: *Anger*. In most cases, this stage is expressed by acting out inappropriately, such as willfully misinterpreting sympathy as condescension, and using imagined insults as a springboard to vent your existential rage. In Hollywood, however, anger is best expressed by doubling your budgetary line items.

Call it Newton's Second Law of Sequels: namely, that every movie premise will get bigger and stupider with each succeeding entry in a franchise. Take for example, *First Blood*, a modest revenge fantasy wherein Vietnam Vet Sylvester Stallone is hassled by the law, so he flips out and kills everyone in town, teaching them a little lesson about the perils of picking on the psychotic. Okay, a bit unlikely, but it *could* happen, if only in a world where Sylvester Stallone wouldn't have been declared 4-F due to severe speech impediments. But in the sequel *Rambo*, Sylvester goes to Vietnam to rescue some MIAs and in the process kills everyone in the country. So now Stallone isn't just a crazed, if beefy loner, he's an invulnerable one-man army who retroactively wins the Vietnam War. Finally, in *Rambo 3*, Sylvester invades Afghanistan to rescue Richard Crenna, and ends up single-handedly killing everybody on the Asian continent. This time he not only won the Cold War, he also took revenge for the Korean War, Pearl Harbor, and the Pokemon phenomena. But it wasn't without cost. No, it cost $58 million, making each life worth about 63¢. If there were a *Rambo 4*, we think it would involve Stallone ripping the heads off every inhabitant of Earth, probably because he received a summons for jury duty, or his neighbor's sprinkler got his newspaper wet or something.

It's clear from *BWP2* that the Blair Witch is working through some of the very same anger management issues. But while denial is a cold emotion, anger is a conflagration, and like most fires, it eventually exhausts its fuel. At this point, the affected person will desperately attempt to negotiate with the forces of the universe, but alas, no matter how assiduously you may have boned up on Trump's *Art of the Deal*, this never seems to go very well. As the Faustian bargain made by Sandra Bullock in our next film so amply demonstrates...

Speed 2: Cruise Control (1997)
Directed by Jan de Bont
Written by Jan de Bont (story) and Randall McCormick

As this sequel begins, Sandra Bullock explains to DMV driving tester Tim Conway that she broke up with her "Speed 1" boyfriend because he gave her pepper spray and she thought it was perfume. Yes, Sandra is still plucky and perky and spunky, but she really should see the Wizard about a brain.

While Sandra chatters on to Tim about her new beau (who is *not* into hazardous stuff, like her last guy), her driving imperils the lives of everyone in her path. She smashes her way into a dangerous high-speed chase being conducted by LAPD SWAT officer Jason Patric, only to learn that her safe, cozy boyfriend is...Jason!

"I don't even know you!" she rages, upset that he was an action hero behind her back. But Jason pulls out tickets to a Caribbean cruise and we cut to...

...The Love Boat, where Gopher is showing Sandra and Jason to their cabin. They're interrupted by the cruise's designated actor, Willem Dafoe, who demands that his golf balls be found *now*. When Jason and Sandra go up on deck, Jason notes that there is a golf tournament on TV but Willem isn't watching it! Willem is no golfer! Jason has cracked the case!

Willem, of course, is a super-villain, and in requisite super-villain fashion, he has a pet that he talks to. But all the good pets were taken, so Willem's stuck with pet leeches, which he keeps in his bathtub. Also, his golf balls are bombs and he has a *fiber optic converter!* Clearly he is up to no good.

Jason and Sandra go to the dining room, where we meet our *Poseidon Adventure* supporting cast members: the Fat Busters Conventioneers (pinch-hitting for Shelley Winters); and some jewelers, who brought along a billion-dollar diamond collection in an effort to score with Kate Winslet. Willem's plan is to blow up a few golf balls, steal the diamonds, and crash the ship into a cliff.

At the first sign of trouble, Jason is champing at the bit to do brave stuff. He informs the incompetent ship's officers that Willem is controlling the boat with his ThinkPad, and suggests they shoot him (Willem, I mean—although shooting Jason would have been *my* suggestion). But Willem is one step ahead of them, and has left his cabin! He taunts them via video camera, saying something about their fathers being hamsters.

Sandra, who thought *she* was the hero of this film, goes looking for her own people to save. She locates the fat folks, who are trapped in their room and stripping so they can use their clothing to block the fumes coming from the vents. Sandra knows she has to hurry, because we don't want to see *this* go any further!

Meanwhile, Jason remembers that in *Speed 1*, Keanu Reeves shot a hostage to prevent a kidnapping, so Jason comes up with the idea of sinking the ship to keep it from running aground, thereby proving the law of diminishing returns.

Willem's laptop computer, HAL, tells him Jason has thwarted Evil Plan A, so he switches to Plan B—crashing the ship into an oil tanker. Willem, who is fed up with Sandra's whining, takes her hostage and flees on a speedboat that was somehow just there.

Jason manages to avert the collision (it involves holding his breath for a long time), but *now* they are headed for St. Maarten's harbor! The rogue ocean liner plows into the town, smashing the pier, the boardwalk, some condos, and a telephone booth. It seems that ocean liners demolishing towns must be pretty common in these parts because nobody pays much attention until the ship actually taps them on the shoulder and says, "boo!" The Love Boat hits a church and finally comes to a halt since, as we all know, cruise ships can only be stopped by crucifixes. So, the movie is over, right? Alas, no, because Jason still has to rescue Sandra, who is trying to sneak off the set to go make *Hope Floats*.

Jason hijacks a cigarette boat from some Jamaican guy and his date, and they head off in hot pursuit of Willem, who has abandoned his speedboat for a seaplane. Willem's plane gets impaled on an oil tanker, he laughs maniacally (Top of the world, ma!), and the tanker and the plane blow up real good.

Jason and Sandra, who fell out of the plane before it exploded, sink into the ocean. Jamaican Guy, who is apparently there to explain the action to the less intelligent audience members, says "I hope they can hold their breaths a long time. Don't run out of air!" Jamaican Girlfriend adds, "Me thinks they're dead." Me wish they were. Instead, they find Willem's bag of diamonds, Jason gives Sandra an engagement ring, and they kiss. The End.

Except we're now back in the car with Sandra and Tim Conway, and it's cruelly apparent that this movie has more false climaxes than a Long Island housewife.

Stage of grief: **Bargaining**. In fact, this movie exists solely due to haggling and the barter system: a star agrees to do a crappy sequel to a successful action movie in exchange for the studio financing a project with great personal meaning to the star, which is a nice way of saying that it's self-indulgent offal that most moviegoers wouldn't touch with an asbestos glove. Ironically, it turns out that nobody wanted to see the crappy sequel either, which goes to show why negotiating with the forces of the universe is always a tricky proposition. You have no way of knowing what cards they hold, you don't speak their language, and you can't figure out their currency without one of those little conversion charts.

Basically, it's the kind of bargaining inexperienced tourists do in Tijuana. They wind up buying the used Sandra Bullock, even though the seller tells them that he's out of the Keanu Reeves upgrade and they'll have to take the cheaper Jason Patric—but they'll still come out ahead if they get the Willem Dafoe option (the same supervillainry as the national Dennis Hopper brand, with only half the sudden, unmotivated bouts of overacting). And the filmmakers walk off, smugly thinking that they did okay. But when they get their movie home, they discover that the high-mileage Sandra Bullock only had her perkiness spray-painted on, that the Jason Patric was just wood in the *shape* of a leading man, and that they *really* got rooked when they traded in their bus for the cruise ship.

At this point, unsurprisingly, depression sets in. Which leads inevitably to…

Star Wars: Episode I: The Phantom Menace (1999)
Written and Directed by George Lucas

Our story begins with crawling titles that tediously establish the back-story (yes, it's the *first* movie of the series, and we already have back-story). It seems that the Fu Manchu Grasshopper People from the Federation have blockaded the planet of Nanoo-Nanoo. Jedi Knight Slo-Jinn Fizz (Liam Neeson) and his apprentice Obi-Wan Kenobi (not Alec Guiness) arrive to negotiate with the Grasshopper Viceroy. Obi-Wan feels a great disturbance in the Force, as though millions of voices suddenly cried out at once, and asked for their money back.

Future-Emperor Palpitation (Whom-Nobody-Suspects-Of-Being-Evil-Even-Though-They-Are-All-Masters-Of-The-Force) orders the Viceroy to kill the Jedi. Escaping to Nanoo-Nanoo, Slo-Jinn meets local irritant Jar-Jar Binks, who looks like a malnourished moose and talks like a Jamaican bobsledder who sustained a crippling brain injury at Innsbruck.

Meanwhile, the Federation forces have captured Amidala, the 16-year-old elected queen of Nanoo-Nanoo. Yes, we know—you never voted for her. But since being queen involves wearing Kabuki makeup and using a voice synthesizer, there probably wasn't a lot of competition for the job. (Do you think she dons this ornate headdress and ceremonial costume to inspire awe in her subjects, or is she just a typical rebellious teen, wearing these crazy fashions because it really bugs her mom?)

Slo-Jinn and company rescue Amidala and head off for planet ChorusGirl. The Fu Manchu people blast our heroes' ship, but everyone is saved by a plucky trashcan that manages to insert the correct cable in the VCR's "out" terminal. And that brave little dumpster was named…R2D2. Now you know…the REST of the story.

The good guys land on Planet Tattooing to make repairs. Slo-Jinn and his posse are heading to town to buy new spark plugs when royal handmaiden Padme informs them that the Queen ordered them to take Padme along because the Queen…I mean Padme…wants to hang out at the mall.

At the garage, they learn that the only vendor who stocks the right brand of spark plugs is Watto, a giant house fly with some sort of accent which members of all ethnic groups find offensive. Watto's slave, an angelic tyke who can see CGI people ("They're *everywhere!*") just happens to be young Anacin Skywalker! Yes, we get to meet Darth Vadar when he was just a 6-year-old Jiffy Lube attendant. I suppose it's true that great oaks from little saplings grow, but you'd think that they might have found one who was a little less wooden to play this role.

Young Ani immediately gets the hots for Padme, and tries to seduce her with lines like, "I'm a pilot, you know." While getting a crush on the babysitter is common enough, you'd think Lucas would be over that fantasy by now. Anyway, Ani invites Padme and company to his house, where he shows them the robot he's building—a robot called C3PO. (Yes, Darth Vadar built C3PO, but apparently nobody thought to mention it in the previous three movies.) Ani informs his guests that C3PO is a protocol droid he's constructing to help his mother, the slave. After all, while most slaves in the Old South dreaded a brutal whipping at the hands of the overseer, their biggest fear was making a faux pas at the embassy banquet.

When Mama Skywalker confides that little Anacin is the result of a virgin birth (yeah, *nobody's* mom ever had sex), Slo-Jinn has Ani's blood tested, and sure enough, his "midichlorian" count is off the chart! "Midichlorians," as we all learned in Biology 101, are microscopic symbionts present in the cells of all living creatures, which reveal to us the will of the Force. Aren't you glad Lucas explained this, so you could appreciate the true grandeur of his belief system? (In the next film, we will see Queen Amidala's own Force powers increase dramatically, since midichlorians are sexually transmitted.)

Meanwhile, Future-Emperor Palpitation sends his apprentice, Darth Maul (a highly skilled assassin with a weakness for the face-painting booth at the Lions Club fish fry) to kill Slo-Jinn and Obi-Wan. Palpitation and Maul represent the Synth Lords, who have vowed to destroy the Republic with German techno-pop.

Anacin volunteers to pilot his home-built pod racer in an upcoming event in order to raise money for the spark plugs. Pod Racing involves blasting through Zion National Park in a highly polluting hotrod, while drunken, disgruntled fans look up from their 32-ounce beers long enough to take pot shots at you. So basically, it's NASCAR. Anacin wins the race, and Slo-Jinn wins Ani in a side bet. He tells Mom that he's taking Ani to teach him the ways of the Jedi. She has his room rented before he's out the door.

After a brief run-in with Darth Maul, we arrive at planet ChorusGirl, home of the Republican Senate and the worst traffic since 5:30 PM on the Beltway. Queen Amidala wears a hat made of whole ox horns in honor of her appearance before this august assembly. But still no one will help her, so she and the Jedi head for Nanoo-Nanoo, where she seeks an audience with the ruler of the Dungans, a giant toad. When he asks her who she thinks she is, a skinny white girl like her wearing too much blush, she announces that she is Queen Amidala of the Nanoo-Nanoo. Then Padme jumps up and says that *she* is Queen Amidala of the Nanoo-Nanoo. It's like an extraterrestrial version of "To Tell the Truth." Anyway, one of the queens asks the Dungans to serve as cannon fodder and the King agrees, because he finds his people really annoying too, and hopes they'll get wiped out.

The Dungans fight the HobbyHorse Droid troops (which look like something you'd buy at Ikea and assemble yourself) by throwing water balloons at them. This works pretty well, but still you worry about the Dungans, fighting such an overwhelming army—until you realize that everybody on screen is a computer generated image, and you just don't care any more.

Slo-Jinn, Obi-Wan, the Queen, some other girl who might also be the Queen ("a long time ago, in a Parent Trap far, far away..."), and about four other people mount an attack on the castle. Since they couldn't get a babysitter, they bring Anacin along too. Slo-Jinn makes him hide in a fighter ship, because what safer place could there be for a 6-year-old?

Slo-Jinn and Darth Maul have a light saber duel, while the Force Tabernacle Choir hums inspiring chords in the background. Since Maul's saber lights up on both sides, he seems to have the advantage. This is confirmed when Jedi Master Slo-Jinn gets brutally kebobed.

Meanwhile, Anacin flies into space, gets through the Robot Control Satellite's impenetrable shield and blows it up from inside! And he accomplishes all this by accident! See, what you or I have always called "dumb luck" is really THE FORCE!

Back at the battle, all the robot troops immediately cease functioning (which is often the case when you buy stuff at Ikea).

Later, Obi-Wan tells Yoda that he wants to make Anacin his apprentice. Yoda, who is cheesed because Jar-Jar is infringing on his "irritating Muppet speech" franchise, tells Obi-Wan that there is grave danger is training the boy, but hey, don't let that stop you.

Then there's a big celebration, with a parade and confetti and stuff, and the Queen presents the Dungan Toad King with a glowing Hippety-Hop. To be continued...in a couple of years, when Anacin grows in ways of the Force, and into big-kids underwear.

Stage of grief: **Depression**. And if you haven't reached this stage before the movie begins, you can pretty much count on Jar-Jar to expedite the process. In fact, the rot of despair runs so deep through *The Phantom Menace* that the film-makers can't even be bothered to hire real actors half the time, and allow long stretches of their film to be hijacked by the Super Mario Brothers. And by the way, is it just us, or does *The Phantom Menace* sound like a film about a little troublemaker with red overalls and a cowlick who dies during a misfired prank, and comes back as a poltergeist to harass his neighbor, Mr. Wilson?

You may wonder how to identify those who are suffering from this stage of grief. One major symptom of depression is apathy, which is evident from that fact that Lucas doesn't seem to care enough to come up with even mildly convincing reasons for anything that happens, as one learns in this imaginary interview:

Mr. Lucas, how did the good guys win?

Um, Anakin accidentally destroyed the bad guys' satellite or something—whatever.

How come Anakin can do all this incredible stuff when he's only a second-grader?

Well, he has lots of…um, hypochondriac cells in his blood. Yeah, that's it.

And why does Naboo have an "elected" queen? And what kinds of idiots elect a goofy 16-year old wearing too much eye makeup as their ruler if they have a choice?

How the hell should I know! Just leave me alone! You think it was *my* idea to make this stupid sequel? I am so tired, so tired. You know, a long time ago, in a galaxy far, far away this might have meant something, but not anymore. My life is a lie. Yes, Jar-Jar does represent my self-loathing and my need to punish myself. Now will you please go away?

Well, clearly we've hit rock bottom, and there's nowhere to go but up. Or *is* there…?

Batman & Robin (1997)
Directed by Joel Schumacher
Written by Akiva Goldsman

Batman & Robin is the most homoerotic thing you are likely to see without actually taking in a screening of *Brothers Should Do It* at the Tomkat Theater on Santa Monica Boulevard. Not a criticism, mind you, we're just saying; it makes Frankie Goes to Hollywood look like the Oak Ridge Boys. It makes *Queer as Folk* look like a monster truck rally. Boy George would likely dismiss it as hopelessly fey.

Our movie begins with rapid shots of polyurethane codpieces and bun-hugging rubber bondage pants with built-in butt cracks. This sequence represents our heroes suiting up as they prepare for a grueling night spent righting wrongs, combating evil, and doing a bunch of amyl nitrate poppers in the parking lot behind the Pleasure Chest. Before climbing into the Batmobile (which now has a rotating disco ball behind the radiator), Batman (George Clooney) and Robin (Chris O'Donnell) pause to contemplate the rubber nipples attached to each other's costume.

Mr. Freeze (Arnold Schwarzenegger) has commandeered the Gotham Museum and is, well, freezing things, as he goes about stealing an enormous diamond. Batman and Robin arrive to foil his plan, and Arnold commands his minions to "Kill the heroes. Yes, kill them. Kill them. Yeah. Destroy everything." But he says it in such a bored, detached way, that he sounds less like a super villain ordering a massacre, and more like a gas station attendant giving a motorist directions to the Interstate. Nonetheless, the Caped Crusaders find themselves under attack by the Mighty Ducks, and suddenly—it's Batman on Ice! You half expect to see our two heroes get the living crap beaten out of them by a giant figure-skating Snoopy.

The sequence ends much as it began—stupidly. Batman hops into Arnold's tank, which morphs into the elevator from the end of *Willy Wonka and the Chocolate Factory*, and blasts through the skylight. With Batman trapped inside, and the capsule headed for space, Arnold jumps out into the night sky and turns into a butterfly. Apparently, Batman loved Mr. Freeze, so he set him free. Mr. Freeze doesn't come back, however, so evidently he was never Batman's to begin with. Anyway, it turns out Robin was clinging to the outside of the capsule, despite the ice and wind shear and G-forces. He frees Batman, and they both escape by kicking out the doors and using them to sky-surf 30,000 feet down to earth, in what some might call the ultimate use of extreme sports as an idiotic *deus ex machina*, but which I prefer to think of as a pretty nice Mountain Dew ad.

Meanwhile, botanist Uma Thurman is attempting to crossbreed a rattlesnake with an orchid, while geneticist John Glover is attempting to splice an Australian skinhead with a Mexican wrestler. John catches Uma peeping on his experiment, and dumps so much acid on her that it eats a hole through the floor, and straight down through the crust of the earth, although the effect on Uma seems to consist largely of tightening her pores and giving her a henna rinse.

Cut to the Bat Cave, where George narrates home movies of Mr. Freeze's origin. It basically involves Arnold falling into some ice water, causing the viewer to reflect that Bedford Falls narrowly escaped being plagued by a super villain when Harry Bailey fell through the ice in *It's a Wonderful Life*.

Anyway, it turns out that Arnold, who requires sub-zero temperatures to survive, needs diamonds because he uses lasers to keep his costume cold. Got that? Or should we just move on?

Let's move on. Alfred, who has been with Batman since the first movie in 1989, can't stand what the franchise is turning into, and starts pretending to die. Meanwhile, Uma pops out of the acid-eaten hole in the ground. She's now got bright red hair, vines wrapped around her arms, and a campy delivery, having mutated into a combination of Bette Midler and Swamp Thing. Oh, and her lips are poisonous (especially when she uses them to speak dialogue.)

Cut back to Arnold, who plans to hold Gotham City for billions in ransom. But the truly evil part of his scheme involves wearing fuzzy slippers like your grandma, and making his henchmen watch a lousy Rankin-Bass animated holiday special. Then he pays a tender visit to his beloved wife, whom he keeps in an aquarium.

Back at Wayne Manor, Alicia Silverstone appears on the doorstep. She's Alfred's niece, and is freshly arrived from an English boarding school, judging by her knee socks, pleated skirt, starched white blouse, and charcoal blazer. Or perhaps she'd just appeared in a Japanese porn video.

Later, Batman and Robin act as celebrity sponsors for a slave auction. Uma, now billing herself as Poison Ivy, shows up in a gorilla costume covered with shiny pink acrylic fur, making her look like the toilet seat cover in Mary Kay's bathroom. Then she strips down, and the crowd instantly finds her irresistible, because she's dressed in a provocative costume like the Jolly Green Giant's mascot, Sprout. Oh, and also because she drugged everybody to like her.

The Dynamic Duo are both trying to hump her when Arnold arrives to steal some more diamonds. Uma tries her pheromone drug on him, but since Arnold is completely blue, including his balls, he's gotten used to the sensation, and doesn't fall for her.

Meanwhile, Alicia is coping with the grief over her parents' death in an auto accident by engaging in unsanctioned motocross events. "I guess all the speed and danger help take me out of myself," she tells Chris. If only it would take her out of this movie.

But with all the money she's won racing, Alicia plans to whisk Alfred away from his "life of dismal servitude" and free him from the "master-servant" relationship in which he's trapped. At last, Chris realizes her true identity: She's Emma Goldman Girl!

Mr. Freeze and Poison Ivy now team up to inflict tedium on the audience, with Arnold vowing to blanket the city in endless winter. "First Gotham," he shouts, "And then the world!" Which is not generally a phrase I enjoy hearing out of the mouth of an archconservative with a heavy Austrian accent. Anyway, after mankind has been turned into Otter Pops, Uma plans to populate the Earth with her genetically spliced reptilian plants, which resemble a sort of Goth Kukla.

Meanwhile, Alfred is dying of the same disease that killed Arnold's wife, so he programs his "brain algorithms" into the Bat Computer, and becomes Alfred Headroom. He also creates some fetish gear for Alicia, so we get to watch the whole crotch/ass/nipple suiting-up sequence again.

Robin tracks Poison Ivy to Busch Gardens, where she kisses him with her poisoned lips, but Robin foils her with the use of a dental dam he borrowed from Lesbo Lass. Unfortunately, he then falls in Uma's koi pond and gets his ass kicked by the little bubbling diver. Batman arrives to save him, but is immediately attacked by the man-eating vine from *The Addams Family*. Then Alicia (now Bat Girl) crashes through the skylight, and she and Uma trade savage blows while engaging in a spirited exchange of ideas about Naomi Wolf's "The Beauty Myth," and the early works of Germaine Greer. Finally, Alicia's stunt double puts us out of our misery by kicking Uma's stunt double into the maw of Audrey II, the giant plant from *Little Shop of Horrors*.

Arnold freezes the city, but Batman pulls some rock salt out of his utility belt, and that's pretty much that. Oh, and it turns out Arnold had a couple test tubes in his sleeve full of some blue liquid (Vanish, I think, or maybe 2000 Flushes) which cures Alfred, thus foiling his escape from the franchise. The end.

Stage of grief: *Acceptance.* At last, we have achieved closure. Feels good, doesn't it? After a long struggle, the psychological and emotional issues are finally resolved as the affected person puts on bun-hugging bondage pants and rubber nipples and says, Hey, This is Who I Am.

Our hypothetical filmmaker understands that Bob—the original film—is dead, and he no longer feels compelled to take Bob's body parts to the baseball game with him. He is released from the grim burden of loss, and is now free to make movies that have nothing to do with Bob. He can finally accept the Biblical advice of "Let the dead bury their dead," and start a fresh new project: maybe another remake of *Night of the Living Dead*.

What I Did for Love

We all want love. But are we truly ready for the sacrifices love demands? Because while you might think that meeting your soul mate and falling into a blissful romance with him or her will be an effortless, magical thing, nothing could farther from the truth. Actually, capturing someone's fancy, forging a relationship with him or her, and then forcing this person to love you is damned hard work, much like winning the presidency. And just like becoming president, your campaign will require that you tell people what they want to hear, pretend to care about their interests, lie about your past, and engineer ballot fraud in Florida—so you'd better start now if you want a date for New Years Eve.

The bookstands are full of self-help tomes that promise to make you so irresistible to the opposite sex that your face will launch a thousand ships and burn the topless towers of Ilium (note: the publishers deny all liability for any burnt towers). Likewise, the subject of attracting and winning a mate is a staple in mass-market magazines. For instance, a recent issue of *Glamour* presents an article entitled "Capturing His Heart: the Same 22 Sexy Secrets We've Featured Every Month for the Past 5 Years." *Cosmo* suggests "Win His Love Through Sluttiness." And *Maxim* submits "Bunches o' Bouncing Boobs." So, obviously the theme of love, the eternal quest to achieve that ineffable union of the physical and the spiritual is very popular, except with men, who just want to see breasts.

But we suggest that the best source of information on how to make someone love you is Hollywood movies. After all, what other segment of society has a better track record at achieving real, lasting, once-in-a-lifetime love than movie stars? And who accomplishes it more frequently? Also, who would know more about the kind of lies that love is based on than moviemakers?

We'll be examining several recent films for tips on navigating the terra incognita of *amour*. Our first movie shows what to do if you're an aging, duplicitous lothario involved with a moribund imp.

Autumn in New York (2000)
Directed by Joan Chen
Written by Allison Burnett

Suggested tagline: "It's 'Lolita' meets 'Camille' in the feel-bad hit of the summer!"

Our movie begins with the gray-haired Richard Gere flirting with pregnant women in Central Park. Clearly Richard is a womanizer who must be taught a lesson—so God decides to make him fall in love with Winona Ryder. Yeah, it seems kind of harsh to us too, but remember what He did to the Cities of the Plain for roughly the same offense.

Richard is a successful restaurateur who has just been named "Sexiest Man Alive" by *The Journal of Industrial Food Service* when he is introduced to Winona by her grandmother. Richard used to date Winona's mother, and Grannie thinks it would make a nice tradition to pass him down through the generations. According to Grandma, Winona is a talented hat maker, and in fact designed the chapeaux that everyone at her table is wearing. Since they look like those pipe cleaner spiders that you made in grade school for Halloween, we begin to suspect that what's so special about Winona is that she attends Special Ed.

Richard asks Winona to design a hat for his date to wear to the big charity ball. When she delivers it, he tells her his date cancelled and she'll have to go with him (because there's nobody else over the age of eight who would be caught dead wearing the Deely-Bopper antenna thing she made as a headpiece). She giggles, stammers, hiccups, and then accepts, telling him that he's not too old for her because she "collects antiques." You can smack her if you want to.

Richard pulls out a dress for her to wear—it's a low-cut, form-fitting sheath with a shawl made of Slinkies; he obviously knows her tastes. Instead of thinking this is creepy, she is charmed and scrunches up her face for a kiss. When he doesn't oblige, she looks into the distance and remarks, "I can smell the rain. When did I learn to do that?" Probably while attending the school where she learned to make hats out of pipe cleaners.

The *Rainman* bit makes Richard hot, and they spend the night together. The next morning the commitment-phobic Richard tells her that there is no future to their relationship, but the wily Winona has the perfect riposte to that line—she says she's dying. Yes, it seems that she's suffering from a fatal movie condition that has no symptoms except for an occasional fainting spell and a lovely glow. (Although these are also the symptoms of "movie pregnancy", we are assured that Winona is afflicted with a chest tumor that will cause her demise within the year—maybe less if we're good, since she has decided to forego all treatment.) Now don't you feel bad for hitting her?

Winona and Richard realize that they are totally wrong for each other, but decide to have a romance anyway since she's dying and it's not like they'll have to spend a lot of time together. Which is a good thing, since Winona says adorable things like, "Your friends like me better than they like you." Then she steals his watch, telling him he can have it back when he forgets she has it. She is just so precious that we don't want her to suffer another minute—let's call Dr. Kevorkian!

Instead, Richard takes her to a costume party. She goes as her heroine, Emily Dickinson, so she can reuse her costume from *Little Women* and quote lines like "Love is a thing with feathers" at us. It's no wonder that while Winona is reading stories to the host's hapless children, Richard is on the roof having sex with the dead A.D.A. from "Law and Order."

But being sick has given Winona super powers, and when she puts her hand on Richard's heart she knows he slept with Claire Kincaid. Richard finally admits it, claiming he did it because "You're a kid and I'm a creep." We certainly can't argue with that.

Richard returns to his apartment, only to find it infested with cards inscribed with Emily Dickinson quotes ("This is the hour of lead" would be an apt description for this movie, except that it lasts way longer than an hour). Winona goes home and actually whimpers like a puppy. Grandma tries to cheer her up by telling her that Richard also broke her mother's heart. The parallels with the Woody Allen story are uncanny!

One day Winona enters her bedroom to find an unkempt bum in there. It's Richard, who has neglected his personal hygiene in an effort to convince Winona to take him back. "Could you let me love you? Please? Please? Please?" he entreats. Just as this kind of tireless wheedling finally persuaded your parents to let you have the illegal fireworks that blew your hand off, his whining causes Winona to relent and let him dote on her.

But now it's winter—and Winona isn't dead! This is clearly a violation of the Geneva Convention! The movie tries to mollify us by having Winona go ice-skating, suddenly remember she has a heart condition, and collapse into an adorable heap. Richard, who is evidently her legal guardian now, decides that she will have the experimental surgery that could save her life. Now he only has to find a doctor who saw *How to Make an American Quilt* and still thinks she should live.

Winona is mad when she finds out Richard tried to save her life behind her back. But Richard explains, "You don't want to die! You want to live!" She'd never thought of that before and agrees to the surgery, eloquently informing Richard that "I don't want to leave you. Ya know?" It's dialogue like this that demonstrates the screenwriter's literary aspirations. Ya know?

Then there are the tense hours of waiting while the surgeon does his stuff. He finally exits the operating room, his head bowed, his shoulders slumped. But he's just funning us, for it's good news—Winona finally died! Richard goes home, finds his watch, and lives happily ever after. The end.

So, what does this movie teach us about winning a man's heart? Oh, just oodles and boodles of stuff! (Sorry, all the Winona cuteness still hasn't worn off.) Anyway:

1. Know what type of guy you're looking for. Make a list of traits that appeal to you, such as intelligence, mutual interests, compatibility of temperaments, being born in the same century, etc. Then throw that list away and fall for someone completely wrong for you. If this person is a serial adulterer with bad personal hygiene who used to have frequent intercourse with your mother, so much the better!

2. Develop a special skill that will bring you fame and success, and will also impress guys with your creativity, talent, and sense of style. We suggest fabricating designer hats that make the wearer look like a Cootie, but you could also try gluing wagon wheel macaroni to a frozen orange juice can and spray-painting it gold, or you could make an ashtray out of clay—the beauty of this approach is that the ashtray can double as a Father's Day gift for your lover in case it turns out he slept with your mom *one too many times*.

3. Be winsome and adorable and as cute as a bug! Practice simpering at least 30 minutes a day.

4. Try employing The Rules. Don't talk to a man first, even if he might be your long-lost dad. Keep things light and fun—only have heart attacks in the cutest, most amusing ways. And above all, be unavailable. Don't see him as often as he wants, deny him your time and attention, and always leave him wanting more. The best way to do this is by dying.

These may seem like old-fashioned, perhaps manipulative guidelines, but if you follow them, we guarantee that you'll be the most popular girl at Forest Lawn. And isn't that what life is all about? For the answer to that question, we now present *Mary Shelley's Frankenstein*, a movie that shows how death not only enhances your allure, but also gives you a whole new range of dating options.

Mary Shelley's Frankenstein (1994)
Directed by Kenneth Branagh
Screenplay by Steph Lady and Frank Darabont, based on the novel by Mary Shelley

The Arctic Sea, 1794. Explorer Aidan Quinn is trying to find a short cut to India through the North Pole when the ship strikes an iceberg—it's *Mary Shelley's Titanic*. Then Kenneth Branagh stumbles across the ice and demands that Aidan and his men listen to a tale which will prove edifying to them. See, he's Victor…Frankenstein. The freezing explorers couldn't care less, but Ken's the director, so…

Geneva, 1773. Kenneth is a tot of 5, and his mother tells him he's the smartest, cutest, bestest boy in the whole world, which, unfortunately, he believes. Then Dad brings in an orphan girl whom Ken is to think of as his sister, meaning that he'll be sleeping with her in a couple of minutes.

Now we jump forward some years, to when Ken is a winsome lad of 35. Mom, who is now younger than Ken and pregnant, tells him to quit being such a scientific genius and meet some girls—preferably ones he's not related to. Then lightening hits a tree, causing her to die in childbirth.

It's now three years later, and Ken is a strapping young man of 35. He visits Mom's grave and tells it, "Mother, you shouldn't have died. No one need *ever* die." He vows that he will stop death or your money back, and commences weird experiments with electric eels and wind-up toys.

Having finally graduated from high school at age 35, Ken is getting ready to depart for medical school. He is sad about leaving his adopted sister, Helena Bonham Carter, despite her Lyle Lovett hair. He asks her, "How do brothers and sisters say goodbye?" then shoves his tongue down her throat. Well, not usually like *that*.

Ingolstadt, 1793. His instructors tell Ken that there is no such thing as original or creative thought, a view that the middle-aged filmmaker takes to heart. Trying to think up a good project for the school science fair, he decides it would be funny to put John Cleese's brain in Robert De Niro's body, so he calls up Ed McMahon and Dick Clark, then starts stitching the supporting cast together.

Now Ken is ready to create life. He removes his shirt (presumably so his patchwork creation can better appreciate his washboard abs). He puts the body into a copper vat full of amniotic fluid (collected from contented pregnant women). He powers up the pinwheels and jumper cables, and then tells the creature to LIVE! The Creature pounds on the vat, spilling amniotic fluid all over the place. It makes a big mess, and Ken decides that he really doesn't want the responsibility of a Creature (sure, reanimating the dead sounds fun, but you have to feed them, clean up after them, and walk them every day).

The Creature turns to crime when rejected by society in *Mary Shelley's Scarface*. After getting beaten up for stealing bread in *Mary Shelley's Les Miserables*, he heads out to the country and lives with the pigs in *Mary Shelley's Babe*. He spies on the nice family that owns the farm, learning to read by repeating with the young daughter "Frr-enn-dddz. Friends." (The Creature is living in a pigsty, so his taste in sit-coms is only to be expected.) Now Creatch can read Ken's journal, discovering that Ken considered him an abomination and not that good in *Mad Dog and Glory*. Creatch is furious, and vows "I will have my revenge!"

The Creature walks to Geneva, strangles Ken's kid brother, and frames Justine, Ken's childhood friend. He also writes some bad reviews of Ken's "Hamlet" for the *NY Times*. The torch-carrying villagers, upset that they don't get to chase any monsters in this version of the story, lynch Justine.

The Creature chides Ken for being a really bad creator, but he offers him a way to make it up to him: build him a friend. A female friend. With really big scars. Ken has mixed emotions about this: how quick kids grow up these days. But he figures two creatures can live as cheaply as one, so what the hell.

Ken returns home and unpacks the monster-making equipment. Creatch, poking around the lab, finds Justine's body and demands *her* as his reanimated bride. Ken refuses, because while he was willing to give the Creature a cadaver to sleep with, he draws the line at close, personal corpses. Creatch is incensed and declares, "If you deny me my wedding night, I will be with you on yours." This bothers Ken, because while he is open to the idea of a threesome, he kinda hoped that Helena would be the one bringing a friend.

But it seems he will have no wedding night, since Helena is leaving him. He begs her not to go, and he looks so cute in his tight knee-britches and puffy shirt that she says he can tell her tomorrow about this horrible evil that he's unleashed on the world. They begin to undress, and Helena murmurs "Brother and sister no more." He replies, "Now husband and wife." Well, actually they are both, as required by West Virginia State Law. Anyway, Ken takes off his shirt and unlaces her corset, then unlaces *his* corset. Then, to the accompaniment of swelling violins, we watch *Mary Shelley's Cinemax After Dark*.

But before Ken can get to the good stuff, the monster alarms go off and Victor runs outside to put out fresh Creaturebane. Helena sulks and returns to bed, only to spot something evil in the room. It's...Emma Thompson! No, actually it's the Creature. He admires her beauty and gently pats her cheek, and it looks like the honeymoon won't be a total loss for Helena after all—until he rips her heart out of her chest. Creatch offers it to Ken, but it's not exactly the kind of Valentine's gift that he was hoping for.

Ken runs to the lab with his dead sister/wife, lops off Helena's head, and sews it to Justine's body, which is still conveniently there in the corner. He puts the hybrid in the vat, turns on the electric eels, and screams "LIVE!!!"

Ken dresses his bald, scarred, creation in a wedding gown, pleased to note that the new body has bigger boobs. The Creature shows up, sees the bride, and it's love at first sight, since her scars compliment his. He grabs her by the arm and tries to make her come with him. Ken is unwilling to lose her to a combination platter of body parts, and pulls her by the other arm. Since those arms were just sewn on a couple of minutes ago, the poor girl is naturally distressed, and sets herself on fire to protest the men's insensitivity to the Vietnam War.

Back on the iceberg, Ken concludes his story and dies. Strangely enough, his audience is still there. They wake up to see Creatch sitting by Ken's body, weeping his eyes out. "He was my father!" the thing exclaims, hoping to get on Rikki Lake. Aiden, irked that he used to star in movies and now only gets booked into framing devices, burns up both Ken and De Niro. The End.

From this movie we can learn a lot about finding love, losing love, and how to keep love alive by putting its head on a body with a better rack.

First, Mary Shelley teaches us that if you are looking for a date, instead of hanging out at the single's bar or under the corner lamp post, you might want to look for eligible partners a little closer to home, like among your coworkers or classmates. Or better yet, actually *at* home, amongst members of your immediate family!

Dating family members can make life a lot easier by eliminating the need to learn new phone numbers, addresses, or names. And they're so conveniently located! Plus, there's none of the awkwardness that comes with trying to make small talk with strangers. You and your family already have a whole life-time of experiences to discuss, so instead of prattling inanely about the weather, you and Mom can relive that time when she made you try the broccoli salad at Olive Garden and you threw up, or the day that she got high on cold pills and put the cat in the dish washer. Now doesn't that sound like a welcome change from the stiffness and strain of the typical first date? And since you regularly read Sissy's diary, you can be pretty confident that she's telling you the truth when it comes time for that chat about sexual histories.

But *Mary Shelley's Frankenstein* took place in the distant past (circa 1793, back when Kenneth Branagh was just 35 or so), and relationships have changed a lot in the intervening centuries. Back then, the man was supposed to wear cleavage-revealing ruffled silk shirts and tight-fitting capri pants, while the woman was supposed to be his sister. Nowadays, society believes that it's okay for the woman to wear the sexy clothes, have the big hair, and get the PMS, while the man is now free to cower without shame. So, let's review the 1998 primer on politically correct relationships, *The Chosen One: Legend of the Raven* and see if we can learn a little something about what broke up the Carmen Electra/Dennis Rodman marriage.

The Chosen One: Legend of the Raven (1998)
Directed by: Lawrence Lanoff
Written by: Sam Rappaport and Khara Bromiley

This movie is a veritable melting pot of plagiarism—from the title, which sounds like a rare collaboration between Chaim Potok and Edgar Allen Poe, to the star, Carmen Electra, who sounds like a Bizet opera of a Eugene O'Neill play. Get ready to spend the next 87 minutes of your life squinting into a Déjà Vu-master.

This rip-off of *The Crow* starts with a rip-off of *Star Wars*, as a block of scrolling text entitled "Episode One: Renewed Hope" informs us that "Good" (embodied by big-breasted women with pubic hair sculpted like topiary) will do battle with "Evil" (represented by the statutes against copyright infringement).

Playboy Playmate Shauna Sand is digging up an ancient tribal talisman that will endow her with superhuman powers. True to the legend, the necklace grants Shauna the highly photogenic ability to counter-rotate her breasts while running; but before she can use her new power to fight crime, she's killed by an evil redneck named Cole.

Shauna's death forces her estranged sister Carmen Electra to return to their ancestral home, Knott's Berry Farm. She immediately picks a fight with her wizened Native American dad, Popi, and is reunited with her true love, a Sheriff's Deputy who makes Barney Fife look like Buford Pusser.

Popi presents Carmen with the super-powered tribal necklace. Shauna's ghost appears, dressed in gravity-defying post-mortem lingerie from the Victoria's Sepulchre collection, and announces that Carmen has been chosen to combat evil.

Her first act as a mystical, crime-fighting superheroine is to wash the dishes with her tongue. But this is only the beginning of her metamorphosis. The necklace has endowed Carmen with the power to make her hair really poofy, which she uses to lure Barney into a sex scene with her body double.

Meanwhile, Cole, the redneck who killed Shauna is holed up in a shack with two other mentally challenged crackers. They've got a big ol' still and, like most gun-toting hillbillies, are using it to make Windex. Hopped up on cleaning fluid, Cole takes a personal inventory and resolves to reconcile with his former lover Nora, the current trailer mate of Deputy Fife. When Barney objects, Nora beats him up and leaves him bleeding and dazed on the ground. Then Cole urinates on him, which excites Nora so much that she and Cole have implied sex in a pickup truck.

They dump Barney in Carmen's yard, after first taking him to the face-painting booth at the Iowa State Fair and getting him airbrushed like a raccoon. Shauna, the Victoria's Shroud model, shows up to remind Carmen that "you have the *power*," which inspires Carmen to wave her hands and make Barney's face paint disappear. So, apparently, the talisman has also endowed her with the power of cold cream.

Popi starts doing voiceovers, and informs us that Carmen's "powers were growing faster than her understanding." But then, so were her toenails.

Meanwhile, the Windex bootleggers are shooting trees, when Carmen suddenly shows up and takes a bullet in the arm (thereby demonstrating her power to attract gunfire).

She runs away, and the rednecks chase her into a night scene as Carmen reveals her awesome power of Bad Continuity. The Chosen One flails ineffectually at her tormentors with a shovel until they shoot her, thereby demonstrating her power to die stupidly. Then Cole shoots and kills Nora, because he's too embarrassed to break up with her again.

Later that night, the two women are raised from the dead by the power of Carmen's accessories. Nora has turned into The Wolf, a creature whose evil lupine nature is betrayed by her predatory bloodlust, and her tendency to curl up on the rug and lick her own genitals.

Finally, Carmen dons her superheroine costume: a silver lamé jumpsuit with see-through knee-high boots. Her ensemble is topped off by a stainless steel catcher's mask with vertical blades that curve far enough past her chin that the first time she looks down, she'll give herself a tracheotomy. This creates an almost unbearable air of tension, as the viewer waits for Carmen's enemies to cry out, "Hey, your shoe's untied!"

The Wolf arrives in *her* costume (which, in keeping with the plot, is assembled from other peoples' cast-offs: Elvira's dress, Audrey Hepburn's cocktail gloves from *Breakfast at Tiffany's*, and Clayton Moore's Lone Ranger mask).

Carmen begins the explosive climax by walking into a western saloon and uttering her now-famous battle-cry, "Hello, Scumbag!" This inspires The Wolf to promptly kick her ass. Fortunately, Barney arrives in the nick of time to save her. He bursts through the door, cocks his shotgun, and declares, "It's over!" Then somebody shoots him and he falls down.

Popi pops back up to tell us that Carmen must call upon "her most formidable power—the power to transform time and space." She uses it to transport herself and her nemesis to the set of a Warrant video, where the two of them have a fierce nipple-jutting contest. (Carmen wins by a millimeter.)

Carmen is now The Raven, The Chosen One, and asks Deputy Fife to join her in her crusade against evil. As they drive into the sunset, they consider new sidekick names for him. Pigeon Boy, perhaps? Maybe The Bleeder. How about Easily Maimed Man…?

So, *The Chosen One: Legend of the Raven*. A perfect example of the old story formula: "Boy meets girl; Girl fights girl; Boy whimpers in the corner."

As this movie demonstrates, ancient sexist stereotypes are no longer appropriate in today's modern world. It's now acceptable for the woman to get into drunken bar fights with lowlife lingerie models, while it's fine for the man to break his heel and fall down. However, it's *not* acceptable for him to borrow your new dress without asking, since he'll inevitably bleed on it, smear face paint on it, or get urinated on while wearing it. Now, here are a few more tips on how you can cast off the chains of traditional romance and turn your relationship into a progressive 21st-century union of equals:

1.   Decide on a gender-neutral term to use when referring to each other. Good examples include "life partner" and "significant other." Also, to assist in pair bonding, come up with gender-neutral superhero names for each other. For *your* dynamic duo, avoid sexist appellations like "Batman" and "Catwoman," or "Boob Babe" and "Power Penis." Instead, follow our movie role models and choose more enlightened titles like "The Raven" and "The Lemming"; or "The Falcon" and "The Snowperson." Or how about "Consumer Advo-

cate" and "Director of Homeland Security"? (Although "Thigh Master" and "Buns of Steel" are sexier, while being equally non-sexist.)

2. Don't try to make your partner conform to traditional gender roles. Men should be able to cry when they feel sad, giggle when they're feeling silly, and pout after they get beat up by the Wal-Mart greeter. And women should feel free to act assertively, use strong language like "scumbag," and get into knockdown, drag-out fights while wearing skimpy outfits that make their breasts poke out.

3. Avoid gendered terminology like "henpecked," "nancy boy," "lacks balls," and "girly man," even when talking about Barney, the hero of this movie.

4. Take turns paying for things like meals, movies, and hookers. And whoever uses the last of the Aqua Net should buy some more.

5. Make sure any sexual acts are performed only with the explicit consent of both partners. Cole should have asked Barney if it was okay before he urinated on him.

We hope this discussion has helped you think of ways to increase the political correctitude of your own relationship, and has convinced you to never make another movie starring a *Baywatch* chick.

But what if you don't have any supernatural powers, but only the power of…Music. And pretty bad music, at that. Well, our next movie shows how women can empower themselves through lip-synching, semi-naked clogging and public sex. So, be prepared to do it for yourselves, sisters, (with the help of a hunky boyfriend, of course), because it's time to get Coyote Uglified.

Coyote Ugly (2000)
Directed by David McNally
Written by Gina Wendkos

Coyote Ugly, the latest in Disney's true-life nature movies, is the story of a homely feral pup that wanders into the big city and, after a series of comic misadventures, develops self-esteem through raunchy dancing.

Okay, actually it's a PG-13 *Showgirls*, combined with a jigger of *Cocktail*, and a splash of that "making their dreams come true" line from the *Laverne and Shir-*

ley theme song thrown in for unredeeming social value. But we think the other one would have made for a better movie.

Anyway, shy, naïve, limp-haired Piper Perabo's dream is to be a famous songwriter. So she leaves New Jersey to settle in a dirty, squalid apartment in New York, and prepare to become the new Jewel (one of them apparently not being enough to usher in the End of Days). When her neighbors complain about her music (basically songs that Neil Sedaka would reject for being too bland) she goes up on the roof to finger her Playskool keyboard and lip-synch to LeAnne Rimes. You see, Piper is the victim of paralyzing stage fright (sadly for us, though, she doesn't appear to be spooked by Panavision equipment).

Piper takes copies of her songs to all the major music labels, which inform her that they don't accept unsolicited demo tapes from unknown songwriters with bodiless hair. She even tries MCA, saying "I just want to leave this for Whitney or Mariah." But surprisingly enough, it seems that even Whitney and Mariah have standards, and they too reject her. Then she goes home to discover she was robbed! It appears that the whole universe is trying to make her abandon her dream of being a songwriter. Having heard her songs, we gotta side with the universe here.

The despairing Piper mopes on over to the corner diner where the kindly counter guy gives her a free burger because she's down on her luck. In the middle of wolfing down her McLoser With Cheese, she sees three beautiful women flaunting their tattoos, licking catsup off their faces, and waving around big wads of cash.

"Are they hookers?" Piper asks the counter attendant.

They wish! No, it seems they only are bartenders/sleazy dancers in a fake redneck bar called Coyote Ugly. But everybody has to start somewhere.

When Piper overhears that Tyra Banks is leaving the Coyote business to go to law school (apparently brain surgery school and nuclear physics school had already filled their supermodel quota), Piper heads over to the bar to apply for a job.

Lil, the owner, is a tough, brassy blonde (with a heart of gold, as required by movie law). Lil thinks Piper is a stupid hick, but hires her because "The average male is walking around with a toddler inside his pants." Um, okay.

When Piper reports to work, the other girls are clog dancing on the bar. Lil rips Piper's T-shirt (producer Jerry Bruckheimer must have had some leftover *Flashdance* costumes he needed to use up*)*, then introduces her to her coworkers: Rachel, a hot-headed, bitchy Hooters girl, and Cammie, a dumb, flirty, Eastern European Hooters girl. But when Piper refuses to hop on the bar and do a bump-

and-grind routine to "The Devil Went Down to Georgia" (and can you blame her?), Lil fires her. However, Piper breaks up a fight by giving the combatants money for drinks (because nothing soothes belligerent drunks like more alcohol), so she gets another chance to wear trampy outfits and do Karaoke on bars for boozy louts. Is this a great country or what? (Since the focus of the movie seems to be our heroine's valiant attempts to make the erectile tissues of clamorous, sodden barflies stiffen with longing, we suggest as an alternate title for the movie, *Piper Picks a Peck O' Pickled Peters.*)

To make up for how mean it was to her before, the universe gives Piper a nice boyfriend to go along with her success as a Coyote. He's an Australian fish gutter who has a dream too—to make it on his own while keeping his dignity. Alas, his chance at realizing *his* dream died when he appeared in this movie. Oh, and Piper suddenly gets full, thick hair, indicating that the secret to bouffant styling is getting sprayed with beer a lot, and bouncing up and down on a bar.

To help overcome her stage fright, Aussie Boy sets up cardboard cutouts of Marilyn Monroe, Abe Lincoln, and JFK on Piper's rooftop, and then makes PG-rated love to her in front of them. Aussie reasons that even if Piper never makes it as a singer, she will now be able to star in live sex shows without self-consciousness.

But then the universe decides that it has been too easy on a girl with a body double, dance double, and singing double, and so Piper's dad disowns her, she gets fired from the bar again, and she spots her boyfriend letting another woman into his apartment. However, God steps in at this point because He thinks Piper is cute as a button, even if she *can't* really dance, sing, or act. He makes sure her dad forgives her, a club owner loves her tape, and Aussie Boy was only showing his place to a potential renter. This happy turn of events demonstrates that you should always hold onto your dreams, even if they are incredibly unrealistic and puerile.

Now it's time for Piper's big singing debut at the club. But as soon as Piper gets on stage, she freezes. Fortunately, she spots Aussie Boyfriend in the audience and remembers having sex in front of Abe Lincoln, and that gives her the confidence to sing. She also struts, gyrates, and shakes her stuff, which can't be easy in her skin tight-leather pants and sequined bra top. And the crowd goes wild! They think she's Britney Spears, of course, but they still like her.

While Piper sings her song we flash forward three months, and now LeAnne Rimes is singing Piper's song. Strangely enough, the two singers sound exactly the same! Aussie asks Piper, "What do you do when you realize that all your dreams have come true?" "Commit suicide," is the correct response, but Aussie Boy doesn't come up with it, showing that he *is* the weakest link. The End.

Most psychologists agree that before you can have a healthy relationship with somebody else, you have to feel good about yourself. Piper developed confidence and became an exhibitionist through erotic square dancing, but maybe this isn't the route to self-actualization that is right for you. Here are some other tips on boosting your self-esteem.

1. Take stock of your strengths, since believing that you are good at a few things will help you feel worthwhile. Even though you may not be cute, young, thin, perky, and a world-class Coyote like Piper, at least you can usually resist the urge to rut in front of two-dimensional representations of assassinated presidents. (And while we're on the subject, why did Aussie Boy insist on doing the nasty for the benefit of only *two* of our martyred chief executives? Does this antipodean fishmonger think he's too *good* to simulate intercourse in front of James Garfield and William McKinley? I think *not*.)

2. Reflect honestly on your weaknesses, then come up with specific things you can do to overcome them. For example, Piper suffered from the heartbreak of limp hair. Instead of succumbing to despair, she thought up ways to combat her disability. She considered getting a hair transplant, joining the Sikh faith so she could always wear a turban, and moving to Mars where the weaker gravity would give her hair more bounce. Finally, she hit on reading the instructions on the shampoo bottle, where she learned and mastered the concept of "rinse." Perhaps some similar scripture holds the secret of fulfillment for you: *The Celestine Prophecy*, Kahlil Gibran's *The Prophet* or the label on a bottle of *Gee, Your Hair Smells Prophetic*.

3. Reduce your fear of failure by imagining the worst possible outcome, as this will reassure you that you can cope with whatever happens. For instance, picture your big singing debut. You're at a club, up on stage, ready to present your tunes to the world. All your family, friends, and coworkers are there. And then you get stage fright and can't sing a note. You sit there in the spotlight, frozen in fear. Everybody boos you and calls you names. The management refuses to give refunds, and a big riot ensues. Several people are killed in the fighting. While the Army is busy trying to restore order, aliens from outer space launch a secret attack and take over the Earth. The human race

becomes Kennel Rations for the Rigelians. And it's all your fault, because you got scared and didn't sing your damn songs. Feel better?

Now that you're self-confident, self-assured, and self-cleaning, you're ready for a relationship. "Yes," we hear you say, "I do love myself now, but how do I get other people to?" And we answer, "What kind of an illiterate moron ends a sentence with a preposition?"

Ha ha. Just messing with your self-esteem. Here, in fact, are some genuine pointers on how to make men fall in love with you, all from noted psychologists, trusted relationship experts, and *Coyote Ugly*:

1. Meet an eligible man through divine intervention. Once you've achieved this…

2. Ask the man about his job. Your interest in his work will flatter him, and he'll think you're a great conversationalist. Plus, there are undoubtedly lots of things you don't know about fish gutting, so your dates will prove educational as well as enjoyable. And if you're the woman who volunteers to spend a Saturday helping him scoop out halibut intestines, then you're the one he'll think seriously about marrying. Or, at least hiring as Assistant Gutter.

3. Have wild, kinky sex with him. As Lil so wisely said, "The average male is walking around with a toddler inside his pants." Meaning, of course, that most men like to keep bawling, untoilet-trained two-year-olds crammed down the crotch of their Dockers. (What, you thought it was a metaphor?)

In conclusion, movies can be a valuable educational resource, and should be consulted often if you want a happy and successful love life. And if you never do find anyone to love you, you can always develop rich, fulfilling imaginary relationships with movie characters or cardboard cutouts.

Deviled Ham
Torments of the Damned,
or Just Overacting?

The great religions have a tradition of enforcing their fiats with threats of post mortem reprisals. Unfortunately, it's difficult for many people to grasp the concept of eternal, unceasing torment, which makes it an inefficient behavior modification tool (even if it is one of the few training methods approved by PETA). Adding to this problem is the lack of any consistent architecture of Hell. Some consider it to be a vast lake of fire, where damned souls writhe and burn until the extinction of time itself. Others envision it as no worse than Alabama in July, where it's not the brimstone so much, it's the humidity. This problem is especially acute for artists who seek to map the netherworld; for in order to portray ultimate suffering, they must assault their audience, transgressing the limits of taste and tolerance. We see this in the paintings of Hieronymous Bosch, in Dante's "Inferno," and in the performance stylings of Howie Mandell. (Who, as of this writing, has grown a goatee, shaved his head, and now bears a startling resemblance to Anton La Vey, founder of the Church of Satan. Coincidence? We think not.)

But how has Hollywood, which for much of its history was under the censorious heel of the Hays Office, dealt with depictions of eternal damnation? By and large, through overacting.

It's no mere happenstance that Satan is often portrayed as a cloven-footed beast, nor that the Jewish and Muslim traditions forbid the consumption of pork, for ham is a powerful symbol of evil. Watch William Shatner's performance in *The Devil's Rain*, and tell us you don't feel the hot, bacon-scented breath of Satan on the back of your neck. Observe Frank Langella's climactic scene in *The Ninth Gate*, and see if you can't smell the pure pork sausage of perdition, frying on the brimstone-fired stoves of Hell itself. And even if the thought of unending darkness and limitless pain is beyond your ken, 100 minutes of Casper Van Dien in *The Omega Code* will make the punishments of a burning underworld all too real.

So Abandon All Hope, Ye Who Enter Here, and keep your hands and arms inside the car at all times. There's some bad, *bad* actin' ahead.

The Devil's Rain (1975)
Directed by Robert Fuest
Written by James Ashton, Gabe Essoe, and Gerald Hopman

It is a dark and stormy night. Ida Lupino is worried about her husband—and she has cause, because when he shows up, he's missing his eyes. Mr. Ida tells son William Shatner to take "The Book" to Ernest Borgnine, then melts into a pile of goop—a thing which apparently happens all the time, since neither Ida nor Shatner are much impressed by it.

Next morning, Shatner rides out into the California desert until he reaches Satan's Subdivision (which, though it reeks of unholy corruption, is convenient to schools and shopping). He and Borgnine exchange fraught dialogue until it's apparent they are equally matched in the overacting department, so they agree to a Faith showdown. As they enter the New England-style white clapboard chapel where the duel is to take place, we notice that the whole congregation is wearing black robes ornamented with Hello Kitty insignias—and they don't have any eyes! Apparently, Borgnine's entire following consists of a Braille Academy graduating class that he recruited in mid-commencement.

Borgnine and Shatner each offer prayers to the deities of their choice, and then Shatner shoots a bunch of parishioners. This is not only improper behavior in a house of worship, but the judges rule that it constitutes illegal use of a foreign object, so Ernest gets his soul.

Meanwhile, over in Hooterville, Shatner's brother Tom Skerritt and Tom's vacant wife Julie are playing the Kreskin Home Game with Eddie Albert. Just then, Tom receives word that his family is missing and presumed damned. Tom and Julie head over to the Satanic Suburbs, where up-and-coming cult member John Travolta (who is listed in the credits as "Danny, the Littlest Satanist") roughs them up. Julie then has a flashback to their previous lives in Colonial Salem. It seems they sold their souls to Satan (through his licensed representative, Ernest Borgnine) in exchange for acting careers. However, the good times ended when Shatner's wife stole Borgnine's book of names and ratted everybody out to the HUAC, which burned them at the stake.

The Satanists are impressed by Julie's uncanny ability to provide exposition, and they kidnap her. A shaken Tom seeks help from Eddie Albert (Arnold Ziffle, was busy). Eddie deduces that "The Book", which has been in Tom's family ever since the flashback, contains the signatures of those who sold their souls back in Salem. Eddie further explains that Satan won't accept delivery of the souls without proof of purchase, which explains why Ernest wants The Book so badly—it's the end of the quarter and he needs to get his expenses in.

Tom and Eddie explore the quaint Satanist chapel, discovering a manhole that leads directly to Hell. While browsing around the underworld, they pick up a lovely souvenir at The Ungodly Giftshop: Satan's Sno-Globe, a vessel containing the souls of Borgnine's followers. These unfortunates are continually subject to the Devil's Rain—which must be even ickier than golden showers, to hear the people in the paperweight moan and groan about it.

But while they were sno-globe shopping, Borgnine grabbed The Book, causing Ernest to hideously transform into the physical embodiment of Satan—which means that he puts on a white fright wig, a sheep's nose, and ram horns. Or maybe he suddenly became a spokesmodel for Dodge Trucks—the movie's a little vague on this point.

Tom puts on a Hello Kitty Satanic cap and gown and infiltrates the coven, but he blows his cover by objecting mildly to Borgnine's plan to sacrifice Julie (allowing John Travolta to deliver his only line in the movie, "Blasphemer! Blasphemer!"). Score so far: Evil 5, Good 0.

Suddenly, the filmmakers spring their horrible surprise: William Shatner is still in the movie! And now *he* has the sno-globe. Fortunately, he succumbs to Eddie's plea to break the cursed knick-knack, assured that this will free his soul (and everybody else's) from the devil's power. *Un*fortunately, this doesn't end the movie, it just causes it to rain—and, as it turns out, devil worshippers are highly water-soluble. So, everybody starts to get gooey and then to melt. For nearly ten minutes. What a world, what a world. While the copy on the video box promises "Absolutely the most incredible ending of any motion picture!" this sequence actually contains all the thrills of watching a carton of Neapolitan ice cream you've left out in the sun. But if you're lactose intolerant, you might feel vindicated by it.

Eventually the landscape is littered with sticky piles of pastel goo that used to be Borgnine and company, and Julie and Tom are free to go on with their lives, released from the curse that has hung over their family for centuries! At last, Good (represented by the star of *Green Acres*) has triumphed over Evil (embodied by the co-star of *Airwolf*), just as it was foretold in the Book of Revelations. The End.

So, what did we learn from this movie? Mainly that the disposition of one's immortal soul depends not upon good works, or mortal sin, but on whether Satan's middle managers turn in their paperwork on time.

We also learned the importance of keeping good records. IRS Publication 552, "Record Keeping for Individuals" makes the same point, albeit without William Shatner or John Travolta, so it's more entertaining. This pamphlet, written for Americans of all ages, asks thought-provoking questions, like "Why Keep Records?" and then provides faith-affirming, weirdly ungrammatical answers ("In addition to tax purposes, you may need to keep records for getting a loan").

IRS Publication 552 also deals with specific situations that may come up in the life of you, the taxpayer. For instance, if you are in the second-hand soul business, and somebody happens to steal your inventory, here is vital information about what records you need in order to file a tax write-off on those souls:

Casualty and Theft Losses of Souls

Before filing a deduction, you must complete form 666-EZ, indicating the amount you paid for each soul. (For intangible payments like "fame" and "power," provide a fair market estimate by checking comparables on eBay; the fair market value of "love" will be determined by whatever the women are willing to sell themselves for on the current version of "The Bachelor.")

To support your claim for a casualty loss, your records should show the type of mishap that destroyed the soul or souls (e.g., "water damage.")

Hint: keep a journal, making note of all the information you will need to file your IRS claim. For example, "Dear Diary, On June 2, 1975, I asked the satanic intern, John Travolta, to check on the souls that I keep in a sno-globe stored in a pit of hell. He said he couldn't find the sno-globe, as it had been stolen. Probably by blasphemers. Those souls were my property that I purchased in a flashback. Before I could get them back, they all melted, so they were a complete loss. (Well, the William Shatner soul had already been depreciated to worthlessness by those Priceline commercials, but the rest were pretty valuable.) I must remember to claim a loss on this year's income tax return, which I fully intend to file in January. Because, as we all know, it's intending to pay taxes that pave hell's roads."

And what else did this movie teach us? Principally, that while the Church of Satan is just a couple of weird guys and some eyeless people who meet Wednesday nights in the old Presbyterian chapel, they do have a cool gift shop where you can buy Hello Kitty ceremonial robes and Tupperware soul containers ("locks in damnedness"). We actually went to their web store (Satanshop.com), and admired their gargoyle planter, Baphomet Styrofoam beverage cooler (very useful for keeping your Coke cold…in HELL!), and satanic car accessories (because if the devil really does look like a Dodge logo, it only makes sense to put one on your truck). But we didn't dare order, for fear of getting on Lucifer's mailing list—and we didn't want to go through *that* again, after having to file a "cease and desist" order to get him to stop sending us all those AOL disks. So, instead we read our bible and discovered it contains a numerical code that tells you to drink more Ovaltine! And that's the plot of our next movie, made by the fine folks at the Trinity Broadcasting Network.

Omega Code (1999)
Directed by: Robert Marcarelli
Written by: Stephan Blinn and Hollis Barton

Tagline: "Not just a movie…It's a miracle!"

According to the opening title card of this miracle, "Scholars seek 'The Bible Code,' a mathematical phenomenon whose hidden messages are said to contain the whole of human history." Give or take the last two thousand years, that is. A few other title cards follow, but basically, the movie's premise is this: Like Playstation 2 games, the bible contains Easter eggs. Such as the "Key to Jerusalem," which brings ultimate power, for whosoever controls Jerusalem in the end days shall control the world, and get power-ups and extra ammo.

Our miracle opens in Jerusalem, where an elderly rabbi is doing some sort of Hebrew Junior Jumble. Suddenly, Michael Ironside shows up with the most unconvincing beard since Lisa Marie Presley, and shoots the old man. He swipes a CD-ROM, but his escape is hampered by Siegfried and Roy, who keep bi-locating around corners until it makes everybody nauseous.

Cut to an infomercial set, where Casper the Friendly van Dien (the poor man's Troy Donohue) has arrived to discuss the Bible Code. After introducing the spellbound audience to a revolutionary hair care regimen, he announces that the bible contains a secret crossword puzzle that foretells the future. Using advanced pink highlighter technology, Casper proves that the Torah predicted Hitler, the Kennedy assassinations, and Isaac Hayes' Oscar for *Shaft*. Then he explains that the murdered rabbi believed the Bible was actually a holographic computer program! And that his shoelaces were actually mind-reading earthworms that could control his feet!

Anyway, it seems we've been reading the Bible wrong all these years, since it's actually intended to be studied in three dimensions; which explains why the rabbi was wearing those paper glasses with the red and blue lenses.

Cut to Rome, where Michael York (the poor man's Simon McCorkindale) has just been appointed "Chairman of the European Union." Since the EU doesn't *have* a chairman, it's probably just something the Europeans told Michael so he'd go away. Meanwhile, the UN presents him with its highest humanitarian award, for single-handedly wiping out world hunger by inventing Pop-Tarts.

Back in LA, Casper's marriage is in trouble, because he's having "visions," bouts of ecstatic imagery that some might call "hallucinations," but others would call "lousy special effects."

Meanwhile, some Russians are using computer technology to decode the Bible, distilling it into a series of cryptic phrases, such as "Ten Horns Unite World Peace," "Houses of Isaac and Ishmael Torn in Terror," and "April: Best Time to Buy a Great Pants Suit."

The Russians blow up a papier-mâché model of the Dome of the Rock mosque, and Casper immediately rushes to Rome to help Michael revive the Roman empire, and to introduce Michael's new line of formal housecoats for men.

Meanwhile, one of the Russians wimps out and tries to warn Casper about…something, but he's gunned down by a unicycle-riding clown.

Michael takes over the world (but in a nice way) and rebuilds the Solomonic Temple. Casper's visions become clearer, and we begin to see that they're actually home videos of the Sacramento Jaycees Haunted House.

Tired of playing second banana, Ironside shoots and kills Michael, but Michael really needs the work, so he comes back to life. Meanwhile, afraid that the audience won't sufficiently recoil from Ironside just because he murdered a man in cold blood, the filmmakers suddenly decide that he's a homosexual, too! It doesn't turn out to have anything to do with the story, but they felt better saying it.

Michael calls the leaders of the world to his bedside, where Sam from "Quincy" wants to know what it was like to be dead. Apparently, Michael's answer goes over big, and the leaders appoint him King of the World, on the condition that he bring about a new Pax Romana, and doesn't make a crappy movie about the Titanic.

The angels Siegfried and Roy reappear, and present Casper with the Final Code. Meanwhile, Michael's coronation takes place inside the new Temple, which has been meticulously reconstructed, based on Old Testament accounts and archeological data, to resemble the ballroom of the Airport Holiday Inn in Burbank.

Michael is crowned King of the World, but when he declares himself god as well, there is a mighty uproar, and Siegfried and Roy must save all humanity by challenging Michael to a contest of overacting. They seem to have the upper hand, when they are suddenly shot dead by Ironside, who prefers a more understated performance style.

Casper is visited by some bad digital effects, which restore his faith, but nobody really cares. Meanwhile, Siegfried and Roy are raised from the dead, and promptly kill Ironside by giving him a bad case of hairballs.

Casper surrenders the Final Code to Michael in order to prevent further bloodshed, and another dull action sequence, and Michael enters it into the computer, thereby unlocking "the DNA of the Universe." This act produces a violent lightstorm, which causes Satan to trip, and fall out of Michael's body. The end.

So, The Omega Code. It helps lower your cholesterol and gives your hair a glossy sheen. No wait, that's omega-3 oil—the Omega Code is the scientific formula proven by Robert Vaughn to restore hair loss in men.

Anyway, this movie is a dramatization of what some people believe the last days of Planet Earth will be like—trouble in the Middle East, wars and plagues, dead Siegfried and Roys coming back to life, and evil Michael Yorks deceiving everybody into thinking the EU has a chairman. Coincidence? Read the book! That is, the Book of Revelation. As you know (and we're just trying to make you feel better by saying that, because we know that you spent your time in Sunday School sniggering at the story of the talking ass), there are several ways to interpret the prophecies in Revelation. This movie (and miracle) uses the futurist approach, which says that most of John's predictions will be fulfilled in the 3 1/2-year period starting…now! However, other groups interpret the book differently, and until God says, "Hey, I was just kidding; are you people stupid or what?" no one can say where the truth lies. But we think we have some pretty good guesses. So let us answer your biblical questions and we'll all go to hell together.

Q: Okay, who is the Beast of Revelation?

A: In our movie today, it was Michael York. But those who take a historical approach to Revelation say the Beast is the Roman Empire, or the emperor Domitian. Others have identified the Beast as Lenin, Hitler, or even Henry Kissinger.

Q: But who do *you* say it is?

A: Pauley Shore.

Q: Seriously?

A: No, we're just kidding you. Actually, it's Rob Schneider.

Q: What's with the 666?

A: It's the number of the Beast—probably his cell phone number, but if you call, you'll just get the voice mail of the Beast, since he's a busy guy.

Q: Is the Beast the same person at the antichrist?

A: The antichrist is believed by most Christians to be Satan himself, or any false prophet, or to be anything that takes us away from God, or to be found in the laughter of small children who won't be quiet while you're trying to sleep. But those who go in for vaguely Christian apocalyptic literature feel that the Antichrist is the offspring of the Devil (to mirror the Christian belief that Jesus is the Son of God). So, the antichrist is actually Tori Spelling.

Q: What exactly is the mark of the Beast? How does the VISA card relate to the mark of the beast? What is the role of computers in the final beast kingdom?

A: "The mark of the Beast" is the UN-mandated barcode that everyone will need to have on their hand or forehead to get PopTarts from Michael York in the final days. VISA cards with computer chips record everything you buy and do, and report on whether you've been naughty or nice—so actually, VISA is the mark of Santa, not Satan. And as we saw in the movie, computers play a very important role in the Final Beast Kingdom, and skilled computer operators are needed to input the universe's DNA. That's why we suggest you enroll in vocational school today, and get a degree in computer science, demonology, black magic, or gun repair.

Q: And who is the Whore of Babylon?

A: Paris Hilton.

And that brings us to our next movie, another apocalyptic story dealing with the personification of ultimate evil; it's also the shocking story of a fast food promotion gone horribly wrong.

The Ninth Gate (1999)
Directed by Roman Polanski
Written by John Brownjohn, Enrique Urbizu, and Polanski; based on the novel by Arturo Pérez-Reverte

Meet Johnny Depp, Rare Book Mercenary—a cross between Paladin, Indiana Jones, and Mrs. Gildersleeve who ran the Bookmobile in elementary school. Book collector Frank Langella wants Johnny to authenticate a volume he bought from the guy who killed himself before the opening credits. This tome, "The Nine Gates of the Kingdom of the Shadows," was published in 1666 (get it?), and led to the burning at the stake of one Aristide Torchia. It seems that Torquemada objected to Torchia co-authoring books with Satan, considering it blasphemy, since Satan's only sanctioned role in literature is as an agent.

But this does bring up the question of how they worked out the billing...Alphabetically? (By Beelzebub and Torchia.) Maybe it was "By Satan *with* Aristide Torchia" (after all, whose name on the cover is gonna sell more books?) Or maybe it was the standard celebrity kind of arrangement: "By Lucifer, Prince of Darkness, as Told to Aristide Torchia."

Anyway, there are only three copies of the book, and Frank wants Johnny to compare his to the other two, because the genuine article can summon up the devil.

Lena Olin, widow of the book's former owner, shows up at Johnny's place and asks to buy the book back. When Johnny refuses, she puts her hand on his crotch and her tongue down his throat. Johnny is puzzled—is she coming on to him? As she strips for action, we notice a tattoo of a snake on her butt. Since Johnny is dealing with occult disciples and satanic arcana, this is obviously a significant clue, and Johnny quickly deduces that she's a herpetologist.

When the book fails to turn up during sex, Lena pulls Johnny's hair and bites him, fighting techniques she apparently learned on the playground from one of Roman's previous girlfriends.

Next, Johnny goes to see the elderly identical twins who sold the book to the dead guy. The monozygotic bibliophiles point out that three of the nine engravings in the book were signed by Torchia's co-author, Lucifer. Johnny is skeptical, recalling how he was duped by that purported Mephistopheles Diary ("Dear Diary, Today I tricked that bimbo Eve into going off her diet. Boy, is God going to be pissed, because his only rule was 'No Fat Chicks!'")

But Johnny heads off to Portugal to examine the second copy of the book, which is found to contain three *different* engravings signed by Lucifer. Apparently, this is some kind of McDonald's contest, where you have to collect all nine game pieces to win a Quarter Pounder. The next day he finds the owner of the second book drowned and his engravings gone! Somebody else is obviously after the free fries, and is willing to kill to get them!

Johnny then travels to Paris to see Baroness Kessler, owner of the third book. She turns out to be a sharp old gal who provides valuable exposition, for which we will always bless her, even if she is a staunch fundamentalist devil worshipper who doesn't hold with Ernest Borgnine's liberalization of church doctrine. She explains that after the death of Torchia, his followers formed a group called The Silver Serpent Secret Friends (or something like that). However, the sect has degenerated into a club for bored billionaires who need excuses to dress up in black robes and have orgies. The Baroness used to be a member, but when she was chosen last for orgying she took her book and went home. Lina, current leader of Satan's Serpents, wants a copy of the book to use at the annual gathering where they try to summon Satan. ("The agenda for our meeting on the 12th includes a reading of last year's minutes, a semiformal orgy, and the raising of Beelzebub, followed by punch and cookies in the fellowship hall.")

Leaving the Baroness's, Johnny is menaced by a scary guy, but saved by Emmanuelle Seigner, wife of the director. She not only demonstrates her slo-mo martial arts moves (she's either bionic or demonic, take your pick), but also flies. About now I'd be suspicious, if I were Johnny. But then, if I were Johnny, I wouldn't have done *Nick of Time* or *The Astronaut's Wife* either.

Johnny wanders around France until he finds Frank Langella at a tower pictured in the book, the nine engravings spread out before him. Frank announces that he's solved the puzzle (it's apparently some sort of satanic Where's Waldo?), and so he will become the equal to God (which, as countless mad scientists have proven, means ignominious death in the next five minutes). Frank intones the rebus prayer to the devil derived from the engravings, brags about having power over all things, and lights himself on fire to demonstrate that he feels no pain. Um, big mistake. Johnny eventually puts the shrieking Demonic Torch out of its misery, grabs the engravings, and runs outside. Emmanuelle appears beside him, and is suddenly nude; they make love to the background of the burning building and the odor of charred Frank Langella.

Emmanuelle reveals that the ritual didn't work for Frank because the ninth engraving was a forgery. She disappears, leaving behind a note saying that the real engraving is at the twin booksellers' shop. Johnny goes there and the engraving eerily falls into his hands. It shows Emmanuelle riding a three-headed dragon in front of the ruined tower at dawn. Johnny returns to the tower. The sun comes up. The screen turns white.

The End.

"NO FAIR!" I hear you shouting. "What in tarnation happened?"

Well, since you asked so nicely, let me explain my theory.

Johnny had collected all nine authentic satanic engravings; he had solved the riddle. (Just be glad this movie wasn't a hit, or kids would have been giving up Pokemon cards and spending all their time trading and collecting 17th Century engravings: "Get the whole set! Impress your friends! Devour your enemies!") He had summoned Old Scratch, who was presumably the spooky chick. So, the judges at Price-Waterhouse determined that he had complied with all the rules set forth by the State Attorney General, and so was entitled to the Grand Prize of omnipotence. And once he was omnipotent, he got the hell out of this stupid movie and started a new life as…I don't know, *Rosemary's Cry-Baby*. The End.

Yes, *The Ninth Gate*: a powerful story about the dangers of entering promotions sponsored by Satan. I hope you'll think twice about Ed McMahon after what you've seen today.

But the movie is also a cautionary tale about cursed books, and how you should probably try to avoid them. The best way to do this is to resist signing up for the Cursed Book Club, despite the two free volumes. As you may recall, there have been several other cases where demonic texts brought suffering to innocent people, such as *The Necronomicon* of Abdul Alhazred. While we don't blame it for what happened in *Re-Animator*, we do hold it culpable for all those nerds who keep blathering about Yog-Sothoth, and how after Cthulhu returns we'll be sorry that we wouldn't go out with them. And of course, there are many other tomes whose very names strike dread in the hearts of the innocent: *Unaussprechlichen Kulten* by Friedrich von Junzt; *De Vermis Mysteriis* by Ludvig Prinn; and *The O'Reilly Factor for Kids*, by Bill O'Reilly. We advise you to stay well away from these damned books, for the sake of your very soul!

So, three movies, three testaments to the fact that Satan is alive and well and living in the multiplex. We earnestly hope that this attempt to justify God's ways to Man has inspired you to take a good look at your life and to repent of your sins. For we believe Sartre was right—Hell is other people, most of them method actors. So, unless you want to spend eternity with Ernest Borgnine and Michael York in a never-ending dinner theater production of "Man of La Mancha," we urge you to shape up before it's too late.

Chick Flicks Versus Ick Flicks

Recent studies suggest that male and female brains have certain structural differences, but does this translate into a difference in the way men and women *think*? As serious social critics, we turn, as always, to the wisdom and insight offered by Hollywood movies, and find that this profound debate can be resolved in two simple words: Body count.

Even a cursory study of Hollywood output demonstrates that both men and women enjoy watching people die. In the average Man's Movie—or what we might call the "Ick" Flick, due to its profusion of airborne viscera—lots of people die in lots of interesting ways. In the average Chick Flick, only one person dies, but they do it slowly and exquisitely. These differences are solely a matter of style and degree, and in the end, both sexes get what they want: human sacrifice.

But are there deeper forces at work here? Let us examine two representative films, one from each genre, and see if content can offer a clue about the differing ways in which men and women satisfy their blood lust.

Armageddon (1998)
Directed by Michael Bay
Written by Jonathan Hensleigh and J.J. Abrams; plus Robert Roy Poole, Tony Gilroy, Shane Salerno, John the Revelator, and Nosteradomus

Before we begin, a warning: This movie is 2 hours and 31 minutes long, so Abandon Hope, All Ye Who Enter Here.

A hail of flaming meteorites bombard New York City, cratering Broadway, decapitating the Chrysler Building, demolishing Grand Central Terminal, and wreaking a toll in human lives and suffering the like of which has not been seen since "Cats" opened at the Winter Garden.

Meanwhile, at NASA headquarters, the homicidal simpleton from *Sling Blade* (Billy Bob Thornton) is in charge, and he announces that an asteroid will strike Earth in 18 days, destroying all life. "Not even bacteria" will survive, he informs the President, implying that the asteroid is a far more effective toilet bowl cleanser than Lysol.

Cut to an oil-drilling platform in the Gulf of Mexico, where Bruce Willis is pelting a Greenpeace boat with golf balls. Bruce represents the last of a vanishing breed of wildcat oilmen, rugged individualists who live life by their own rules, as they carelessly rape the fragile ecosystem. And yet, when he finds his daughter (Liv Tyler) in bed with Ben Affleck, he shows a surprisingly sensitive side by attempting to blow Ben's head off with a shotgun. This tender scene is interrupted when black crude starts gushing all over the cast in a series of dizzying, rapidly-edited images intended to convey that they've just struck oil, or maybe to induce epileptic seizures in Japanese schoolchildren.

Billy Bob decides to send Bruce and his team of handpicked stereotypes into space, where they'll land on the asteroid, drill an 800-foot hole, and explode a nuclear warhead. There follows a series of light-hearted scenes in which Bruce and his crew of dullards comically exasperate the NASA brass with their sociopathic fetishes, gross ignorance, and inappropriate body-fat content.

Now comes the scariest part of the film, as Bruce secretly watches while Liv and Ben make out. Granted, their necking consists largely of Ben licking her left shoulder blade, but still—he's her *father*! and he's just *standing* there! *Watching*! I once dissected a fetal pig in a poorly ventilated classroom when I had the flu, and felt less queasy than this.

That is, until the *next* scene, when we watch as Ben attempts to seduce Liv by molesting her with animal crackers, and talking in the voice of that Crocodile Hunter guy from the Discovery Channel. For some reason, this actually works.

Cut to Shanghai, where a gigantic meteorite kills millions. But the previous two scenes have left the audience so shaken and depressed that we can't help envying the dead.

Cut to Cape Canaveral, where Bruce and company are suited up and heading for the launch pad. But first, Ben and Liv pause to sing an off-key rendition of "I'm Leaving on a Jetplane," and suddenly, the audience shakes off its mood of apathetic despair and begins actively rooting for the asteroid.

The team has to take two shuttles, because everyone whined about wanting to sit by the window. They strap in, heroic music starts to blare, and the shuttles blast off! At last we've got some action! Which comes to an instant halt as they pull into the Mir for gas. (You'd think they might have thought of that before they left.)

Ben screws up the refueling, sets everything on fire, and blows up the space station. On the ground, Liv pensively removes her engagement ring and entertains second thoughts.

Finally, the two shuttles approach the asteroid from upwind. Predictably, Ben's ship crashes headlong into it, while Bruce's shuttle lands in the wrong place.

Ben loads the survivors in their self-propelled drill rig, which is also equipped with a high caliber gatling gun (apparently, they expected the asteroid to fight back). "I'll show you how we do things where *I* come from," he bellows, and fires off five thousand rounds from the machine gun while inside the shuttle, then drives the drill rig through a wall. So apparently he comes from Texas.

Cut to Bruce and crew, who are saying things like "Drop the hammer!" and "Let's chew this iron bitch up!" in an effort to make digging a hole seem exciting. But all they manage to do is blow the drill rig's transmission, and the audience is filled with dread by the prospect that at any moment, James Brolin may appear on behalf of Aamco.

Some of the cast members stage a coup, and try to save their careers by just detonating the nukes and ending the movie right here. But, as with everything else, they screw it up, and we've got another 42 minutes to go.

Eventually, Ben shows up in the second drill-rig and finishes the hole. During all the ruckus and horseplay, however, they damage the bomb, and can no longer detonate it by remote control. Unsurprisingly, Ben is chosen to stay behind and blow up the asteroid, since he's destroyed just about everything else in the film. But Bruce, who hasn't really had much to do, is so sick of it all he decides that *he* wants to stay behind and touch off the nuke. He and Ben cry and scream that they love each other, in a moment reminiscent of two fishwives performing a scene from *Spartacus*.

The survivors lift off, and Bruce presses the button that controls the bomb (it also apparently controls a slide projector, since along with the explosion we get a montage of Bruce's vacation snaps.)

The crew returns to earth as heroes, the saviors of mankind. Despite this, their shuttle gets a crappy parking place, and they have to walk all the way back to the terminal.

Armageddon has been dismissed as a typically mindless summer movie, but serious critics regard it as the most tender tale of man-on-man love since Hyacinthus and Apollo. The story describes the classic love triangle; in this case, the Athenian paradigm of a mature man besotted with a callow youth, who is in turn tempted by the soft and relatively unwhiskery flesh of Woman (it's basically a remake of the intimate 1971 British drama *Sunday, Bloody Sunday*, except with asteroids and space shuttles).

After a shocking opening in which flaming orbs fall from the sky and emasculate the Chrysler building (a likely reference to Freud's concept of the "castrating mother"), we cut to a drill rig (probably the name of a gay bar on First Avenue) where Bruce finds Ben in bed with Liv, and nearly commits a crime of passion by chasing Ben all over the place with a shotgun in a scene that screams "If I can't have you, *nobody* can!"

Later, with the world in peril, the two lovers are unexpectedly reunited. Ben coquettishly teases Bruce by letting him peep while Ben makes out with Bruce's daughter; skillfully leavening a common male fantasy—watching while your girlfriend heavily pets with another woman—with a refreshing splash of incest. Alas, the reconciliation fails when Ben can't go through with the sex, and is reduced to desperate attempts to satisfy Liv by using Animal Crackers as sex toys (the Bunny works best)...

Realizing that the heterosexual subplot is fooling nobody, director Michael Bay thankfully allows Liv to pull off her beard (and her engagement ring). The two unsuccessful lovers finally bond Will and Grace-style as they bring NASA's desperate, last ditch effort to save humanity to a crashing halt with a campy musical comedy number that makes *Dames at Sea* look like *Battleship Potemkin*.

While the director continues to throw the occasional bone to the straight members of the audience (huge drill bits plunge deep and hard and "chew this iron bitch up!" in an obvious metaphor for rough sex with Margaret Thatcher) the remainder of the movie is dedicated to resolving the Bruce-Ben love story. And like all great love stories of *amor* and passion, it ends tragically, with one lover sobbing and moaning like *La Llorna*, and the other blowing himself up with an atom bomb so he can get some peace.

Beaches (1988)
Directed by Garry Marshall
Written by Iris Rainer Dart (novel) and Mary Agnes Donoghue

Bette Midler is rehearsing for her big concert at the Hollywood Bowl when she gets a message that causes her to abandon the gig and head to San Francisco. As she drives and cries, we flash back twenty or thirty years (depending on how old we are supposed to believe Bette Midler is); voila, we're at Atlantic City, and Bette is TV's Blossom. Back then she was a foul-mouthed, histrionic, whiny show business brat—and a much more interesting performer. She's smoking under the boardwalk when she meets a lost little rich wuss named Hillary. Blossom forces Hillary to watch her bump 'n grind version of "Glory of Love" before she'll take her back to her hotel. Hillary likes Blossom's singing. Blossom likes it that Hillary likes her singing. So, the two girls become friends for life.

They are the best of pen pals until they're 21, when Hillary turns into Barbara Hershey and comes to New York to escape her sheltered life. Bette invites Barb to share her squalid apartment, and it's a festival of sisterhood as the two women dye their hair together, sing Christmas carols, do each other's laundry, and synchronize their menstrual cycles.

To pay the rent, Bette dresses up like a killer rabbit from "Night of the Lepus" and delivers singing telegrams to John Heard. He is so impressed that he invites her to audition for the play he's directing. Despite the fact that John's production is so off Broadway it's actually in the Hudson River, Bette falls in love with him. But he only has eyes for Barb (actually, his character seems kinda light in the loafers, but the movie *claims* he's smitten by Barbara). Following Bette's triumphant debut in John's weird musical about evil mimes, Barbara helps John celebrate by sleeping with him. Bette shouts at Barbara, "So much for you and your feminist principles!" and tells Gloria Steinham to revoke Barbara's NOW membership on account of hussiness. Barbara explains that she couldn't help herself, since John Heard was "the most attractive man I've met in my life." It seems she really *did* live a sheltered existence.

Barbara returns to San Francisco, so, it's back to letters and over-dubbed narration to let us know what's happening in their lives. Bette becomes a Broadway star. (It seems surprisingly easy—one day she just *is* one. I don't know why more people don't do it). Barbara becomes a socialite and marries a jerk. Bette counters by marrying John Heard.

Barbara visits New York to see Bette's musical about the invention of undergarments, and to be bitchy. John Heard is still attracted to Barbara, which infuriates Bette, but since he is also suffering from "A Star is Born Syndrome," we already know this marriage is doomed. The two women have a shouting match in a department store, and the friendship is *over*.

Life goes on. Bette goes home to mother because John wasn't paying attention to her. Mother tells her that *everybody* is tired of paying attention to her, and she should just get used to it. (No, this doesn't mean the filmmakers realized that the audience is bored and ended the movie—it just means that you have Bette's mother's permission not to pay attention to Bette anymore.)

Bette's career goes down in flames when she punches a director who says she has a fat ass, and she's reduced to singing at a boarded-up disco. Barb finds her and apologizes; she explains that she was just jealous because she can't yodel. (Really.) Bette's still mad until Barb confesses that her husband left her and she's pregnant. So, with Barbara's life officially worse than Bette's, Bette forgives her and the two have a baby-prep montage.

But when Bette's agent finds a role for her, she's outta there! The two women scream at each other, but a diva's gotta do what a diva's gotta do and Bette returns to New York. She learns that the job is in John Heard's new production, and he gave it to her out of pity. So, now *she* is James Mason and *he* is Judy Garland! But then Barb has her baby, which makes everything okay for everybody. (Remember, babies solve all problems—have one today!)

Barbara's daughter, Victoria, is now about six. Bette is a Broadway star again (as demonstrated by doormen congratulating her on her Tony wins). Barb is a noble lawyer (as demonstrated by other lawyers chiding her for high morals). Everything is going great when Barb gets dizzy and has trouble with drinking fountains...

Yes, she has a fatal disease. Bette volunteers to accompany Barb to the beach for her last summer (she just didn't know how long this summer was going to be). Bette and Victoria don't get along at first, because they're both bossy, self-involved drama queens, and they're both six. But Bette teaches Victoria how to smoke, cuss, and sing in bath houses, and the two bond, leaving Barbara feeling left out and unloved. Barb tries to get back at them by looking pale and sickly, but they don't notice. So, she escalates her aggressive dying by refusing to speak, move, or bathe. She and Bette have *another* fight, which causes Barbara to snap out of it (the moping, I mean—not the dying), and they braid each other's hair, play cards, and do other girly stuff for the rest of the summer. Bette even agrees to not sue Barbara for failing to die as scheduled, and goes back to being Bette Midler, Super Star.

She is preparing for her Hollywood Bowl concert when Barbara finally starts to get somewhere with the dying (this is where we came in). When Bette gets to the hospital, Barbara tells her that she wants to die at the beach in order to make the whole movie so gosh-darned poignant that *nobody* will be able to stand it. So, Bette sings "Wind Beneath My Wings," we see some lovely sunset 'n surf images from a K-Tel commercial, and Barbara finally bites the sand.

The film seems to heave a sigh and wipe a tear as it treats us to a final flashback of the 11-year-old girls vowing eternal friendship while Bette belts out another musical tribute to aerodynamics.

Unlike *Armageddon*, *Beaches* goes fairly light on natural disasters. There are fewer gay men on screen and more in the audience. And there's only one death, but they milk the crap out of it. But the most important difference is that while the protagonists of *Beaches* clearly love each other, they aren't *in* love, and so aren't permitted to settle their spat with a nuclear weapon. So what is the ultimate lesson of this film? Well, its message is as old as time itself: that although we may fight with our friends, although they may steal our men, belittle us, let us down, and try to sabotage us, eventually they die, which makes it all worth while.

So, what do these conflicting movie preferences say about the differences between men and women? Primarily that both sexes seek vicarious experience in order to deal with physical and psychological stress. Both men and women yearn to witness tender and bittersweet love stories. However, men also want to see New York obliterated by meteors in *Armageddon* in order to satiate an atavistic blood lust, while women want to see Barbara Hershey die in *Beaches* so that they can have a good cry and eliminate free radicals, and because she deserves it for getting those puffy collagen lip implants that make her look like a duck-billed platypus going into anaphylactic shock.

MSNTV
The Leading Fictitious Channel Providing Learning Through Movies

Back in the days of tea parties, white gloves, and finishing schools, well-bred young ladies received their formal education the old-fashioned way: via a PBS channel broadcasting from the local agricultural college. Of course, our educational needs were simple then: some French chefing, the farm report, and a little Masterpiece Theatre (which helped us to pass as a duchess at the ambassador's ball).

Nowadays, people need to know more! And so basic cable provide us with The Learning Channel, The Animal Mating Channel, The Crime Scene Voyeur Channel, The Guerilla Decorator Channel, The Gory Operation Channel, and many, many more. The execs at these channels quickly realized that while mildly edifying fare was fine for previous generations, today's extreme TV viewers demand real-life, cheap-to-produce human drama along with their dull facts.

So, instead of a cheery Julia Child preparing *Duck a la Booze*, today we have *Surprised by Design* and *While You Were Out*, programs where people write heart-rending letters telling why their loved one deserves to have TV personalities secretly turn a room in their house into a set from *Masque of the Red Death*. (Okay, in our day we did have reruns of *Queen for a Day*, in which women wrote pathos-filled letters telling why they deserved to get a new Mixmaster, but no civilians were harmed during the making of it.)

But we don't think that the various learning and watching-others-labor chan-nels have fully exploited the potential for educational reality TV programming. So, we have come up with a few suggestions:

Surprised by Adultery: A husband comes home from a weekend business trip to find that something's new in the master bedroom—it's a film crew and carpenter Ty Pennington, all naked and in bed with his wife.

Trading Organs: Where patients swap body parts with the person in the next bed. Since contestants are semi-conscious from the morphine drip, they don't actually have to vote each other out of the hospital—player attrition is taken care of through transplant rejection and peritonitis.

Joe History Professor: In the hopes of getting a good grade, twenty coeds com-pete to sleep with the guy who teaches their Western Civilization 101 class. But the joke's on them, because he's really just the TA.

While it may seem that mockucational TV is the source of all knowledge, in truth, Hollywood movies offers scads of handy hints for the homeowner or how-to buff. And many (okay, two-thirds) of these movies are about expeditions to Mars. We think NASA is missing out by not being part of our new cable channel, MSNTV (Mars, Space & 'Nowledge Television). Not only is MSNTV trusted by more Americans who think it sounds like a real cable channel without actually being one so we can't get sued, it also provides educational fare like *Mission to Mars*, a film about how ancient astronauts made the human race from snacks.

Mission to Mars (2000)
Directed by Brian De Palma
Written by Lowell Cannon, Jim Thomas, John Thomas (Story) Jim Thomas & John Thomas, Graham Yost (Screenplay)

"Mission to Mars" was a fairly dull ride at Disneyland, consisting mostly of canned narration, vibrating seats, and the sight of adolescent riders shifting their mouse-ear hats to their laps in an effort to conceal the resulting erections. The motion picture *Mission to Mars* offers largely the same experience, except without the engorged tissues.

It's the year 2020, and Man is still alive, and Woman has apparently survived. It's the night before the first of two staggered flights to Mars are about to blast off, and judging by the beer-swilling barbecue that's in progress, NASA has recruited its astronauts from some of the finest trailer parks in America. Don

Cheadle with be leading the first mission, Tim Robbins will be leading the second, while veteran astronaut Gary Sinise will be doing pretty much what he did in *Apollo 13*—staying on Earth and sulking.

One year later. Don and crew think they've found water on Mars, but in a startling twist, it turns out they've actually discovered some unconvincing special effects. And whatever force is generating the CGI can apparently read the astronauts' minds, because it assumes the form of the one thing that most terrifies trailer park denizens: a tornado.

Cut back to Earth, where we finally get a glimpse at all the cool stuff we have to look forward to. According to the visionary filmmakers, in 2020 we'll have a giant wheel-shaped space station, like we were supposed to have back in 2001, our hot-shot pilots will drive T-birds like they did in the 1950s, and our space program will be run by an elderly Nazi, just like it was in the 1960s.

Okay, the visionary thing isn't working out, so how about some plot? Mission Control receives a faint transmission from Mars. It seems that Don somehow survived the twister, but he's bruised and traumatized, his spacesuit is spattered with the blood of his dead comrades, and a witch is trying to steal his ruby slippers.

Gary demands that project director Armin Mueller-Stahl authorize a rescue mission to Mars. Armin is reluctant, observing that any rescue attempt would be expensive, dangerous, and ultimately pointless, since all Don has to do is click his heels together three times. Then Tim Robbins demands that Armin assign Gary to Tim's flight, even though Gary's wife died, and his personal tragedy is causing friction with the other crewmembers, who demand their own lachrymose backstory. Finally, the British demand that Armin stop talking in that heavy German accent, because it's giving them all flashbacks to the Blitz.

Tim and his wife Terry are off to Mars, with Gary and Jerry O'Connell, who eventually get bored with the entertainment potential of their rhyming names, and pass the time by creating a free-floating double helix out of M&Ms. "That is the exact genetic composition of my ideal woman," Jerry says. This news arouses Gary, who eats two M&Ms from the middle of the ideal woman, in the cinema's first example of molecular porn.

The gods apparently take offense at this idiotic scene, and pelt the ship with meteorites. The imperiled astronauts heroically attempt to repair their ship, in a taut action set piece that packs in all the drama and excitement of watching your older brother replace the water pump in his AMC Gremlin.

Our heroes fumble the repairs and blow up the ship, which doesn't speak terribly well for NASA, since your brother managed to properly install the water pump even though he was listening to Gentle Giant at the time and totally baked on half a bag of Maui Wowie.

Tim leads his crew on a desperate space-walk to an orbiting supply satellite, but then he slips and falls into the atmosphere, and burns up. Then Gary, Terry, and Jerry crash the satellite into Mars, bringing to a climax the most inept rescue attempt since that episode of "Gilligan's Island" where the Professor programmed a robot to walk to Hawaii.

Don, after expressing disappointment that NASA sent a bunch of self-immo-lating goons to his rescue, introduces them to his neighbor, The Giant Face of Mars. Intrigued, Gary turns the radar gun on the Giant Face to check its fastball, and discovers that the beams act like a good mud mask; it causes the Face's pores to open wide enough for the astronauts to walk inside, where a planetarium show is in progress.

A tall, thin, flame-shaped alien appears, revealing to the awe-struck humans that Mars was once populated by a race of Goya etchings. It seems that a billion years ago, Mars was like Earth, until it was struck by an asteroid that turned the planet into an icy wasteland. So the technologically advanced inhabitants boarded spaceships and rocketed toward a distant galaxy in search of a new, Earth-like home, although it seems like it would have been a lot quicker just to go to Earth. Maybe they were afraid they'd look like out-of-towners, and the native trilobites would pester them to buy baskets and folk art, and the cab drivers would take them to clip joints. Anyway, far be it from us to question the wisdom of god-like aliens shaped like those twisty orange bulbs you see in the wrought iron chandeliers of Mexican restaurants.

One alien stayed behind, however, to seed the Earth with Martian DNA, resulting in the evolution of everything from amoebas to Ann Coulter (appar-ently they were keeping the good stuff for themselves). The astronauts are so moved by this news that they join hands with the Martian around a holographic image of Earth, and sing a selection of camp songs. It's an inspiring moment of interspecies understanding, although one gets the impression that the Martian is just mouthing the words to "Kumbaya."

Don, Terry and Jerry prepare to blast off in Don's repaired rocket. But Gary realizes that the Giant Face of Mars is not only a planetarium and a source of National Enquirer cover stories, it's also a space ship, and he decides to ride it to wherever the ancient Martians went. So he enters the Martian command module, which locks him in and rapidly fills with water. And as Gary drowns, the entire movie flashes before his eyes, including scenes that happened just thirty seconds ago, so we get to enjoy it all over again, except this time with a sappy fanfare blaring at us. Terry and Jerry lift off for Earth (where they will presumably resign from NASA and pursue careers as an animated cat and mouse team), while the Martian spaceship rockets away toward that distant galaxy, carrying Gary's bloated, drowned body to a rendezvous with our alien ancestors, in what must be the most elaborate payoff to a practical joke in history.

We hope you enjoyed our "Hicks in Space Theater" presentation of *Mission to Mars*. Tomorrow's double feature will be *Ma & Pa Kettle Blow Up Venus* and *The Hee Haw Honeys Vs. the Queen of Outer Space*.

Keep watching MSNTV for even more quality educational programming. Up next:

The Galaxies Goofiest Pranks, Pratfalls, and Practical Jokes
Inspired by Gary Sinise's gag in tonight's movie, Suzanne Sommers and Ryan Seacrest mail their corpses to the plasma beings of Alpha Centauri 12.

Followed at 9:00 Eastern (8:00 Central) by:

9:00: *The Real World: Mars*
In this episode, straight-laced Terry tells Gary that he's a pervert who will burn in hell for eating the green "private parts" M&M from the helix; stoner Don punches Jerry in the face "for that last season of *Sliders;*" and the flame alien comes out of the closet. He then gets pissed at the whole group for leaving their dirty socks lying around, and accuses them of being a waste of good DNA. The episode ends with the flame alien leading the group in a show tunes sing-along.

But now, stay tuned for MSNTV's second feature, *Red Planet*; it's another film about cretinous clodhoppers who travel to Mars and lower property values. It's also an instructional video demonstrating how you can make movies out of those worthless Val Kilmers and generic. sci-fi cliches you have lying about the house.

Red Planet (2000)
Directed by Antony Hoffman
Written by Chuck Pfarrer and Jonathan Lemkin

It's the future, and we've got the usual apocalypse in progress: pollution, over-population, ozone layer, reality TV, etc., etc. On the bright side, we've been sending algae to the Martian ice cap for twenty years, where it's supposed to grow and produce oxygen. Suddenly, however, the O2 levels have begun to drop, and a team is assembled by the international community to fly to Mars and determine if the algae is being killed off by global climate change, meteor strikes, or a visit by the pool guy.

Now let's meet that team, shall we? Carrie Ann Moss is "Mission Commander Bowman," just like Keir Dullea was in *2001: A Space Odyssey*, except she doesn't get old and become a baby. The chilly, dead-eyed Terrence Stamp is Chief Science Officer, and "the soul of our crew." (Maybe it's just me, but casting Terrence Stamp as your "soul" is like casting Christopher Walken as *The Singing Nun*). Along with the Tang, NASA has also stocked the ship with dehydrated beefcake in the form of co-pilot Benjamin Bratt, who's apparently the testicles of our crew. Carrie claims that her team represents humanity's "finest minds," although it plainly contains Val Kilmer, who is some kind of space janitor, and the "descending colon" of our crew. Rounding out the cast is AMEE, a larger, meaner version of the Aibo, that stainless steel robot dog from Sony. AMEE is on loan from the Marines, and is supposed to help them navigate on Mars—but since she's a military killing machine, and worse, has been programmed to recognize bad acting, things are likely to get gruesome.

In an amazing case of synchronicity, the filmmakers of *Red Planet*, like the creators of *Mission to Mars*, envision a future in which NASA is staffed entirely by hillbillies. Earth's "finest minds" spend the entire trip making moonshine, getting plowed, and baying like hound dogs at their shapely commander. Once again, the gods are displeased, and just as in *Mission to Mars*, the ship promptly blows up once it nears the eponymous red planet.

Commander Carrie sends the boys down to explore the planet so they won't get in her hair while she watches *This Old Plot Contrivance* and tries to renovate the spaceship. She also conducts an illuminating symposium on Newton's Third Law (for every action there is an equal and opposite reaction), which Carrie demonstrates when she tries to use a fire extinguisher in zero gravity, and it sends her pinwheeling down the hall.

The guys predictably wreck their vehicle ("Mom said not to play ball in the landing craft"), and must now wend their way across Mars to the Motel-6 where they have reservations. But Terrence decides he's creeped us out enough, and thoughtfully fakes a spleen injury so the others will leave him behind. Meanwhile, AMEE climbs out of the wreckage, and boy, is she pissed.

The survivors reach their lodgings, but like in *Mission to Mars*, it's also apparently been hit by a tornado, and looks like an Oklahoma mobile home park. So they all sit down to die of suffocation, each man privately mourning the lack of foresight that would have allowed him to fake a ruptured spleen and get out of the film twenty minutes ago. Val is the first to run out of oxygen, which is surprising—considering the lackluster performance he's been giving, he can't have been using much—and looks like we can all go home shortly, when he opens his visor and finds that he can BREATHE!

Well. Apparently that whole the-oxygen-is-gone thing was NASA's way of dropping 50 trillion dollars on an interplanetary snipe hunt.

So, everybody's okay! But just then, AMEE shows up and starts kicking the crew's ass with Northern Crane-style Kung Fu before padding off into the bushes to do her business.

Carrie has now repaired the ship, and decides to have semi-nude flashbacks to scenes that never happened. Seems she and Val got a bit flirty in the locker room—kind of like Val did with Tom Cruise in *Top Gun*. There's apparently something about the smell of damp towels and old jockstraps that lights his fire.

Meanwhile, the filmmakers borrow a plot twist from *Marooned*, as Carrie informs Val that there's an old Russian probe they can jump start to get back to the ship, but only two of them will fit inside. So, predictably, we spend the next half an hour thinning out the cast.

Sensing that our interest is flagging, Carrie skins out of her space suit and sits around in a thin tanktop, letting her painfully erect nipples carry the plot for awhile. Finally, one of the cracker astronauts catches a bad case of subcutaneous moths, which sizzle and burst out of his carcass like so much Jolly Time Popcorn. (Actually, if the bugs weren't so obviously computer generated, this would have been a horrifying scene. As it is, it's sort of like watching a grown man devoured alive by the little dancing mushrooms from *Fantasia*).

At last, the mystery of the oxygen is solved. It seems the bugs have been eating the algae and, well, breaking wind. Enough wind to create an atmosphere. So according to the filmmakers, mankind's ultimate salvation will depend upon flatulent fireflies.

Eventually, Val reaches the broken Russian probe, and AMEE, Hound of HAL, reaches Val. He devises an elaborate deathtrap using liquid oxygen, rocks, and a parachute, and manages to slay the rabid Teddy Ruxpin. He then uses its Duracells to jump-start the probe and blast off. Still, even with the assistance of a solid-fuel rocket engine, Val's escape momentum is measurably less than the velocity achieved by the audience in exiting the theater. The end.

So, Red Planet. Not just a deeply felt paean to flatulent fireflies, but also a meditation on Carrie Ann's nipples. Following the movie, MSNTV's panel of experts (master carpenter Norm Abram, Heloise impersonator Mary Ellen Pinkham, homemaking felon Martha Stewart, and trash-to-weapons-of-mass-destruction guru McGyver), answer your questions about tackling home and garden projects like those in the movie. It goes a little something like this:

First Caller: Hi. I'm a beautiful young woman and I like to lounge around in my skin-tight T-shirt, my breasts straining against the material, nipples jutting…

Norm Abram: I'll handle this one!

Mary Ellen: I don't think she's asked a question yet.

Caller: Well, my question has to do with repairing my spaceship after a solar flare caused it to explode.

Norm: Use high quality lumber, and Old English furniture polish.

Caller: Um, okay.

Norm: And call me at home, anytime, if you want me to come over and show you wood…

Mary Ellen: Let's hear from another caller!

Second Caller: Hi. I'm Bob from the Department of the Exterior. I'm trying to terraform Mars, and just don't seem to be getting the results I'd hoped for. I keep sending rockets full of algae, but lately the oxygen levels are going down. What am I doing wrong?

Martha Stewart: Bob, lush, green algae is a Good Thing, but it isn't enough to make an entire planet interesting and inviting to guests. Have you considered farting bugs? They not only add oxygen, they also eat any surplus astronauts you no longer have a use for.

Caller: Sounds great, Martha! Where do I get some?

Martha: They will just evolve. From rocks or something.

Caller. Thanks!

Third Caller: Greetings. Much like what happened to Val Kilmer in today's film, my Furby is trying to kill me. I wonder if McGyver could share some ways to kill it, using common household objects?

McGyver: Have you tried putting a potato into its exhaust pipe?

Caller: Yes, but it doesn't seem to have an exhaust pipe and my wife won't let me have any more potatoes—she says they're for dinner.

McGyver: Then I'm stumped. Sorry.

Mary Ellen: Caller, did you do anything to cause the Furby to have hard feelings towards you?

Caller: Well, I guess it could be annoyed because I stopped it from mating with the Dust Buster.

Mary Ellen: I suggest polishing it with Wonder Bread, to get a sparkly shine for just pennies! This will also relieve its sexual frustration.

Caller: Thanks, but my wife won't let me have any Wonder Bread. She says it's for lunch.

And that's all the time we have today for this installment *of The Experts Answer Your Home and Garden Questions About Mars.* But stay tuned for our next feature, an exciting movie about water conservation. In the future! Since this movie will count for half of your "Alien Ecosystems" grade, if you get confused or have any questions as we proceed, be sure and raise your hand.

Dune (1984)
A Dino de Laurentiis production of a David Lynch film. Written and directed by David Lynch. Produced by Raffaella de Laurentiis. Based on the novel by Frank Herbert. Everything else by David Lynch or a de Laurentiis.

Our story begins as some blonde girl floats against a backdrop of stars and tells us stuff. This establishes the theme of the movie, which is: the marvels of exposition! Other men quailed at dramatizing a 500-page novel with its own language, mythology, and technology, but not David Lynch! He decided that if he couldn't film it all, at least he could film people *telling* you about it all. When the characters aren't casually mentioning the average yearly rainfall on Arrakis (zero), they're narrating everything that happens to them (even though you're sitting there and just *saw* what happened to them). They are also wont to share every thought that passes through their heads (you can tell the thoughts from the dialogue by the fact that they whisper their thoughts, but SHOUT their lines.)

The blonde chick, who's the daughter of Emperor Jose Ferrer, tells us that it's now 10,191 AD, and the most precious substance in the universe is Spice. Apparently, Spice is vital to space travel, since it lets the Navigators (gigantic, free-floating Ball Park Franks) "fold space", which involves traveling without moving. Everything clear so far? Oh, and Spice is only found one place in the whole universe, the planet Arrakis. And apparently in the future they've done away with all other seasonings, since everybody just calls it "the Spice," and not once does anybody think maybe they're talking about paprika, or cumin.

Meanwhile, Emperor Jose has a secret plan to destroy House Atreides. It seems that Atreides has developed new amplifiers (and really big speakers), and their neighbors, the Harkonnens, are upset because they have to get up in the morning.

Now let's watch as the Emperor's bald, telepathic secretary schemes and plots. It seems that she is a Mother Superior in the Mary Kay sisterhood, a mystical group that has spent 90 generations practicing eugenics in order to produce the QuitThat Baccarat, the galaxy's super-being. Jessica, the concubine of Duke Leo Atredies and the mother of Paul Atreides, is one of these Mary Kay women. Still with us?

Now let's meet young Paul, who will be Agent Dale Cooper when he grows up. The Duke's posse (Jean-Luc Picard, and Al from *Quantum Leap*) has just arrived to test Paul's fighting prowess, having realized that a boy with Farrah Fawcett hair is going to need to know how to defend himself.

After beating up a turnstile, Paul goes to bed, but continues to narrate in his sleep. He murmurs, "Arrakis. Dune. Desert planet", and then he is awakened by the Reverend Bald Lady, who wants him to take the Messiah SAT, which involves sticking your hand in a weasel cage. Paul thinks (out loud, of course), "Fear is the little death." The Reverend Mother thinks, "Could he be the one?" Paul lives through the test, and Jessica thinks, "My son lives!" The audience thinks, "I thought *orgasm* was the little death."

Meanwhile, over at House Harkonnen, everybody is evil and has hair like Carrot Top. The Baron is obese, unpleasant, and (judging by the mound-like growths that sprout from his flesh) has a face infested with prairie dogs. And as if that weren't enough of a burden to bear, his nephew is Sting.

The Duke, Jessica, and Paul dress up in Nazi uniforms, and take off for Arrakis. The giant floating kielbasa "folds space," and suddenly we're there: Dune. Arrakis. Desert Planet. The original Spiceworld. Be sure and check out our giant worms.

Max Von Sydow shows up to do some exposition about "still suits", which are basically sauna suits, except they capture your sweat, urine, and feces, and recycles them so you can drink the results. Apparently, they're all the rage amongst the aboriginal Fremen, and Max is astonished that Paul instinctively knows the proper way to wear a still suit. But then, Paul's so thin, he can wear *anything*. I just hate him.

Paul takes his first hit of Spice and starts tripping. He has a few mystical dreams before realizing that a hypodermic needle has sprung from the bed and is trying to kill him, probably jealous that he picked Spice over heroin. He foils the hypo just before it stabs Linda Hunt, the housekeeper, who came to warn him that there is a traitor in their midst, but she doesn't know who it is, and would he like turn-down service?

It turns out the traitor is Al from *Quantum Leap*, who deactivated the "weirding modules" (the brand name of their amplifiers). Baron Harkonnen captures the city, and Jessica and Paul are told that they will "die in the innards of the worm." A pretty horrifying threat, until you remember that they're sealed into sauna suits and chugging their own urine like Gatorade.

A couple of soldiers take Jessica and Paul out to the desert to be eaten by giant worms, in a scene that exactly mirrors the story of Snow White, except for the giant worm part. They escape, but the Spice in the sand makes Paul trip-out again. Paul thinks, "They will call me Muad'Dib," (and they *do* call him Muad'Dib, because that's what he *asks* them to call him. He must be psychic!) He also thinks, "The sleeper must awaken." Apparently he's talking about the audience.

Paul plants a "thumper" to divert the giant sandworms that live in the deserts of Dune (the annoying rabbit from *Bambi* probably would have worked too). See, the worms are attracted to rhythm, and so most white folks are safe. But this one keeps coming, and we finally get to see one of the fabled sandworms of Dune—it looks like an aardvark snout that's inhaled a picket fence.

Then Paul and Jessica conveniently fall into a cave, and into the midst of the whole Fremen Militia. Paul hides while his pregnant mom beats up their leader. The Fremen honcho is impressed, and says to her, "Your water shall mingle with our water." Which apparently means that on Saturday nights they stick straws down one Fremen's suit and have a kegger.

The Fremen leader tells Paul that from now on he will be called Ursula among the tribe, but he can pick his secret name. He picks Muad'Dib, which means "mouse turd," or something. The Fremen then take him to their basement, which, like all basements, is flooded. Paul thinks, "The Fremen have water! When they have enough, they will change the face of Arrakis!" Yes, and then they can stop drinking from each other's underpants, too!

Paul meets the girl of his dreams, Sean Young, and we share a tender ten-second scene depicting their great love. She says, "Tell me of your world, Ursula."

He thinks, "Tell me of your world, Ursula." This is pretty much the high spot of their romance.

Meanwhile, the Fremen ask Jessica to be their new Reverend Mother. To accept, she must drink the "Water of Life." This is actually sandworm juice, and is contraindicated during pregnancy, so Paul's sister Alia is born with a severe birth defect—knowledge. It seems she has all the powers of a Reverend Mother, but only half the calories, or something like that.

Paul teaches the Fremen warriors how to break limestone by using an amplifier and singing at it (Toto songs appear to work best). He explains that, "Some thoughts have a certain sound, that being equivalent to a form." Um, okay. He tells them that they will be able to use sound to break bones, start fires, and suffocate people—so apparently he's given them the power of Festival Seating.

However, before Paul can lead the Fremen, he has to ride Moby Worm. He does. The Toto music blares triumphantly. A choir sings. It seems like this would be a good place for the movie to end, so naturally it doesn't.

Bimbo narrator tells us that two years have passed (yeah, honey, and we've felt every minute of them), and the Fremen have managed to stop Spice production.

A 3rd Level Navigator (whom we can immediately tell is high ranking, because he's smothered in chili and onions) pays another visit to the Emperor. Through his badly dubbed assistants, the irked frankfurter tells His Imperial Screw-up that he has only one more chance to stop Muad'Dib. So, Jose decides to kill everything on Dune—where's your Messiah NOW! He starts by giving Dune City to the Carrot Tops.

Paul fights back by sending his six-year-old sister against the bad guys. She sneaks into town dressed like an Italian widow, and lowers the defense shields using her Jedi mind tricks. Then the Fremen attack, riding sandworms and shrieking like adolescent girls. In the midst of the battle, Alia yanks out Baron Harkonnen's pacemaker, causing him to fly straight into a worm's mouth.

The Fremen win, but Sting isn't ready for the movie to be over, and he challenges Paul to a fight. Alas, even his leather Speedo and trick poisoned-kneecap are no match for Mouse Turd's mystical powers. Paul kills Sting, then cracks the linoleum by shouting at it. Paul has evolved past the need for amplifiers, and has clearly won the battle of the bands!

It starts to rain. Paul has an ocean in his eye. Alia lisps, "And how can this be? For he *is* the QuadStackPartypack."

Any questions? We didn't think so.

That concludes our "Hebrew National Franks Theater" presentation of *Dune*. Stay tuned for this week's episode of ***Don't Wear That, You Idiot*** in which our stylists visit Arrakis to perform some much-needed makeovers. Young Alia is counseled against wearing head-to-toe black on the first day of kindergarten, and Sting is sentenced to death for wearing cowhide bikini briefs in public. However, our fashion fuehrers find Paul Atreides' still suit trendeliciously fab after he treats them to a warm drink from it that he made himself.

And on tomorrow's very special episode of ***Interplanetary Idol***, we watch young hopefuls put their hands in weasel cages to see if they have eerie mental powers, a high threshold for pain, and a complete lack of sense. This will be followed at 9 by ***Celebrity Consternation Factor***, where top stars compete to see who will do mundane chores without calling for a personal assistant. On this week's episode, Donny Osmond and Fantasia have to apply Thompson's Water Seal to the Fremen's flooded basement, and then wait around all day Tuesday for the guy from Arrakis Plumbing & Heating to fix the leaking water heater.

MNSTV now concludes our broadcasting day.

Sex, Lies, and Direct-To-Videotape: The Rise and Fall of the Erotic Thriller

The Age of Erotic Thrillers officially began in 1987 with *Fatal Attraction*, the movie that taught women to more openly express their sexual feelings through boiled rodents. But the genre really took off in 1992, when Joe Eszterhas's *Basic Instinct* captured the public's attention, as Sharon Stone's pantyless pudenda and Michael Douglas's flabby buttocks competed in a "Survivor"-style test of the audiences' gag reflex. This triggered an explosion of movies starring women named Shannon, or occasionally Shauna, usually with the word "Body" in the title.

But by 1995, the trend was pretty much over—we saw the end of the *Body Chemistry* series, the *Body Of Influence* series, and even the venerable *Night Eyes* series, forcing Shannon Tweed and Andrew Stevens to find work which involved wearing clothes, even on casual Fridays. While there were still a few Erotic Thrillers being made for the direct-to-cable venues, these starred Julie Strain instead of Sharon Stone and Joe Estevez instead of Michael Douglas, which—on the Hollywood Food Chain—is roughly at the level of those microbes that live in your intestines and convert metabolic wastes into Vitamin K.

And yet, any genre which held society in such thrall for so long must have expressed some deeply held fear or longing. In an attempt to expose the psychic wound that drove America to embrace this almost medieval parallel between sex and death, we shall examine three movies from the days when the Erotic Thriller, like the bison, roamed proud and free across our nation. Because we believe it's about time that these movies also get made into sloppy joes and sold to tourists at Fake Old West Days. Let the healing begin.

Body Chemistry (1990)
Directed by Kristine Peterson
Written by Jackson Barr

Our movie begins with a close-up of a nipple, then cuts to a shot of an eye. No, this isn't meant to signify that the viewers are boobs—it's just Marc Singer doing cutting-edge porn research at the Smut Institute. And he has just made the revolutionary discovery that men get more excited by watching *Debbie Does Dallas* than "Two Fat Ladies."

But just as he's on track for the Nobel Prize in Porn, Marc meets Dr. Claire Archer, who is trying to prove her own theory that kinky sex is boffo at the box office. Marc is working late at the office when Dr. Archer takes off her lab coat to reveal that she is only wearing a silk teddy, thigh-high stockings, and a garter belt. Claire places her breasts in Marc's face and throatily whispers that latent psychopaths often enjoy S&M—and the first one's free, kid! Marc half-heartedly demurs, stating that he is a married man with a prestigious career in scientific porn. Claire assures him that that their casual affair won't jeopardize any of that, since she is not Glenn Close, just an incredible simulation.

So, his mind at ease, they hop into a bed that resembles a jail, and Marc Singer demonstrates that he *is* the BeastWithTwoBacksMaster! He slips away while Claire is still asleep, and heads home to takes a milk bath, hoping to wash away the sin and to make his skin smooth and soft for the many nude scenes to come.

Marc fails to return Claire's post-coital phone call, so Claire cancels her project—and the Smut Institute loses its big research grant from the President's Council on Getting Physical. Marc asks her to reconsider, and they end up doin' it in the shower; Marc takes this opportunity to press his butt up against the steamy glass, proving that Michael Douglas has nothing on him!

Thanks to Marc's prowess at showering, the lab gets the contract back and Marc gets promoted to Institute Director. But when Marc goes home, who should be there in a van but Claire! She offers him candy, and when he falls for her ruse and gets in, she undresses him, ties his arms above his head, and, um, interns him.

Marc tells Claire that it's over. She has a differing view, and orders him to come to her house for dinner on Friday night. He's flustered and flummoxed, and...another "f" word. When Friday comes, he rebels by staying home and having good, clean married sex with Mary Crosby. But Claire will *not* be ignored! We feel a mixture of apprehension and horror when she puts a boiling pot of water on the stove and throws in...a lobster! (While the movie doesn't elaborate, we assume this was Pinchy, Marc's beloved pet crustacean.) Claire then trashes the dinner, smashes the china, and generally acts out. Someone needs a nap!

When Mary Crosby opens the mail, she finds a package containing broken crockery and the squished remains of a lobster. "Who would want to send you a box of garbage?" she asks Marc. Well, maybe the viewers of *Beastmaster 2: Through the Portal of Time,* who thought turnabout was fair play. But Marc blames it on animal rights activists (who often send lobsters to sex researchers); meanwhile, his son plays with a lobster claw. Little Jason really loved Pinchy!

Claire's next act of revenge is to send Jason a video of his father, nude and whimpering in the van. Jason seems strangely unaffected by seeing his dad in a porno flick—but after sitting through *If You Could See What I Hear,* the kid can probably stomach anything.

Marc confronts Claire. They have a tussle that ends with him ripping off her clothes, tying her up, and taking her brutally from behind. He shouts, "This is what you want!" She replies, "It's what *you* want." He is shocked and horrified to realize that she is right—he *does* want to star in *Basic Instinct*! Although he left her bound and naked, Claire continues to phone him about 100 times a day (presumably dialing with her nose).

Realizing the lobstergram didn't have quite the impact she was hoping for, Claire ups the ante and burns down Marc's house. Marc retaliates by breaking down Claire's door and trying to strangle her. They fight in slo-mo for a while, then Claire grabs a gun. They stare at each other, hoping even now for something original to happen—but it doesn't, so she shoots him.

And we the viewers are left to contemplate the sad moral of the story: That flaunting the conventional academic wisdom in porn leads inevitably to professional ruin, murder, and a mailbox that reeks of seafood.

The basic premise of *Body Chemistry* is that adultery is wrong. This may seem like a fairly obvious piece of moral wisdom, going back at least to the Ten Commandments. But the filmmakers go even further than the Old Testament, proclaiming that adultery is wrong even if you're a porn researcher whose boss orders him to have *Last Tango in Paris*-style sex with a hot blonde in order to get a government S&M contract. It's wrong, and it will be punished by death! Glen Close's death, if you're Michael Douglas; however, if your last big role involved gadding about in a loincloth and tiara, then it'll be your death. The lesson? Before you fornicate, check your resume.

Besides helping men keep their pants on, *Body Chemistry* and its ilk also provide valuable information to women. For instance, single girls are taught creative ways to terrorize men who fail to call after sex. You say that guy who was so eager to "make the crustacean with two carapaces" last week can't seem to remember your name now? Well, do like Dr. Archer, and mail him a squashed lobster. (A cooked octopus or boiled manta ray will also work, but only if they were close, personal marine life). Bet he'll never forget you after that!

If he claims he's too busy for sex games, what with his family responsibilities and porn research, then get busy yourself and expand your social life. Try meeting new people—like his 10-year-old son! Yes, a relationship with a younger man will be just the thing to restore your self-confidence, even if he'll want to play SpongeBob SquarePants, while you want to play SpankBob NoPants.

And if your partner in Mixed Doubles Showering seems to be losing his enthusiasm, then kill him. It will help you move on, and it might even open the way for you to meet somebody new. Like a nice prison matron.

And speaking of hard-faced, sexually aggressive women with a lot of upper body strength, our next morality tale comes to us from Madonna. It also teaches valuable lessons about obsession, adultery, and murder, and how they result in bad movies. The twist this time is that for once, the fishy smell isn't coming from a dead lobster.

Body of Evidence (1993)
Directed by Ulrich Edel
Written by Brad Mirman

Tagline: "This is the murder weapon. Her name is Rebecca."

As our picture begins, it's raining. This is so we'll know we're watching a *film noir*, and not just a tawdry excuse to see William Dafoe's chest develop a dull waxy build-up of candle-drippings. But let's be honest—when the sexiest part of your leading man's performance is his impersonation of a Chianti bottle, your erotic thriller *may* be in trouble.

Anyway, elderly millionaire Andrew Marsh has died of heart failure, and the police quickly deduce from the tagline that Marsh's girlfriend Rebecca (Madonna) killed him with her BODY! And when the police learn that Marsh left her $8 million, she is tried for murder. Madonna hires shyster Willem Dafoe to defend her because she saw him in that Scorsese movie and figured he was easily tempted.

Presiding over the trial is Black Judge Judy, who hates everybody, but reserves her special contempt for the audience. Well, we *do* have it coming.

D.A. Joe Mantegna declares that Madonna "is the murder weapon itself." He compares her to a knife or a gun. Clearly, stricter Madonna control legislation is called for, but the NRA counters that "If you outlaw Madonnas, only outlaws will have mediocre pop stars."

At a billable dinner, Madonna relates a suggestive story about getting scratched on the thighs while stealing strawberries as a child. This excites Willem, who realizes he has solved *The Caine Mutiny* mystery. They rip off each other's clothes, then she takes a candle and drips hot wax on his chest. Willem whimpers. Then she heads south with the molten paraffin, while Willem whines. And we see that Madonna, slut though she may be, is actually furthering the feminist agenda, since it's about time that a man had to experience a bikini wax. Meanwhile, Willem wails.

Back in court, the prosecution calls to the stand Jürgen Prochnow, Marsh's former doctor. He testifies that he and Madonna used to be lovers, and that he had told her that the old guy would die if he ever had wild sex with a self-promoting exhibitionist. But Willem brings in surprise evidence proving that Jürgen was in *Dune*! The plot congeals!

Since he didn't screw up in court that day, Madonna gives Willem a hand job in a crowded elevator. The other lawyers and the Japanese tourists finally get off (ha ha), leaving Madonna and Willem free to engage in *really* public sex in the parking garage. Madonna climbs on Willem's car and the camera shoots from between her legs, revealing (purely by chance) her black garter belt. She smashes the overheard light, then hangs from the pipes and wraps her legs around Willem's head. She looks like Mary Lou Retton in heat.

Madonna tells Willem that the jury hates her (a lucky guess on her part). She adds that the women think she's a whore and the men think she's a bitch (another lucky guess). So, she *has* to testify, to explain that it wasn't her idea to be in this movie, it was Sandra Bernhardt's. Her plan works, as the jury reasons that if the defendant was bi, she doesn't have to die. She goes free.

So justice has triumphed, right? Not really, for when Willem arrives at Madonna's to present his bill, he finds Jürgen there, discussing how they killed Marsh. Willem bitterly announces that he would have defended Madonna even if she hadn't, um, boinked him. Jürgen is surprised to learn that Madonna *isn't* like a virgin. She says (not an *exact* quote), "Don't look so hurt, Jürgen. I boinked you, I boinked Marsh, I boinked Willem. That's what I do: I boink. And it made me 8 million dollars!" And that was just in tips!

Jürgen is miffed and tries to kill Madonna. She and Jürgen fight over the gun, and she gets shot. Then Jürgen and Willem get to roughhousing and Jürgen falls over a railing and dies. As Willem tenderly ministers to Madonna, Jürgen comes back to life, shoots her again, and re-dies. D.A. Joe Montegna arrives to deliver the moral of the piece: "People usually get what they deserve."

Thanks, Joe. Not exactly "Twas Beauty killed the Beast!" or "Keep watching the skies!" In fact, it sucks about as bad as the rest of the movie, but at least it's a better coda than "Madonna will be back in *Body of Evidence 2: Body on Tap!*"

But what would this movie have been like if, instead of Willem Dafoe, Madonna had engaged Perry Mason to represent her?

Well, obviously Perry wouldn't have slept with his client—he's too principled for that. And too gay. And he damned well wouldn't have let D.A. Hamilton Burger deliver the coda!

And if Mason had defended her, Madonna would have been innocent, no matter how damning the evidence, and no matter how many people she boinked. We think the climatic courtroom scene would have gone a little something like this:

> D.A. Burger: So, not only is the defendant guilty of murdering an innocent dirty old millionaire for his money, but she herself was the murder weapon. For proof, we offer into evidence the movie's poster. The prosecution rests.

> Mason: Your honor, while it may appear that my client killed Mr. Marsh by forcing him to have kinky sex with her until he died of Viagra poisoning, I submit that the real killer was…Willem Dafoe! He seemed to have nothing to do with this crime. Nobody suspected him. Therefore, he's clearly guilty! If the police had conducted even a rudimentary record check they would have found that Dafoe was the nefarious boat-crashing terrorist in *Speed 2*, the murderous psychopath Green Goblin in *Spiderman*, the depraved Bob Crane-killing pornographer in *Auto-Focus*, and a really unconvincing T.S. Eliot in *Tom and Viv*. It's clear that he killed Marsh in order to land the role as the villain in the new Bond movie.

> Willem: Yes, I did it! I did it and I'm glad! I also committed those ice pick murders Sharon Stone got blamed for. I really did it to open the way for my fellow male actors (who are always unfairly stereotyped as dupes and patsies in these films), to play the sexy femme fatale roles! But I would like to be the new Bond villain, yes.

Burger: Your honor, I object! *Speed 2* was not made until four years from now.

Judge: I refuse to rule on your motion because maybe *I* am the murderer. Nobody *ever* suspects us plump black woman. Hey, we can be treacherous, erotic killers too, you know!

Mason: Then my client is free to go.

Burger: Not so fast! She still has to answer those *Swept Away* war crimes charges!

Mason: Oh…right. Say, Hamilton, why don't you just boink her and we can call the whole thing even?

Cut to a shot of the lonely, hardworking Burger lying dead in a parking garage, bludgeoned by a SUV owner who didn't appreciate the D.A. having gymnastic sex on his hood. A discarded newspaper beside his body proclaims "Willem Dafoe, Psycho Killer, to be New Bond Villain." Meanwhile, a TV in the attendant's booth shows Madonna making additional millions with her Gap commercials and children's book. Mason strolls in to proclaim, "People usually get what they deserve. Except in *real* film noir." The End.

Or is it? Maybe Perry Mason was the real killer, like O.J. Simpson always maintained. And that leads to the chilling question: what if Bruce Willis was a psychiatrist who lost his red, and he met up with a mysterious nympho who lost her panties? Lost them in a MURDER! For the answer, turn to our next film, *Color of Night.* It also features nude frying.

Color of Night (1994)
Directed by Richard Rush
Written by Matthew Chapman, Billy Ray, and Richard Rush.

An agitated patient tells shrink Bruce Willis that she hopes his "cock shrivels up," thus introducing the main theme of the movie: Willis's willie. She is so upset by Bruce's penis that she jumps through the window and plummets 200 stories to her death. Through a clear panel in the sidewalk we watch her blood pool artistically. When the blood turns gray we realize that Dr. Bruce has been stricken with hysterical color blindness! He has lost his red!

Bruce is all broken up about causing the death of a patient with litigious next of kin, so he slinks off to L.A. to stay with fellow psychologist Scott Bakula. Scott introduces Bruce to his therapy group, which consists of sexaholic Lesley Ann Warren, dorky Brad Dourif, dour Lance Henriksen, masochistic artist Casey, and big-eyed, bucktoothed, effeminate Richie.

On the drive home, Dr. Bruce diagnoses the members of the group, based on his five minutes of contact with them. Scott gets chills from Bruce's uncanny insight, but Bruce modestly claims that he was "born with it, like a psychic tuning fork." Scott confides that he has been getting death threats, and he thinks they are coming from inside the group! He hopes Dr. Bruce, the Amazing Kreskin of the A. P. A., can help him pick out the genuine nut job from the people who just need lots of expensive therapy.

Sadly, Bruce's metaphysical flatware failed to tell him that a killer really is after Dr. Scott. After the next session we hear high-pitched giggling as a figure dressed in black leather stabs Scott repeatedly. Yes, Scott has been killed by Olivia Newton-John from *Grease*!

The following day, the sexist, racist, and obnoxious Detective Hector Martinez, the most likable character in the movie, questions Bruce, asking whom he thinks killed Dr. Scott. Bruce declines to answer due to doctor-patient confidentiality, which he likens to "the Miranda Oath" (you know, the vow cops take to never recite lines from *The Tempest* to suspects). Hector says that if *his* friend had been murdered, he would perform anal sex on Miranda. Not that it would help, of course, but I guess that it would take his mind off his grief.

Bruce is on his way to break the news about Dr. Scott to the group when his car is rear-ended by Jane March, a big-eyed, bucktoothed lass. She says her name is Rose. (Rose! Get it? It's a color in the red spectrum!) Rose begs Bruce to not report the accident. She refuses to give him her last name, address, or phone number—which might make a lesser man suspect her reliability, but since Bruce's amazing "tuning fork" indicates she doesn't wear panties, he agrees to let her "make it up to him."

The group invites Bruce to be their new therapist (notwithstanding how he killed his last patient, and can't see red, and is crazy and everything). When Bruce tells Hector he is taking over the group, Hector expresses concern for Bruce's dick, which he predicts will get chewed off if Bruce keeps sticking it in with barracuda. Bruce accuses Hector of wanting him. Clearly Bruce's dick is quite the coquette.

Bruce goes home to gaze moodily at the swimming pool. Rose appears, wearing a bright red dress. She kisses him, they fall into the pool, and her dress just kinda dissolves (due to high chlorine levels) to reveal a decided lack of underwear. Bruce's clothing also melts (except for his socks and shoes). As they squirm and flop in the water, you can see Bruce in all his splendor (at least in the unrated version). Um, for a movie designed around a penis, it isn't really all you might have dreamed of.

Rose cooks dinner in the nude (gaining an unfair advantage over the other contestants on "Top Chef"), and then she and Bruce take a shower. We see that Rose has a rose tattoo on her butt. We also see that Bruce's butt is pallid and rather repellent (one of these butts is a plot point, so pay attention)!

Bruce decides to visit Leslie Anne, who has just returned from a shopping trip with her friend Bonnie. Bonnie has big eyes, buckteeth, and wears a red wig—but doesn't wear underpants (apparently L.A. was suffering from a major underwear shortage back in '94—some rock groups should have done a benefit or something). Bonnie seems vaguely familiar...

Bruce continues his house calls by visiting Casey's studio. He steps in something gray, then looks up to see Casey's body strung from the ceiling, his blood pooling on the floor. Bruce looks sick, thinking that his damned color blindness has caused him to ruin a perfectly good pair of shoes!

Meanwhile, Leslie Anne and Bonnie are titillating the audience with their naughty lesbian antics. Bonnie pops out of her clothes, and a close-up of Bonnie's butt reveals...a rose tattoo! What could this mean???

When Bruce gets home that night he finds Rose in the kitchen, cooking up a storm while wearing only a frilly apron. Clearly this girl has a thing for nude food preparation—her secret life probably involves working as a fry cook at TGI Naked.

At the next therapy session, Bruce finds Dr. Scott's hidden journal. Bruce reads Scott's last entry, which says that he was right about somebody in the group posing a threat to his life, since he's now dead and all. Bruce also finds a nude photo of Rose with a note on the back rating her as "Pretty hot for a sociopath." Bruce passes the photo around, since sharing is what group therapy is all about. It turns out that Rose (or Bonnie, as they knew her) was sleeping with each of them! What are the odds of that?

Bruce deduces that Richie, the only one who didn't sleep with Rose, is the key to the mystery. Bruce takes off Riche's glasses and wig, and...he's Rose! She tells him that when her little brother Richie died, their older brother Dale started calling her "Richie" and this caused her to develop multiple personality disorder. When the therapy group became her family, she created "Bonnie," a personality who could strengthen those familial ties through sex. Then she met Bruce, and was free to be Rose again, thanks to his amazing penis!

Alas, before there is time for more cuisine au natural, *real* sociopath Dale comes after Bruce and Rose with his nail gun! It all ends in an homage to *Vertigo*, with Rose frantically climbing a spiral staircase in a storm, and Bruce following her onto the roof. They fall off several times, but catch each other before hitting the ground. This continues until Bruce can finally see red again, and so they live happily ever after, in perfect mental health. The End.

So, *Color of Night:* probably the best movie ever made about the tragic problem of hysterical colorblindness. As you may recall, Bruce Willis was asked to host the telethon for the affliction, but he had to decline since he was already heavily involved in the "Men with Bad Toupees and Mediocre Wieners" charity.

But besides being a disease-of-the-week nudie flick, this movie also offers lots of valuable information to you, the credulous viewer. First, it provides actual psychological information, such as the fact that if you repeatedly call somebody by the wrong name, you will cause him or her to develop multiple personality disorder. So, it will be all *your* fault when that nondescript guy in the next cubicle whose name you can't recall takes to speaking with an English accent and asking to be addressed as "Miss Nancy." Also, this movie teaches us that neurotics are really unobservant, and can easily be fooled by Jane March wearing a wig and glasses. Of course, psychiatrists are no better…at least, that's what they'll claim when investigated by the medical board for sleeping with their patients. ("How was I to know she was that teen I've been treating—she wore glasses, for God's sake!")

Secondly, this film presents ideas for adding more carnality to your life. For instance, put clothes-dissolving chemicals in your swimming pool and invite sexy strangers over for a dip! If somebody hits your car, instead of swapping insurance info, exchange bodily fluids! And add excitement to boring tasks like cooking by doing them in the nude! Of course, this can result in grease burns in sensitive (and embarrassing) places, but if done carefully, it can make life more interesting for you and those around you—especially if you're a lunch lady at the junior high.

But *Color of Night* also illuminates the dark side of love, and raises the question: how can those of us who aren't psychic, under-endowed, hysterically colorblind mental health professionals tell if we're sleeping with a homicidal psychopath? Well, you can begin by taking this quiz from *Cosmo*: "Is Your Main Squeeze a Dangerous Loony?"

1. When you show a naked picture of your boyfriend to your therapy group, they say:

    a. "My lover *also* has Bill O'Reilly's face tattooed on his hinder! Who knew that design was so popular?"

    b. "You know, if you took off his glasses, he'd look just like *my* boyfriend, Superman."

    c. "What a disappointing penis."

2. Your chick has shared everything with you but:

    a. Her name, address, phone number, and gig as TV's "Stark Naked Gourmet."

    b. Her gender.

    c. The fact that her brother kills everybody that she sleeps with.

    d. The fact that she's actually dead.

3. When the people around you start dropping like flies, your honey is:

    a. The number one suspect, having means, motive, opportunity, and buckteeth.

    b. The number one suspect, since she's spooky, secretive, and much too young and attractive to be dating you, if she were in her right mind.

    c. The least likely suspect, since she doesn't wear underwear.

4. Your guy claims to have:

    a. A "psychic tuning fork" that allows him to instantly spot and diagnose the mental problems of others.

    b. A "psychotic salad fork" that gets him free side dishes at Sizzler with the purchase of any meal.

    c. A "schizophrenic forked tongue" that permits him to tell you your pants don't make you look fat, but later complain to his friends about your big butt.

And that concludes our review of the genre *thrillerum erotica*. What have we learned from our study of these movies? First, that when sex scientists sleep with

Glenn Close impersonators, it's always the lobsters who suffer. Secondly, that sexual intercourse, far than propagating life, only brings death. And thirdly, that the root word of "erotic" is "rot."

And just why was this genre so popular just a few years ago? One theory is that it echoed society's fears of AIDS.

A good guess, but wrong.

Actually, the entire genre was part of a calculated eugenics program by former Nazi scientists. Using the powerful medium of the motion picture, they sought to associate sex with death in the public mind, and thereby persuade stupid people not to breed. (Or at least, not to breed with Madonna.) With sufficient aversion therapy, the genes that lead people to watch Madonna movies in the first place would eventually die out. The neo-Nazis were well on their way to perfecting their new breed of Reichkinder, when the project received a fatal blow in 1995: *Showgirls*. With its release, the genre swiftly imploded, and the whole "You Must Be At Least This Smart to Have Sex" project was quietly shelved.

Satan: A Career Retrospective

In the age-old battle between Good and Evil, there comes a time when every soul must ask of himself one burning question: Why is Evil doing so much better in Hollywood, despite a spotty record at the box office? One need only skim the history of cinema to see that for every *Greatest Story Ever Told* or *Ben-Hur*, there are a dozen *End of Days* or *The Devil's Rain*. Is there a conspiracy afoot to promote an unholy agenda at the expense of the Gospels? Or is this vast disparity in screen time simply due to the fact that Satan is less choosy about his projects? We believe the latter is more likely the case, and also helps to account for why Dolph Lundgren has made three times as many movies as Daniel Day Lewis.

But this trend has increased wildly of late, with the recent re-release of *The Exorcist,* as well as pictures such as *Stigmata, Lost Souls,* and *Bedazzled.* Why this sudden explosion of interest in the Father of Lies? Perhaps it's because over the years, Beelzebub, like Drew Barrymore, has matured and developed right before our very eyes on film. To paraphrase Bobby Goldsborough, the movie-going public has been "sittin' here, smiling, watching Satan grow."

Let's take a look at three films spanning the Devil's most fecund period, the 1970s through the millennium, and see how Satan has handled his transition from the low budget teen flicks to overblown summer blockbusters. Benjamin McKenzie, take note.

Satan's Cheerleaders (1977)
Directed by: Greydon Clark
Written by: Greydon Clark and Alvin L. Fast

Our movie opens with John Ireland leading a Take Back the Night March in his bathrobe. Then we cut to the beach, where a group of bikini-clad pom-pom girls from the local high school are performing cheers for the female P.E. teacher. Horrified by the frank sexuality of the girls' routine, she urges them to replace the offending choreography with moves stolen from a minstrel show.

Suddenly, the movie delivers a shock: One of the cheerleaders—blonde and bland teen goddess Patti—is spotted sitting alone on the sand, staring out to sea.

Fearing that she's not feeling fresh, her friends rush to her aid, only to learn that Patti has been "thinking."

"About what?" they ask, flabbergasted.

"I don't know," she replies.

Meanwhile, the high school custodian (Wilfred Brimley Lite) is attending John Ireland's al fresco pajama party and satanic kegger. Wilfred pledges his soul to Satan, so those darn kids will finally quit annoying him and stop TPing the chain-link fence around the school.

The next day, Wilfred is pulling toilet paper off the chain-link fence and having second thoughts about that chalice of goat's blood he drank last night (was it *really* the right thing to do?) On the bright side, the Lord of Darkness *did* apparently come through with a Ronco Rhinestone and Stud Setter, since Wilfred's highly ornamented janitor's uniform would likely be dismissed as wretched excess by Liberace.

Realizing he's failed to give any of the characters a shred of distinguishing personality, director Greydon has the girls change into tight white t-shirts with their names emblazoned on the chest in block letters—exactly like the Mickey Mouse Club, except for the visible nipples. (And now that you're picturing Cubby's highbeams, we should probably point out this movie *does* contain a shower scene, and you do see breasts. But since they're the sort of breasts you usually see only on very young girls, or very old men, it left us feeling kind of queasy.)

While the girls are showering, Wilfred sneaks in and curses their shorts and baby tees.

The cheerleaders pile into the PE teacher's car and head off to an away game, followed by Wilfred, who has himself been cursed with a leisure suit the color of tomato bisque. Furiously rubbing his talisman (probably not what you're thinking) he curses the PE coach's Country Squire, causing it to come to a safe and complete stop. Wilfred picks up the stranded pep squad in his camper, and laughs maniacally as he reveals that they are now helpless, and completely in his *power*! Then he loses control of the pickup and stalls in a vacant lot. Fortunately for him, it's a *satanic* vacant lot. As the girls emerge from the truck, Patti is suddenly overcome by an unnatural passion, and exposes her boobs to Albert Finney's doorknocker from *Scrooge*. Then she lies down on a barbecue and has an orgasm, while Wilfred has a heart attack.

Teach and the cheerleaders get in Wilfred's truck and drive until they see John Carradine, who is dressed in rags and wandering the roadside with a burlap sack, picking up discarded cans, bottles, and cameos in Jerry Warren movies. Now the filmmakers deliver another big shock, as we learn that John's not actually in this film. Apparently, it was some sort of clerical error, or maybe the camera crew just caught him puttering around on his day off.

Teach and the cheerleaders seek out the local sheriff (John Ireland), who goes by the name "B.L. Bubb" (get it?). The guileless girls don't yet realize the full significance of this strange name, but they're pretty sure it means he used to be on "The Dukes of Hazzard."

While Sheriff John goes to check on their story about a dead satanic custodian near a giant doorknocker, the unspeakably sinister Yvonne De Carlo shows up dressed like Howdy Doody. When the Sheriff finds Wilfred napping on the barbecue, he beats his oddly spangled disciple to a pulp, then gives him a piggyback ride. Unsure how to react to this, Wilfred decides to die again.

Back at the Sheriff's house, the girls sense that Something Is Not Right. They try thinking, but once again, it makes them feel unfresh. Then they overhear Sheriff John's plan to sacrifice a "pure maiden" (yeah, right) and they run away.

Meanwhile, Patti is muttering mumbo-jumbo in the living room and going all satanic on Yvonne's ass (apparently, flashing her knockers at a knocker has endowed her with the ability to browbeat washed-up contract players).

The girls are recaptured, then promptly escape again, giving us yet another chance to enjoy long scenes of them jiggling over hill and dale. Gathering a posse of demonic hicks and bumpkins, Sheriff John puts on his pajamas and hunts down the fleeing pep squad. Yvonne helps by pulling out the Satan Home Game and saying a prayer for her Audi. (Well, that's what it *sounded* like—I suppose she could have been facing a satanic altar and saying "Howdy," but that would seem to undercut the moment.)

Catching up to the Semi-Naked Prey, Sheriff John dresses them in graduation gowns and brings them to the consecrated barbecue. But it turns out that Patti is now going steady with Lucifer. As she shouts some more nonsense, Wilfred rises from the dead again and stabs Sheriff John in the bladder with a trowel. The demonic "Hee Haw" extras bow down and worship Patti as the Devil's intern.

Cut to a football game. The cheerleaders, now sponsored by Satan, are hopping around and shaking their pom-poms, when one of the players is felled by an injury. But Beelzebub has endowed his Bride with the power to repair groin pulls, and she commands the player to rise, and the team to *win*! So, for those of you dreading the coming of the Anti-Christ, you can relax. The Horned Beast doesn't have time to engulf the world in darkness, since he's busy fixing high school football games.

Satan's Cheerleaders: not just a shocking expose of how football imperils innocent groins, but also a Betty Freidan-inspired call for female empowerment through Satanism and shower scenes.

Our director, Greydon Clark, is also responsible for *Angel's Revenge*, another movie about skimpily dressed women who jiggle and giggle their way through a battle with the forces of evil (represented by cast members Arthur Godfrey and Alan Hale, Jr.). So, we might consider Greydon the John Milton of '70s cinema, showing the armies of God battling the legions of Lucifer, with sexy results. It's just that his heavenly hosts have Farrah hair and wear skin-tight t-shirts, while his hellish battalions are composed of inept janitors, John Ireland, and Lily Munster. In fact, the Satan of these films would most likely have the motto "Better to reign in hell than to serve lunch specials at TGI Fridays."

And speaking of rain, Anton LaVey, founder of The Church of Satan, was a technical advisor on *The Devil's Rain* (which is why those melting sherbet scenes seemed so authentic). However, he was touring with Bread when it came time to film *Satan's Cheerleaders,* so the moviemakers had to rely on a copy of *The Devil's Cliff Notes* and the instruction manual from a Weber grill for their info about Satanism. And while a cursory knowledge of the occult leads us to believe that real devil worshippers don't actually wear rhinestone-studded leisure suits (except to the Academy Awards), what about the rest of the film's demonic theology? Do Satanists really sacrifice virgins, pray to doorknockers, and impersonate Howdy Doody?

To find out, we interviewed Anton LaVey (via Ouija board, since he's passed over and is with Satan now). At least we think it was Anton LaVey we were talking to—it may have been Anton Chekhov, or possibly Lyndon LaRouche. Anyway, it was somebody with a funny name. Here is a transcript of our interview (send $29 to *Dateline* if you want a transcript of our séance with Dick Cheney):

Q: Mr. LaVey, when we tried researching Satanism on the Internet, we read that Satanists kidnap children for rituals, and eat at least 3000 babies a year. Is this true?

A: No, of course not! In fact, the ninth of my "Eleven Satanic Rules of the Earth" is "Do not harm little children." Modern Satanists are not like the ones you see in horror movies, always sacrificing goats and terrorizing Mia Farrows. Besides, babies are too fatty for today's active Satanist. After a busy night of reading from the Satanic Bible, ritual magick, and a nice orgy, we usually have something light, like a salad, followed by some baby-flavored Jell-O.

Q: Is it also untrue that there's a massive ritual network, which kidnaps virgins and makes them participate in weird sexual ceremonies—all headed up by the British royal family?

A: Well, *that's* true, but it has nothing to do with us!

Q: Many coaches and players thank God for their sports victories; shouldn't they be blaming Satan for their losses?

A: Yes. Because the stadium, gym, or arena is the *real* playing field of the ultimate battle of good or evil. Every time one of God's teams wins a game, the Almighty wins. However, when these teams lose (due to the evil machinations of the devil), then Satan comes that much closer to ruling over the Earth. And, while Lucifer doesn't actually have any teams, since athletes are too pious, humble, and pure to have anything to do with him, Satan does own the league officials, the refs, and, as you saw in the movie, the cheerleaders. So, it's pretty balanced.

Q: Wow, we never realized that sporting events were so cosmically important!

A: Why else would men spend so many Sundays watching them? I'll let you in on a little secret: the Battle of Armageddon, the combat that decides the ultimate fate of the planet, will be Super Bowl XXXVI. Buy your commercial spots now!

Q: One last question, Mr. LaVey: some Christians believe that Harry Potter is the Pied Piper of the Antichrist, leading kids to Satan, and that having a Harry Potter book in the house gives Satan "legal authority" over it, so he can, say, eat all the Frusen Gladje or hide the TV remote with impunity. Is this true?

A: Hey, I'm heading back to Hell, where I don't have to put up with this kind of nonsense. May I just say that this is why the first of my "Nine Satanic Sins" is "stupidity."

Well, I guess now we'll never know the truth about Harry Potter. So, let's turn instead to young Damien Thorn, who was also raised by foster parents who didn't understand him, sent to a boarding school, and who bore a mark of his magical heritage on his head. Of course, Damien isn't a good role model for kids, but his movies are a lot easier to find at the video store on a rainy Saturday afternoon. So next time the offspring are driving you crazy, rent *Omen III* and tell them it's *Harry Potter and the Death of Millions.* It should keep them quiet for an hour or two.

The Final Conflict: Omen III (1981)
Directed by: Graham Baker
Written by: Andrew Birkin

As a scary-looking machine drills a tunnel beneath Chicago, a worker discovers a dirt clod transfixed by a dagger. He withdraws the blade, and is rightwise declared King of England, or Employee of the Month, or something.

A swing choir invades Sotheby's, and sings upbeat selections from the Satan Big Note Songbook during a cutlery auction.

A bald guy delivers a complete set of steak knives to a monastery in Italy, where the utensils are French-kissed by a Friar.

Suddenly, we cut to a Bell Laboratories instructional film on the Ice Age.

Damien Thorn, spawn of the devil, sits in a private screening room, where he bitterly critiques the Ice Age footage because it will not advance his campaign for world domination, and because it reminds him of rainy days in the junior high Cafetorium, and the smell of Tater Tots and Sloppy Joes.

Back in his office, Damien predicts the Second Coming, and attempts to conceal his total ignorance of scripture by quoting at length from a previously unknown chapter of the Bible, "the Book of S&H Green Stamps."

In London, the United States Ambassador is uneasy, convinced that he's being followed through Hyde Park by a dwarf with a Handycam. Panicking, he turns the wrong corner and comes face-to-face with a vicious rottweiler. The demon dog hypnotizes the ambassador, promising to help him quit smoking, but instead compels him to commit suicide in a ridiculously baroque manner, involving guns and doorknobs and typewriter ribbons, and the unexpected arrival of Up With People.

Back in Washington, the guy who did the voiceovers for those Smuckers jam commercials has been elected President of the United States for some reason, and he appoints Damien ambassador to Great Britain, and president of the Young Republicans for Satan. Meanwhile, somewhere in England, two astronomers discover an amazing—even biblical—convergence of three celestial bodies, which is pretty impressive considering they were just playing "Asteroids."

Back at the Italian monastery, the monks distribute the steak knives, the only weapon on Earth that can kill the Anti-Christ, and vow that they will hunt him down and slay him, and *still* be able to slice a tomato so thin you can see through it.

In Britain, Damien is a huge success as Ambassador to the Court of St. James, and earns kudos from the entire diplomatic community for not killing himself. Determined to win over the press, he seduces a BBC newswoman by giving her son a slavering hell-beast and some valuable tips on how to achieve the Dry Look.

The monks begin their holy quest, but as hunters, they turn out to be slightly less effective than Elmer Fudd. ("Be vewwy quiet…I'm hunting Anti-Chwists!"). They track Damien to a television studio, but the assassination goes awry when the killer-monk accidentally sets himself on fire and winds up hanging upside down by one ankle and swinging around the room like a wrecking ball as he knocks over the set.

Damien immediately deduces that something is amiss. Either a band of incompetent, Ginsu-wielding monks are attempting to assassinate him, or else the *Cirque du Soleil* auditions were an abysmal failure.

Damien goes into his Secret Fort to play with his My Size Jesus, but gets into one of those my-Dad-can-beat-up-your-Dad arguments, and then he cuts his hand on the crown of thorns and has to go in early.

Meanwhile, the three stars noticed by the video game-playing astronomers have aligned over London, signaling that England—so often snubbed by the International Olympic Committee—has won the competition to host the Second Coming.

With Christ now returned to Earth and time of the essence, the monks make another attempt on Damien's life, this time by accidentally stabbing each other, then locking themselves in a tomb and dying of starvation.

To thwart the Second Coming, Damien decrees the death of every male infant born on the day of the harmonic convergence. But first, he goes fox hunting, giving the monks yet another chance to assassinate him. They fail, but do succeed in assassinating the fox.

Rallying, a monk on horseback pulls his dagger and charges Damien, but almost immediately falls off the horse, and then off a bridge. The remaining assassin is torn apart by Springer spaniels.

In a cave somewhere, the Antichrist conducts an Anthony Robbins-style seminar for a covenful of Satanists, and charges his pale, doughy disciples with the task of slaying "the Nazarene." But first, he makes them walk on hot coals and buy his complete set of self-motivation tapes.

The surviving monk pays a visit to the BBC newswoman. He reveals that Damien bears the devil's mark on the back of his head, which is concealed by the Anti-Christ's cunning use of a volumizing shampoo.

Through a process of elimination, Damien deduces that the Christ child was born to his own private secretary. Irritated that it's always in the *last place you look*, Damien orders the disciple to slay his infant son. But the man refuses, defying his demonic master because Damien didn't get him anything for Secretary's Day.

Meanwhile, the newswoman gets into a battle of wills with Damien over her son, whose Dry Look is now preternatural. In exchange for sole custody, she offers to lead Damien to the Christ child, who is sheltering in a cathedral.

Damien starts searching the nave for a baby. Fed up with the whole thing, the newswoman stabs him in the back with the sanctified Ginsu, producing a terrifying *shriek* as the wound releases Damien's inner James Brown. There's a prolonged bit of shaking, jittering, and scenery-chewing, followed by the sad but inevitable death of the Hardest-Working Anti-Christ in show business.

So, *The Final Conflict*: a film about American diplomacy in action! Like *The Omega Code*, this movie is loosely based on the book of Revelation, as well as other Christian eschatology about Antichrists and hair-care products. It also is a lesson about the importance of reading the Bible, especially if you're mentioned in it. See, the Bible (specifically Acts 1:11, as the movie thoughtfully points out), specifies that Christ will return the same way he left: not by rebirth, but through special effects. But Damien spends all his time looking for a baby in a manger; so, it's pretty obvious that Our Little Antichrist never bothered to read the Good Book, which is like having a copy of the enemy's war plans but never looking at them because you're too busy watching *She's the Sheriff*. Clearly, Damien got into college on the strength of his family name, and not his SATs. Learn from his mistakes.

What else does this movie teach us? To start with, the importance of having a really good set of cutlery. The monks in our film utilized the Seven Sacred Knives of Megiddo, a set of holy shish kabob skewers that Gregory Peck picked up in the first movie, just in case he ever needed to kill an antichrist. As we learned in that film, you must make a cross formation with the seven daggers in order to kill the son of Satan. However, this was too difficult for the average warrior monk (they really seem to have gone downhill since the days of "Kung Fu"), so the rules were modified so that you only had to stab Damien with one of the knives in order to defeat ultimate evil and win the game. And these knives are so easy to use that even a TV Weather Girl can kill demonic beings with them! How much would YOU pay for knives that can cut through a tin can, slice tomatoes paper-thin, and also dispatch the spawn of hell? Don't answer yet, because these knives are authentic Megiddo® blades, made by the same people who brought you *Megiddo: The Omega Code 2*. Yes, Michael York is back, and this time Armageddon is personal! It seems Michael only became The Beast because his brother stole his girlfriend, and Satan promised to help him get to second base with her. Which makes us wonder: just what *would* the Mark of the Breast be? Oh, and here's part of the "They Call Me Trinity Broadcasting" description of the film: "From the rise of the Antichrist and false prophet, to his seizure of world power, to that last great confrontation between good and evil—God and Satan—MEGIDDO, the movie, will keep you on the edge of your seat! The end will leave you breathless as Satan." Which makes us wonder: just how breathless *does* Satan leave Paul and Jan Crouch?

Anyway, buy good knives.

And that brings us to our next glimpse at Satan's home movies, *End of Days*. This one is about that big Y2K disaster that never happened, and how we all bought lots of bottled water, guns, and inflatable women, and it was all for naught! And it turns out it was the devil's fault, not Jimmy Carter's, as previously announced.

End of Days (1999)
Directed by Peter Hyams
Written by Andrew W. Marlowe

It's December 28th, 1999 and Jesus Christ…I mean Jericho Cane (Arnold Schwarzenegger) is an atheistic, suicidal former cop. His disdain for life is evident when he picks up old pizza off the floor, mixes it with coffee and raw eggs, and blends it into a nutritious shake (one in the morning, one for lunch, and a sensible dinner out of the McDonald's dumpster at night). These days Arnold works as a bodyguard, protecting scummy investment bankers. As bad as that sounds, it gets even worse, as his latest client, "The Man" (Gabriel Byrne), is Satan.

It seems that Lucifer hath risen from hell on a matter of cosmic importance—he's got a hot date. See, it was predicted that at the end of a thousand years (starting a thousand years ago, conveniently enough) a woman would exist who could bear the devil's child—and Christine (Robin Tunney) is That Girl! If her EPT strip turns blue, it will usher in the End of Days, which is not only the prophesied End of the World, but also a switch in the cosmic power structure, with the Devil becoming the Supreme Being and everybody on Earth going to hell. Left unexplained is whether everybody in hell comes to Earth. And if so, does that mean that horned demons and scorched, flayed, brimstone-scented souls in torment would be driving busses, selling insurance, and working the counter at Subway? (This whole premise was spawned by the misinterpretation of a sentence by the apostle John—we would hazard that our screenwriter has never actually *read* the Book of Revelation, but still thought it might make a good action movie.)

So, the Prince of Darkness, using the body of Gabriel Byrne, must impregnate his foreordained bride or lose his chance to take over. But to make it a *challenge*, he has to get busy and fertilize her deviled egg between the hour of 11:00 PM and midnight on December 31, 1999. Talk about performance anxiety!

Christine, as we learned earlier, was born in a public hospital with the loving assistance of a Satanist obstetrics staff. Immediately after her birth they made her suckle snake blood (the reason for this is never explained—maybe because it tastes better than Similac). Then they killed her parents and raised her in a gorgeous brownstone in the lap of luxury, where she was lovingly cared for by a demonic au pair who made sure that Christine did her homework, ate her vegetables, and drank her snake blood.

Meanwhile, as Arnold is protecting The Man, a frail old priest named Thomas Aquinas tries to mow him down. In an action sequence that endangers almost everyone in the city, Arnold barely manages to overcome the 90-year-old cleric, and desperately hopes he isn't called upon to face even *more* fearsome assailants, like Grandma Moses, or Lambchop.

For the rest of the movie, everyone tries to either kill, kidnap, or rescue Christine, to variously prevent or further her little tryst with Satan, and the Unblessed Event that will result from it. But everybody is so intent on stopping the sex that apparently they forgot about *birth control* as a way to foil the devil's plan. (Yes, this *is* the Catholic Church we're talking about, but we doubt even the Pope would advocate the Rhythm Method when Lucifer turns up as your Mystery Date).

Then a lot of action-y stuff happens, most of it involving explosions, fires, and noise. In the course of all the violence we learn that all members of the NYPD are Satanists (big surprise).

The Man gets shot, burnt, thrown off a subway, etc., but it doesn't really bother him because he's made of liquid metal. Eventually, though, the bullets give him a rash, or he just gets tired of being Gabriel Byrne, because at 5 minutes before midnight on the 31st, while Arnold and Christine are holed up in a Cathedral and Arnold has *just* gotten his faith back, Lucifer possesses him. He *still* hasn't given up on making the Beast With Two Backs and is going to use Arnold's body to do it (but it's going to have to be a quickie, since he doesn't even begin to rip her clothes off until about a minute before the deadline). But wait—the movie told us that the devil had to father the child using Gabriel Byrnes' pre-ordained body—so having Arnold rape the girl would *make no sense!* However, I guess it's anything for a climax (no double entendre intended).

Just when it looks like we're all going to hell, the girl tells Arnold to not give in to Satan and to just say no to drugs and stuff, and in a stunning *deus ex machismo*, Arnold manages to impale himself on the bric-a-brac. Having failed to get a date for New Years Eve, the Father of Lies returns to hell, where he spends the rest of the night sulking on the couch in his boxer shorts, knocking back tallboys of malt liquor and watching Shannon Tweed movies on Cinemax. Meanwhile, Arnold, who began the story as an atheist with a history of unsuccessful suicide attempts, has traveled a long, hard road to redemption, and is now a believer with a *successful* suicide under his belt. He goes to heaven, even though suicide is a mortal sin, thus proving that there's an exception for people who commit suicide to avoid having sex. Unfortunately, this means that Arnold will be spending the rest of eternity with Robby Benson's character from *Ode to Billy Joe*.

So, what lessons from this movie can *you* apply to your everyday life?

Well, that if you're too picky about whom you are willing to date, you will never have sex—especially if you only make yourself available one hour every thousand years (Satan's Mom told him the same thing, but he would never listen). If he had just joined a dating service, he might have found a girl with a good personality who would have accepted him for who he was. We can recommend Stygian Expectations or DatesFromHell.com.

Secondly, we have learned that while Cathedrals can't keep out Satan (because that would violate Equal Housing regulations), they do have nice knick-knacks that you can kill yourself with, if needs be. And, as we learned from personal experience, those knick-knacks could be made from the remains of the last person who used them to off himself! Let us now tell you of our afternoon of true-life horror in…

The Bone Church of Kutna Hora!

First, some background. During the Crusades, the local abbot brought back some dirt from the site of the Crucifixion, and from then on Kutna Hora (a village in Bohemia) was *the* happening place to be buried. By the 19th century, the monks had a basement, attic, and rental unit full of human bones, and were running out of storage space. So, they turned the skeletons into lovely bone candle holders, darling skull pyramids (topped with cherubs), a striking eight-foot-high bone chandelier ringed with skulls, and even a whimsical bone bird. All in all, the church at Kutna Hora is decorated with the skeletal remains of 40,000 persons.

Some years ago when we were visiting the Czech Republic, our guide dropped us off at an old building, telling us only that it used to be a monastery, and he'd wait in the car. We strolled around with that blasé attitude of world travelers who, if they've seen one elderly pile of stones, have seen them all. But after a few moments we realized…hey, this place is *built from human bones!* And then we began to speculate about what kind of people would have constructed a monument like this. Were they satanic monks, who invited pilgrims to retreats, and then killed them so they could use their blood for diabolic black masses, their bones to make bread and/or bibelots?

Of course, they might not have been satanic monks per se—maybe they just had a different notion of the monastic ideal. Instead of a life dedicated to asceticism and self-denial, maybe they were dedicated to aesthetics and design. Maybe they were Martha Stewart monks.

("Look, Brother Matthew, I *know* it's an ossuary, but that doesn't mean it has to be so boring. *Look* at this—limestone boxes full of bones, stacked from floor to ceiling. It might as well be a shoe store! As long as we've got these old bones lying around, why can't we do something kicky and fun with them? We could use some of the phalanges and metatarsals for a sort of filigree effect along the molding—sort of like Victorian gingerbread. We could use cracked ulnas and ribs to make decorative sconces. And what about taking some of the major bones—your femurs and skulls, say—that are just lying around taking up space, and using them to make a beautiful, functional, but oddly chilling chandelier?")

Whatever the explanation, it's clear that Kutna Hora represents a rather extreme dichotomy—the holiest of consecrated ground, containing soil filched from Golgotha, overlooked by a church filled with the desecrated remains of thousands. Talk about going out of your way to appeal to every demographic!

And that is what we learned from *End of Days*. And it made us better people and gave us some great ideas for what to do with grandma's remains.

But now, let's take a moment and review the way Hollywood depicts Ultimate Evil, shall we? In *Satan's Cheerleaders* (1977), we meet Lucifer when he was just starting out, a hungry young go-getter with a business plan that involved middle-aged has-beens and really small breasts. But as the "Me Decade" melted into the Greed-is-Good 80s, Satan's ambitions would grow larger (and so would the breasts). In 1981's *The Final Conflict: Omen III*, Lucifer has become a Yuppie, using junk bonds and infanticide to engineer a hostile takeover of the cosmos. But the time we get to 1999's *End of Days*, Satan is a middle-aged burnout who just wants to score with a hot young chick. Therefore, according to Hollywood theology, it won't be an army of sword-wielding archangels that finally defeat the Arch-Fiend. It'll be male menopause.

Ziggy Stardust, Action Hero!

The 1980s were a manly time for motion pictures; an age when movies about muscular men with speech impediments signaled an end to the agonizing introspection of the Post-Vietnam era. In the *oeuvre* of Stallone and Schwarzenegger, we saw the birth of a new breed of hero, a brawny man untroubled by malaise or moral relativism; a modern legend, with the physical strength and spiritual purity of a Hercules, and the accent of a shoemaking dwarf from the Black Forest.

And yet, for every Stallone or Schwarzenegger, there was also a Kurt Thomas, or a Barry Bostwick: fey and elfin heroes who fiercely bitch-slapped their enemies on behalf of the American way. Judging by the action movies of the 1980s, it wasn't only testosterone and body grease that brought down the Berlin Wall—it was dance belts and bilevel haircuts, too, as can be seen in the following, quintessentially '80s action flicks.

Gymkata (1985)
Directed by: Robert Clouse
Written by: Charles Robert Carner, Dan Tyler Moore (novel)

This movie was based on a book, *The Terrible Game*, and probably the filmmakers' worst misstep was changing the title to *Gymkata*. Not to say that *The Terrible Game* isn't a lousy title in itself, but we would have opted for a more modest adjustment, and called it simply, *The Terrible Movie*. (Actually, saying this cheeseball of a script was based on a novel is like saying that Count Chocula cereal is based on Le Fanu's *Carmilla*.)

The Terrible Game is actually *The Most Dangerous Game*, as designed by the President's Council on Physical Fitness. It requires the player to run around and climb a rope, and we're told that only a select few people in the world can meet this grueling challenge: either world-class gymnasts, like American champion Kurt Thomas, or 11-year olds who've passed sixth-grade gym.

The movie opens with an angry white man—Kurt's dad, who's apparently playing on the Terrible Game Senior Tour—attempting to cross the rope bridge at Camp Snoopy. Richard Norton (who we know is evil because he's wearing

Sonny Bono's sheepskin vest from *Wild on the Beach*) shoots an arrow into Kurt's dad, who falls to his death.

Cut to the United States, where the Olympic Games are being held in a high-school auditorium. American champion Kurt Thomas dismounts the parallel bars, and is immediately recruited by the CIA to play The Game, which is held in Parmistan, a mountain kingdom ruled by "the Khan." Kurt will be trained by Princess Ruballi, the Khan's daughter, and even though she spends the first half of the film attempting to do grievous harm to his groin (knee it, stab it, rope-burn it, etc.), Ruballi eventually becomes Kurt's love interest, because she's the only person in the film who's shorter than he is.

Kurt and the Princess white-water raft into Parmistan, where they're promptly attacked by Himalayan ninjas, who object to his mullet. Dressed in black Dr. Dentons and black Ku Klux Klan hoods, topped off with those red plastic hats from Devo's "Whip It!" video, they present a fearsome sight. Hopelessly outnumbered, Kurt unleashes the secret martial art of *Gymkata*, and manages to overcome his assailants using the deadly power of Mary Lou Retton's compulsory floor routine from the '84 Olympics.

Once in the capital, Kurt and the other competitors meet the Khan, who is apparently a member of The Davy Crockett Hair Club for Men, and who explains the rules of "The Game." Basically, you run around and climb on various pieces of playground equipment until someone shoots you with an arrow. If Kurt wins, the U.S. will be allowed to build a "Star Wars" satellite-tracking station in Parmistan. If Kurt loses, he will be killed in the traditional way: shot with an arrow while playing the "Smack the Mole" game at a Chuck E. Cheese.

The next morning, the Khan announces that Sheepskin will wed Princess Ruballi after the game, with a reception to follow at Medieval Times restaurant. The peasants respond by saying "Yock-mallah!" in unison, and listlessly waving some giant candy canes. Then the competitors are off and running.

Amazingly, Kurt makes it across the rope bridge *without* getting shot by an arrow, and enters "The Village of the Damned," a planned community for the criminally insane. No one has ever escaped alive from this blood-soaked bedlam, and it is soon apparent why. In short order, Kurt is attacked by a man with a sickle, beaten to a pulp by a pack of Italian grandmothers, and mooned. Finally, the entire populace converges on Kurt, shrieking and waving various farm implements as they surround him in the village square. Fortunately, next to the communal well is the communal pommel horse. Leaping onto it, Kurt manages to kill the axe-wielding maniacs with a quick and deadly series of Magyar and Sivado cross-travel variations. The surviving villagers give Kurt a 9.2.

The crazed peasants chase Kurt into a blind alley, forcing him to climb a sheer wall, but he's too much of a pussy to reach the top. Surprisingly, one of the Himalayan ninjas reaches down and pulls Kurt to safety. He then peels off the black mask and reveals that he's really…Kurt's dad! It turns out that he *wasn't* killed in the fall, just maimed. Their tearful reunion is interrupted when Sheepskin shoots Kurt's dad with an arrow again. Springing into action, Kurt heroically jumps on a horse and rides away.

Sheepskin catches up to our fleeing hero and gives him a well-deserved thrashing. But Kurt cleverly goes into "rope-a-dope," outlasting his opponent until they get to the page in the script where it says he wins. Sheepskin takes a dive, and Kurt proudly rides back into town with Dad, who's been maimed some more, but is otherwise fine. Now, at last, everyone knows the truth: Sheepskin is a traitor, and Kurt's dad is Rasputin.

Oh, and Kurt won The Game, all right. But if you ask me, he won ugly.

And what lessons about being a hero should you take from the film? Well, here are a few, courtesy of myth-master Joseph Campbell:

1. The mythic hero is an everyman who receives a call to adventure while living his everyday life. Gymnast Kurt was minding his own business, competing in the Olympics at the local high school, when the CIA asked him to go on a mission having profound national security implications. Likewise, someday you might be going about your daily routine (i.e., eating a Hungry Man dinner while watching a "24" rerun), and the CIA might ring the doorbell and ask *you* to destroy the atomic weapon housed over at Burt's Feed 'n Seed. That's how these things work.

2. As he proceeds on his journey, the hero will meet a mentor who will teach him what he needs to know to complete his quest. Kurt's mentor was Princess Ruballi. Luke Skywalker's was Yoda. The similarities are clear—Yoda was the only person in *Star Wars* shorter than Luke, and so their romance was also inevitable. The lesson you should take from this is: pick your mentor with care, since this relationship might get closer than you intend and you could find your quest interrupted by a reach-around from Fozzie Bear.

3. The hero will eventually reconcile with his father—even if his father is dead. So, if you suspect you're a mythic hero and you have unfinished business with Dad, you should constantly be on the lookout for ghosts, zombies, and children or pets who might be your reincarnated progenitor. In recent years

a consensus has coalesced around two discrete works in the Western canon which scholars believe most fully realize this theme: *Hamlet* and *My Mother the Car*.

4. At his journey's end, the hero obtains a boon for humanity. Gilgamesh brought an understanding of mortality to his people (thanks, Gil). Luke brought freedom to the Galaxy. Kurt got us a satellite-tracking base, a crappy electroplated trophy, and a dwarfish member of Himalayan royalty.

And speaking of weird cinematic pairings, our next movie offers us John Stamos and Gene Simmons—who, in their day, were known collectively as "Stammons" until they broke up over Gene's indiscretions with Bob Saget.

Never Too Young To Die (1986)
Directed by Gil Bettman
Written by Anthony Foutz

John Stamos first achieved notoriety as "Blackie," the sensitive, cycle-straddling delinquent on *General Hospital*, before finally rising to a flaming, Phoenix-like apotheosis of fame as "Uncle Jesse" on *Full House*. In between, he made a lame stab at snatching the action hero tiara from Kurt Thomas in a contest that resembled two old women struggling over a discounted bra at a Woolworth clearance sale.

But John was no mere simulacrum of Kurt. No, he forged his own unique character in *Never Too Young to Die*, playing a champion gymnast with a mullet whose Dad worked for the CIA…

Hmm. Anyway, this time Kurt—I mean John—is called "Lance Stargrove," a name so manly that every actor working in male porn films in the1980s must have been kicking himself that he didn't think of it first. John's dad is George Lazenby, who comes bearing impeccable spy film credentials, having thoroughly stunk up *On Her Majesty's Secret Service*. As the movie opens, George is trying to foil arch-criminal Gene Simmons (yes, the guy from KISS), who is playing an evil hermaphrodite with a super-powered middle finger.

George infiltrates Gene's headquarters with a group of commandos who eventually get bored and frag him. Then Gene shows up and shoots George too. A puffy fellow sporting six-inch stiletto boots, Mr. Spock's eyebrows, and Roseanne Rosannadanna's hair, Gene artfully evokes the inherent duality of his character by working himself into such a flamboyant, cackling tizzy that he makes Caesar Romero's Joker look like the farmer in "American Gothic."

At George's funeral, Vanity shows up to make soulful goo-goo eyes at Lance through her veil. As a former Prince protégé, Vanity has quite a bit of experience in feigning attraction to slight, androgynous men, and is therefore the perfect choice for Lance's love interest.

Seeking a break from the film's relentless pace, Lance retreats to his dad's farm in Ojai. But Vanity is already there, prancing around the barn in jodhpurs and one of Prince's lacy blouses, and shooting it out with two of Gene's thugs. (They don't introduce themselves, but they appear to be Duke Nukem and the Artful Dodger from "Oliver!") Lance is utterly confused, and for the first time, we're on his side.

Later, Vanity meets with her superior, CIA spymaster Carruthers, who's played by Gene Simmons in a red wig and fake beard. (Shhh! We're not supposed to know.) Gene orders Vanity to find Gene at a nightclub where he's performing, and kill him. Lance dons the Miami Vice look—blue t-shirt, and a shiny sport coat with the sleeves hitched up—and follows her to the nightclub, which turns out to be a cross between Fellini's *Satyricon* and the Riverside County Sheriff's Department impound lot.

Inside, a paunchy Gene sashays around in a sequined body stocking, batting his false eyelashes and shaking the long plumes of pink feathers that trail from his elaborate headdress as he shrieks out a song. It's not the most entertaining musical number ever filmed, but remember, it's an action movie, so they had to work in at least one macho character.

Next on our tour of Southern California spots where you can shoot a movie without expensive filming permits, Lance hops on a motorcycle and follows Vanity into the desert. She tries to lose him, and thanks to the editing, there are several implied car stunts. Then, suddenly, John is attacked by some homeless guys on motorized carrousel horses, who use wicked-looking battleaxes to gently poke at him as though checking to see if a pot roast is tender.

Vanity and Lance get captured by the *Mad Max* cast, and Lance wakes with a start back in Ojai (which actually *is* kind of scary—take it from one who knows). In the best scene of the film, two of Gene's henchmen torture Lance by banging his head around the insides of the kitchen sink, like a bell clapper. They try to break his spirit by squashing a cherry tomato against his cheek, then they spank him until he cries, and throw him into the bookcase.

But Lance spots a broken picture of he and his dad amongst the wreckage, and it apparently has the same effect on him that spinach has on Popeye. He leaps to his feet and suddenly starts kicking ass Gymkata-style, while a Jan Hammer wannabe plays listless, yet vaguely triumphant music on a synthesizer.

Realizing that Vanity is in mortal danger, and no doubt being tortured at this *very instant*, Lance must race to her rescue! But not right now. First, he decides to change his shirt and wander around the house for awhile.

Meanwhile, Gene is now being aided in his evil master plan—whatever the hell it is—by Freddy Krueger from *Nightmare on Elm Street*, who for some reason is dressed like one of the Archies.

Eventually, Lance goes off to infiltrate Gene's secret headquarters, which is located in an abandoned foundry in Fontana because there's no lock on the gate and the crew could film there for free. Our hero finds Vanity chained down and spread-eagled on a cement slab, with the camera pointed at her crotch. Surprisingly, her crotch gives a very nuanced performance, but all good things must come to an end, and Lance rescues her by…Well, pretty much by just showing up.

Safely back home, Vanity tries to kiss Lance. This makes our hero visibly uncomfortable, and he promptly retreats into the house to watch TV, having suddenly remembered that Christopher Lowell is doing a fabulous program on marbleizing techniques.

Vanity refuses to take a hint, and strips down to her bikini. Lance wrings his hands, and gazes anxiously skyward. Vanity doggedly rubs oil on her chest and thighs, licks her lips, doffs her top, and basically does everything possible to seduce Lance short of slipping him a roofie. Eventually, she's stark naked and shivering under the spray from a garden hose, and Lance abruptly stumbles toward her. Perhaps he was suddenly overcome by passion, although my theory is that the director was crouching just off-camera, and jabbed him in the ass with a hatpin.

Mercifully for everyone involved, the sex scene is cut short by terrorists. Lance and Vanity are kidnapped and whisked aboard a helicopter, where Gene pulls off the beard and wig and reveals that Gene is actually…Gene! As surprises go, it's not exactly *The Crying Game*.

Gene takes them to a Junior College amphitheatre where they can shoot on weekends and nobody will know. Here we get the only actual sex in the film, as Gene flaps his prehensile tongue and shoves it down Vanity's throat like a plumber's snake. Lance challenges Duke Nukem to a one-on-one fight "with a *real* man!" Surprisingly, he means himself. Duke agrees, but it turns out that Lance's definition of "a *real* man" is rather elastic, and includes a hysterical pussy who will grab the Uzi from a slack-jawed spectator and gun down his unarmed opponent. Before he can embarrass himself further, however, the U.S. Army Special Forces arrives, having apparently secured transportation by renting the Long

Beach Harbor excursion helicopter for a few hours. Lance fires indiscriminately into the extras in an effort to clear the set, since time is money.

Gene climbs into a big rig truck and tries to flee by passing himself off as Large Marge. But Lance catches up to him, and in the climactic battle, they literally scratch and bite each other's nipples, until Lance suddenly throws a CPR dummy over a dam and declares victory. The Director of the CIA offers Lance a job as a secret agent, but he's too much of a puss, and runs away. The End.

And what lessons does *Never Too Young to Die* teach us about being an '80s action hero?

First, that if you're big and beefy, you can get by with just one two-syllable name, such as Rambo, Rocky, Conan, or Roseanne. However, if you're kinda delicate and boyish, you'll need a strong, masculine moniker to give you gravitas: you know, something like "Lance Stargrove" or "Savage Beefrod" or "Dick Cheney."

And second, that while being an action hero may sound cool, it's not all fun and games. You might have to withstand torture, such as water-boarding, electro-shock, or having to watch a dumpy, aging rock star perform in *Victor/Victoria*. And the job could entail indignities, like cherry tomato facials, or wearing Don Johnson's hand-me-downs. But worst of all, naked starlets might follow you around, demanding that you make out with them, thus exposing you to biohazards such as cooties!

So, think the whole thing through before you sign up for that PCDI correspondence course in Criminal Justice and Action Hero Vocational Training. Admittedly, their spokesman makes it sound exciting. ("I'm Simon MacCorkindale. You might remember me as Jonathan Chase, the man who solved crimes by changing into animals in the TV series 'Manimal.' And if *you* want a great career in the exciting fields of crime fighting, accounting, PC repair, or shape shifting, call now for our free information packet.") But Simon doesn't tell you about the embarrassing wardrobe requirements, the torture, and the icky, old girls!

For more about girl cooties, we go to glam mercenary Barry Bostwick, for some Amazing Discoveries about safe movie sex (all covered in our exclusive free pamphlet, *Giving the Digit to Gidget*).

Megaforce (1982)
Directed by: Hal Needham
Written by: André E. Morgan, Albert S. Ruddy

A profoundly personal film, wrenched deep from the soul of stuntmeister Hal
Needham, *Megaforce* stars Barry Bostwick, Persis Khambatta, Edward Mulhare,
and Henry Silva. (Suggested ad copy included, "Needham? There's plenty in *this*
cast!")

Based on a painting by Jackson Pollock, the plot of *Megaforce* goes something
like this: Edward Mulhare (as "The General") and Persis Khambatta (as "The
Major") are dropped off in the middle of the desert by a limousine. They remain
there for a really long time while nothing happens, giving us plenty of opportunity to admire their wardrobe. Edward is sporting a beige polyester shirt, double-
knit slacks, and the shortest tie this side of Oliver Hardy. Persis is wearing a
gauzy, rust-colored gown that matches her rouge, and sitting on a rock with her
legs spread at right angles like a truck driver. This attracts a huge rattlesnake,
which attempts to recreate the climax of *North By Northwest*, where the train carrying Eva Marie Saint and Cary Grant goes into a tunnel. However, Persis and
her scaly love interest are stopped just *inches* from turning this whole thing into a
John Waters film by the intervention of Michael (*Xanadu*) Beck, who shoots the
snake, then poses while Needham treats us to a long, loving, lingering look at his
bun-hugging Sergio Valentes, his musky T-shirt advertising SKOAL smokeless
tobacco, his Linda Blair-style shag haircut, and his straw cowboy hat. Clearly, this
is Persis's *new* love interest, and she reacts accordingly: She sits on a rock, and
spreads her legs. Edward is apparently aroused by this, because his tie suddenly
gets longer.

They all pile into a sport utility vehicle with a ThighMaster on the roof, and
drive through the desert. Eventually, they stop to watch some guys on motorcycles pop wheelies and gun down a bunch of giant beach balls that were apparently
going on an Outward Bound trip with Rover from "The Prisoner."

One of the cyclists dismounts, and Persis meets her third love interest of the
film. It's whippet-thin, frost-and-tipped action hero Ace Hunter (Barry
Bostwick). Sporting a skin-tight gold lamé bodysuit and a sky-blue headband stolen from Olivia Newton John's "Let's Get Physical" video, Barry introduces himself as the commander of an elite special-forces unit, despite the fact that he's
dressed like a chorus boy from *Starlight Express*. He leads the party into his super-
secret underground matte painting, where he changes the skintight bodysuit for a
skintight velveteen cutaway coat and a sky-blue ascot the size of a lobster bib.

Edward Mulhare explains that he needs an elite force of professional killers for a *blitzkrieg* assault on a fortified target, and he believes that Barry's cadre of highly trained Edwardian fops are just the men for the job. Barry consents, and gives a high-tech briefing on the mission—the effect of which is somewhat compromised by the fact that he looks like Barry Gibb in *Sgt. Pepper's Lonely Hearts Club Band*, and the briefing consists of him and Michael Beck playing "Pong."

Persis is persistent about wanting to go along on the attack, so Barry runs her through Megaforce basic training, which involves a trip to the Driver's Ed. simulator, and a rear-projected skydiving sequence, in which the two of them attempt to mate in mid-air like eagles until Barry prematurely deploys his chute, if you know what I mean. Persis passes the training with flying colors, which convinces her that Barry was right: She's just a dumb ol' girl, and she ought to stay home. As they tenderly part at the airport, Persis kisses her thumb and shows it to Barry, who kisses *his* thumb and shows it to *her*. This is as hot as the sex ever gets.

Megaforce attacks the target, which turns out to be a strip mall in San Bernardino. While a red digital clock counts down in the corner of the screen, the killer motorcyclists ride through and blast all the buildings. Then they ride through once more, and we watch all the same stuff blow up again. And again. And *again*. Apparently, it's a *Möbius*-strip mall.

Meanwhile, Mulhare conspires with some off-screen politicians to double-cross Megaforce.

Trapped in the middle of the desert, Barry and his men have but one chance of escape: They must stage a Super Bowl Halftime Show. This plan works for some reason, and everybody reaches the rescue plane except for Barry. Fortunately, just as the aircraft lifts off, Barry's motorcycle turns into Chitty Chitty Bang Bang, while Barry himself turns into a cross between Margaret Hamilton in *The Wizard of Oz* and Henry Thomas in *E.T.*

Flushed with triumph, Barry is met at the airport by Persis, and they run off to spend a romantic evening together, Frenching their own barely opposable digits. The End.

Ace Hunter: yet another mythic hero. As Joseph Campbell said in *The Hero's Journey*, "Each of us has a Hero, a Sage, a mercenary, a Princess within. Each of these pulls and pushes as we journey through the story that is our life." And that's why Barry didn't need to get inside Princess Persis: he had his own inner Princess.

But what was that thumb-kissing all about? Well, palm readers call the base of the thumb "The Mound of Venus," and say that it's an indicator of our ability to love, as well as our capacity for playfulness. However, a woman's *mons pubis* is also known as the Mound of Venus. So, it's apparent that while Barry's heart is in the right place, he just has a really crappy sense of direction.

Anyway, we've now looked at three of the finest action heroes that the '80s had to offer—what else can they teach us? Well, deep textual analysis of these films reveal a startling truth: Girls go for femmy guys. In the Rambo or Arnold movies, most everybody is dead by the end of the film, including the disposable female lead. But you'll note that in *Gymkata*, Kurt won the hand of Princess Ruballi, Lance wound up burdened with Vanity, and Barry won—if not the hand of Persis—at least her thumb. Ultimately, the message of Reagan-era action films seems two-fold: On the one hand, America must adopt a strong and uncompromising stance *vis-a-vis* our ideological opponents in the international arena. On the other hand, steroids will make you impotent, and short, effeminate men will get all the chicks.

But what will the action movie hero of the next decade be like? It is our expert opinion, based on the trends we have identified from the past twenty years, that the hero of future popcorn movies will be strong enough for a man, but made for a woman; tough enough to make a tender chicken, but now with wings! Oh, and not very bright, kind of ineffectual, and with pouffy hair. So, in conclusion, we predict that the action hero for the New Millennium is going to be Richard Simmons.

BIONIC BOOTY:
Hollywood's Enduring Love Affair with Man-on-Machine Miscegenation

What's the first thought that springs to mind when you hear the word "robot"? Most people would define it as the stuff of science fiction. Others might reflect on the capacity of robots to standardize output and reduce repetitive motion injuries in light manufacturing. But to Hollywood, robots have always meant one thing, and one thing only:

Hot steamin' *love*.

From the mechanized seductress "Maria" in Fritz Lang's silent masterpiece, *Metropolis*, to Robin Williams' chrome-plated horndog in *Bicentennial Man*, filmmakers have always been fascinated by the romantic possibilities of robotics. Just as early Man watched birds in flight and yearned to take wing, so do the geeks who saw *Westworld* at an impressionable age now look at their inflatable lovedolls and long to take that next step into power-assisted self-abuse: the android.

And yet, if we were to achieve intimacy with a machine, would we not surrender a bit of our soul to it? Or would we simply gum up its moving parts with our viscous secretions? Over the years, a brave handful of filmmakers have dared to ask what would happen if man and machine were to become one. Not metaphorically, as in the act of love, but literally, as in a stupid movie. Let's now look at three of these meditations.

Colossus of New York is about a man who turns into robot, kills dozens of people, and then dies. *Bicentennial Man* is about a robot who annoys dozens of people, turns into a man, and then dies. *Saturn 3* is about the unfortunate effects of exposing a cyborg to *Charlie's Angels*.

The Colossus of New York (1958)
Directed by Eugène Lourié
Written by Willis Goldbeck (story) and Thelma Schnee

Humanitarian Jeremy Spensser (Ross Martin) has just returned from accepting a Nobel Prize for being Princess Diana's cousin when his son Billy throws a toy airplane in front of an oncoming truck. Jeremy, a certified genius, dives after it, is run over by the truck, and dies. The End.

Well, it *would* be the end except that Jeremy's father is one of the world's foremost brain surgeons. So, despite Jeremy's terminal case of death, Dad performs an operation that results in him still being dead. Jeremy's eulogy is given by his oldest friend, John Carrington, one of the world's foremost *Dynasty* characters, who says that Jeremy's tragic death was all part of some divine plan, in that God hated him. Dad disagrees loudly, and after the service he and Carrington have a debate on the subject of brains. Dad argues the "pro" position, stating that the brain contains all of man's glory, plus a creamy center. Carrington takes "con," delivering the movie's thesis: "A brain divorced from human experience becomes a monster." Dad smartly rejoins, "You are an idiot!" but the judges award the match to Carrington because he looks more like Snidely Whiplash.

After Jeremy's tragic passing, his younger brother Henry loses no time putting the moves on Jeremy's widow, Anne. Dad interrupts the lechery to show Henry what he's been working on—raising a brain in an aquarium. (Dad got the idea from an ad in the back of a comic book: "Raise Brains at Home. Make Good Money.) And guess what? It's Jeremy's brain! Henry is resentful at this latest example of Dad's favoritism—after all, Dad never saved *his* brain.

Dad asks Henry to build a mechanical body to house the brain of his supergenius brother. Henry puts aside his resentment and soon has constructed a 9-foot tall papier-mâché robot with headlights instead of eyes. And best of all, it has an off switch for when it's time to end the movie!

When Colossus experiences a WAOL protection error, Henry wants to destroy the automaton, since having a robot brother didn't turn out to be as much fun as he thought it would be. Colossus also votes for destruction, but Dad says no, declaring that Jeremy can't die until he ends world hunger and finishes his homework.

Colossus has almost perfected his inventions—Arctic-growing wheat and edible underwear—when he sees images of a sinking ocean liner. Dad turns on the TV, and indeed, an ocean liner *is* sinking—and it's taking Leonardo DiCaprio down with it. But the important thing is that the robot has telepathy and can control minds!

It's now been a year since Jeremy died, and in celebration Colossus trudges over to the cemetery and reads his headstone: "Jeremy Spensser: Brilliant Scientist, Really Moronic Pedestrian." His son Billy arrives, chats up the hideous cardboard creation, and trustingly jumps into his arms after Colossus promises him a present. Billy is quite the little present-slut.

That night Colossus stealthily clomps into Anne's bedroom to ogle her while she sleeps. She awakens and decides to stroll around the grounds in her low-cut, slinky nightgown to see if she still has what it takes to attract giant robots. At first, all she gets is Henry, who forcibly nuzzles her. Then there is the sound of arcing electricity, and Colossus lumbers into view. Anne faints, and Henry runs away, figuring that Anne will be protected by her sexy nightie. Colossus tenderly carries her to bed, cursing his brother for having pawed his wife, and even worse, for giving him mesmerizing headlight eyes but no penis.

Henry flees to Manhattan, and Colossus pursues him by walking under the Atlantic Ocean. Well, actually Colossus walks behind a vinyl shower curtain with waves drawn on it to *suggest* that he's walking under water, since an electric robot made from papier-mâché really shouldn't get wet. He plods up the pier to where the oblivious Henry is waiting. Sparks fly from his eyes, and Henry is toast.

Colossus returns home and tells Dad that raising crops to feed the weak is a waste of time, and that he's tired of keeping "human trash" alive. So in addition to becoming a murderer while in New York, Colossus also became a Republican.

But he continues to meet innocent, greedy little Billy. When Anne asks Billy where he got the plane that looks just like the one that he threw into traffic to kill his dad, Billy tells her he got it from "Mr. Giant," whom he's been seeing behind Mom's back for weeks now, the little tramp. Billy adds that today Mr. Giant said the cutest thing—he asked Billy to call him Daddy. Anne looks concerned, realizing that judges traditionally side with giant robots in custody battles.

Colossus uses his strobe-light mind control to force Dad to take Anne and Billy to the U.N. Colossus uses the underwater route again, walking in slow motion to simulate water resistance and match the movie's pace (a better title for this thing might have been "Molasses of New York").

At the U.N., a spirited game of human chess for world dominance is going on when Colossus enters and starts shooting death rays at everybody. They all just panic and die, so little Billy takes charge. He runs up to the giant killing machine and yells, "I hate you! You're bad!" Billy's message gets through to the inhuman creation, which tells Billy that if he touches him in *just* the right spot, he can make Colossus stop his rampage. "Push harder!" he orders. Yes, he has Billy turn him off (not turn him on, as *you* probably imagined). Colossus tumbles over a balcony and lands with a horrible clatter for papier-mâché. Dad surveys the smashed robot and the carnage it caused, then remarks to Carrington, "You were right—without a soul, there is only monstrousness. I guess I owe you a Coke."

What did we learn from *Colossus of New York*?

First, the reason why the United Nations passed a resolution strongly condemning the construction of weapons of mass destruction without souls.

Second, that if you plan on doing the nasty with your brother's wife, then perhaps building him a large mechanical body that can shoot death rays from its eyes is not a good idea. Actually, it might be wiser to make him a nice Nerf body—and even then, you probably shouldn't play with him in the house.

And lastly, that an adviser to the lovelorn mechanoid is badly needed. So, we decided to fill that niche, and provide romantic guidance to our robotic readers. Here are some of the many letters we've received, plus our responses:

Dear Android Landers,
   I am a single, silver robot who suspects his humanoid life partner is cheating on him. Recently my man has been living away from the ship, hanging out with a brunette bimbo and her insufferable son. Anyway, he died yesterday, but instead of doing the decent thing and telling me himself, he sent his floozy with the message "Klaatu Barada nicto!" What do you think it all means?
   Signed, Gort

   Gort, it means "Wake up and smell the WD-40." Maybe you've let yourself go over the years, and aren't the cylindrical killing machine he first fell in love with. But whatever the reason, it's clear he's found another, and now he'd rather be dead than be with you. But if you set off an atomic explosion and blame the Earthlings, you'll get to vaporize the entire planet—and then the little mantrap will get hers!

Dear Android Landers,
   I am a giant space-age robot who feels like my boytoy actually has all the power in this relationship. What should I do?
   Signed, Gigantor

   Gigantor, you let the kid touch your joystick, and now he controls you. It's a common problem. You have to find a way to regain your dignity (and your remote), and then crush him like an ant. And next time keep it in your pants, or in a handy remote control caddy.

Dear Android Landers,
    I am a general domestic robotic aide whose creator designed me to look like a ten-year-old girl. He made me stupid and docile, dresses me in Mary Jane pumps and a lacy red pinafore, and has me live in his house. Isn't this wrong?
    Signed, Vicki

Yes, it's deeply wrong. While robot pedophilia can't be cured, it can be treated. Use your superhuman strength to break his "small wonder"—that should slow him down. And watch out for that creepy pervert "brother" too!

Dear Android Landers,
    Danger, danger! My lover is verbally abusive, always calling me things like "Bubble-Headed Booby" or "Nattering Ninny." I know he means it in fun, but it really hurts my feelings. How do I get him to stop?
    Signed, The Robot

Dear The Robot.
    You could change your programming and stop being a babbling bird-brained baby who cares about such things. Or, you could just do us all a favor and kill him. It's all the same to me.
    But if you still have questions about matters of the artificial heart, you should watch the following very special episode of *Saturn 3*, in which a young robot learns his first lessons in love from Farrah Fawcett. A high death count ensues.
    Emotionlessly yours, Android Landers

Saturn 3 (1980)
Directed by Stanley Donan
Written by Martin Amis

This film was created by a trio of literary and cinematic titans: legendary director Stanley Donen (*Singing in the Rain*), distinguished novelist Martin Amis, and Hollywood icon Kirk Douglas. And guess who got top billing? Farrah Fawcett. Don't *ever* let *anybody* tell you the Eighties didn't suck.
    Our movie begins inside a spaceship. A pasty Brit named Captain James is suiting up for his flight when Harvey Keitel walks into the locker room, dressed in a space suit and wearing a weird black helmet that makes his head look like a cross between a microwave oven and a ball peen hammer. "So, you failed the mental test, huh," the Captain joshes him. "Potentially unstable," he adds with a chuckle. Given that Captain James has apparently *passed* the mental test, it seems

obvious that it doesn't test for stupidity. Because seconds later, Harvey opens the air lock, and James is sucked across the room until he hits a cable and shatters like a porcelain figurine. It's a bold prediction, but Time may yet vindicate the film-makers' vision of a day in which manned space exploration is conducted entirely by Hummels.

Harvey blasts off and flies through the rings of Saturn, which turn out to be composed of dust, ice, Fiddle Faddle and popcorn balls. He dives toward a moon and flies low over somebody's skin condition before landing at the Saturn 3 installation, which is comprised of an omnidirectional microphone and some Speidel watchbands embedded in nougat. Farrah and Kirk are the resident staff of this "experimental food station," and are striving to perfect a vending machine that will work in zero gravity without having to shake it really hard.

Anyway, in the future, it seems that Earth is hungry for snacks, and Harvey has come to help. He's strangely terse and aloof though, and won't let anyone touch his lunchbox. He *is* willing to share his stash of hallucinogenic "Blue Dreamer" pills with Farrah, however, and after briefly examining her dog's anus, asks if he can use her body. When she declines, he looks aghast and retorts, "That's penally unsocial on Earth." So this film envisions perhaps the darkest dystopia yet—a future in which it's illegal not to have sex with Harvey Keitel.

Harv starts to unpack and reveals that he's brought them an enormous robot. "It's the first in the Demi-God series," he says, eliminating any annoying guess-work about what's coming next. Then we cut to a tense scene in which Harvey takes inventory, while the soundtrack creates a sense of impending doom by play-ing the music from "Pac-Man."

Harvey hits on Farrah again, and again strikes out. In order to put things on a more professional footing, Farrah dresses up like a pirate, while Harvey finally opens his lunchbox, and pulls out a three-foot Thermos full of brains. Once he's installed the gray matter in the robot, it will take the place of Kirk, who is nearing his "abort time," despite being in his 240th trimester. Now Kirk's only hope to remain on Saturn 3 with Farrah is Operation Rescue. Or he could just flush Har-vey into space. After all, he tells her, "People are being flushed all over the solar system," implying that Man's knowledge of toilet technology has advanced far beyond his wisdom in using it.

Cut to Harvey, whose efforts have produced "Hector," an 8-foot tall robot with human brain tissue, which Harvey begins to program directly from his own psychotic cerebellum via a serial port in the back of his neck. Unfortunately, as Harvey is transferring his consciousness to Hector, he suddenly remembers Far-rah's swimsuit poster, and gives the robot a virtual boner.

Harvey tries to push more drugs on Farrah—this time, "Earth greens," which, while not hallucinogenic, are an important source of roughage. Meanwhile, Hector pretends to be nearly out of power so that Harvey will plug a suggestive-looking hose into its groin.

Kirk goes outside to collect nougat samples, and Hector makes a pass at Farrah by killing her dog. When it then tries to comfort her by dislocating her shoulder, Farrah hits the Horny Robot alarm. Kirk and Harvey hogpile Hector and pull his brain out, a technique that was earlier used on the screenwriter.

Hector lies dismantled and brainless, but as soon as the humans leave he somehow persuades the kitchen appliances to reassemble him.

Harvey empties his pillbox and swallows the whole pharmacopoeia—Earth greens, yellow moons, pink hearts—then barges into the bedroom and announces that he's taking Farrah back to Earth with him. Kirk and Harvey stage a lame re-enactment of the nude wrestling scene from *Women in Love*, then Harvey knocks Kirk out with a cardboard wrapping paper tube, grabs Farrah, and whisks her away for six days and seven fabulous nights on Earth. But Hector suddenly amputates Harvey's hand and offers it to Farrah in marriage. Meanwhile, Kirk realizes he was hit with a piece of cardboard, so he slips on a pair of bun-hugging polyester bellbottoms, and takes control. He devises an escape plan that involves duck-walking like Chuck Berry, while Farrah tries to help by falling down and screaming a lot.

Kirk switches to Plan B, and uses Farrah as bait while he cowers behind a desk. This doesn't work too well either, but they do manage to knock Hector into the cesspool. Unfortunately, the robot succeeds in climbing out with no ill effects, except that he's now flocked like a Christmas tree.

Intrigued by this heretofore unknown concept of accessorizing, Hector takes to wearing Harvey's severed head as a hat. But Kirk is outraged by this ostentation, especially on a Casual Friday, and blows up the robot (and himself).

Farrah is grief-stricken, but goes on that cruise to Earth anyway, since the tickets were nonrefundable.

So, *Saturn 3*—evidence that Michael Douglas's butt baring compulsion is probably genetic. But this film is also an allegory about adolescence, with Hector the Robot representing all those clumsy boys on the verge of manhood who saw Farrah's swimsuit poster and felt strange longings they didn't know how to deal with, and in their confusion killed their dad and used his head as a fashion statement.

Besides *Saturn 3*, Farrah is also remembered for starring in *Charlie's Angels*. This '70s TV series about three female private detectives was a breakthrough for working women, since the lead characters were portrayed as strong, competent professionals who could hold their own in a man's world. It's true that each of their cases required them to go undercover as lingerie models, strippers, or topless stockbrokers, but this was not gratuitous T&A, since male private detectives of the time, like Cannon and Barnaby Jones, had to wear the same outfits.

However, Farrah is best known among robots for being the wife of Lee Majors, the Six-Million Dollar Man. As you may recall, Majors played Col. Steve Austin, an astronaut injured in a plane crash. But fortunately for him, during the opening credits some government scientists announce, "We can rebuild him. We have the technology." And hey, what good is technology if you can't use it to play god? So while Steve is in a coma, he is given nuclear-powered legs, a super-strong arm, and a peeping-tom eye. When Steve wakes up and gets the bill, he tries to commit suicide. There's no way he can afford a $6 million medical bill on a government salary—especially since his HMO has ruled that bionic enhancements are "cosmetic surgery." Steve protests that he never agreed to these options (bionic parts, rust proofing, extended warranty), they weren't on the initial estimate, and he won't pay a lot for this muffler, so OSI repossesses him and he is forced to become a secret agent.

But Steve was smashed up pretty badly in that crash. Is it possible that more than his limbs and eye were damaged? Well, since Steve is soon given a bionic girlfriend, there seems to be more to the story than we were told as kids. We located Oscar Goldman and asked him for the truth. After telling us that we can't handle the truth, and later, that we couldn't afford the truth, Oscar finally confided what we suspected all along: Steve was also given a bionic penis. (Yes, OSI stands for "Office of Sexual Implants"—Oscar now works for the Vice President's Office, making bionic penises for Bob Dole, and keeping cyborg Dick Cheney in good working order.).

Per Oscar, Steve's first wife, Farrah Fawcett, just couldn't handle the bionic sex, and, as we saw in the movie, hooked up with an elderly Kirk Douglas who wasn't nearly so energetic in the sack. So, to keep Steve happy, the OSI guys rigged a sky-diving accident for tennis star Jamie Sommers, and while she was unconscious, gave her nuclear legs, a super-strong arm, a Miracle Ear, and a bionic vagina (able to withstand up to 4000 ergs of torque, and exert 1200 p.s.i. of suction without a significant loss of viscosity). They used generic parts on her, but she too was forced to become an indentured spy (protecting America's tennis courts and fighting off Vegas's fembot armies) in order to pay for her surgery.

Eventually she and Steve got married, acquired a bionic boy, bionic dog, and bionic Sandra Bullock, and lived happily ever after until Steve contracted cyber clap from one of the fembots.

As for Farrah Fawcett, she went on to achieve critical acclaim in *The Burning Bed*, and later to become crazy and scary. But in her day, she had what it took to sell a million posters (and launch a thousand wet dreams), and to win the hearts of both Steve Austin and Hector the Robot. Clearly, there's just something about Farrah that appeals to men who are mostly mechanical. Probably her acting.

But not every robot who becomes obsessed with a human woman and buys a bionic penis is evil like Hector. Some of them are evil like Robin Williams, who in *Bicentennial Man* plays the hairiest automaton since Country Bear Jamboree.

Bicentennial Man (1999)
Directed by Chris Columbus
Written by Nicholas Kazan, based on writings by Isaac Asimov and Robert Silverberg

In the not-too-distant-future, robot Robin Williams is delivered to Sam Neill's palatial seaside home. As he makes his first appearance, clanking around in a bad Tin Man costume, Sam's younger daughter sensibly backs away, with a whispered, "Scary!" The elder daughter retorts, "It's not scary—it's *stupid*," demonstrating that this film employs the same advanced technology as the self-cleaning oven—it lambastes its own idiot conceit, so you don't have to.

Anyway, Robot Robin is so gentle and benevolent that he removes a spider from the house rather than kill it, but Sam's wife doesn't seem convinced, and always looks as though she's waiting for Robin to re-enact the computer/human rape scene from *Demon Seed*.

Unable to bear the strained atmosphere of whimsy wherever Robin goes, the Older Daughter orders him to jump out the window. The robot complies, sustaining damage to his delicate and sophisticated microprocessors, which causes him to talk like Charlie Callas.

To prevent further destructive pranks, Sam orders that everyone start treating Robin as a person—a mistake people have inexplicably been making ever since "Mork and Mindy."

Younger Daughter lets Robin hold her favorite possession, a glass figurine of a horse, but he breaks it in an effort to convince the bored audience that they're actually watching "The Glass Menagerie." Robin then shocks the family by carving a tiny horse out of wood to replace it, causing Sam to wonder if his robot is in fact showing signs of human-like behavior. This leads to a hilarious and heart-warming scene, in which Sam awkwardly explains the birds and the bees to Robin, presumably to facilitate that upcoming *Demon Seed* sequence in the second act.

Years go by. Older Daughter becomes a sullen, foul-mouthed cycle slut. Mom becomes a jumpy, ill-tempered wino, while Younger Daughter develops an inability to relate to her own kind and a severe erotomania directed toward the robot, who will apparently vibrate for you if you give him a quarter. Yes, it's clear that Robin has had a profound effect on his adopted family.

Younger Daughter, who is now inexplicably older than Mom, receives a marriage proposal from her boyfriend, but hesitates because he lacks the Magic Fingers attachment. She makes it plain to Robin that she's got a yen for some android booty, but he rejects her by symbolically severing his thumb with a band saw.

12 years later. Robin is sick of picking up after Sam's family, and offers to buy his freedom. Sam is so relieved to be rid of the weird-faced golem that he tears up the check and kicks him out on the spot.

Robin finds himself sitting alone on the beach. He is on his own at last, no longer a slave, and free to pursue his dream of becoming human. Unfortunately, the first human he becomes is Martha Stewart, and proceeds to build a gorgeous Craftsman bungalow out of driftwood and kelp.

16 Years later. Sam dies, and Robin celebrates by going on a quest to see if other robots have also evolved toward consciousness and developed the personality of an overrated comic obsessed with dick jokes.

Another ten years go by, and we've finally got those flying cars they've been promising us ever since the October 1939 issue of Popular Mechanics. But Robin has failed in his quest, discovering that all the robots like him have been deactivated, dismantled, and had their operating systems deleted, proving that not everyone in America is as stupid as Sam.

Just as it looks like we're heading for a happy ending, Robin finds a female robot dancing in a fruit market and blasting Aretha Franklin's "Respect" out of her pelvis. She leads him to Oliver Platt, who gives him a face made from Silly Putty.

Now looking exactly like Robin Williams, he goes home to horrify Sam's survivors. He finds that the actress playing Younger Daughter is now playing her granddaughter, so we're *still* not through with her. Younger Daughter, now a crone, dies with Robin's hand-carved wooden horse figurine in her hand, inspiring him to want to have sex with look-alike Granddaughter.

Robin hooks up with Oliver again, who solves the dilemma by installing a penis. (Mercifully, Robin wears a T-shirt during the subsequent sex, so we don't have to wonder why an android has the thick, oily pelt of a beaver. Just so we don't get cocky about our good fortune, however, he climaxes the love scene with a fart.)

Robin wants to wed Granddaughter, but even in the future there remains a social prejudice against human beings marrying household appliances. So Robin takes his case to Artificial People's Court, but Justice Antonin Scalia (whose deal with Satan is apparently working out quite nicely for him) declares that Robin is legally a machine.

Many years later: Granddaughter is 75 now, and getting a little too brittle for Robin's jackhammer-like sexual technique. She understandably longs for death, so Robin transfuses his system with a chemical solution that will cause his body, over time, to acquire age make-up and a white wig.

Many *more* years go by. Now wizened, he goes before the U.N. (whose members are composed entirely of chorus boys from Janet Jackson's "Rhythm Nation" video) and asks to be declared a mediocre actor. Then he dies. Granddaughter asks to be unplugged from her life support, and dies beside Robin, secure in the knowledge that at least she won't be seeing him in the afterlife.

Bicentennial Man: a thought-provoking exploration of just what it means to be human, but also a sociological fable which asks the important question, "Just what kind of screwed-up future society would manufacture robots modeled on Robin Williams?" More than one, apparently, since *Bicentennial Man* wasn't Robin's only robot movie. No, he also lent his voice to *A.I.: Artificial Intelligence,* the film which showed us that in the future, abandoned Haley Joel Osment mecha-sons, Jude Law brand "Gigolo Joes," and other feral androids will infest our national parks. It apparently started when Bush rescinded the Clinton-era regulation banning snowmobiles in Yellowstone—and the next thing you know we've got kevlar-plated androids using Old Faithful as a bidet. Remember to take plenty of 'bot repellent on your next vacation.

There is a bright side, however. Most movies portray robots as libidinous monsters, always terrorizing our women and pulling the heads off our men. *A.I.,* on the other hand, indicates that in the future, women will be the ones exploiting the robots, using them as mere walking, talking vibrators that look like Oscar

Wilde's lover. So, ladies, decide who you'd rather do: Twiki, Robby, or the Cylon's Imperious Leader.

Now, to conclude our lesson on robot/human relations, let's review what we've learned from the three movies we've studied today: *Colossus of NY* taught us that robots are inflamed by negligees, are against humanitarian aid to Third World nations, and are prone to vote Republican. In *Saturn 3* we discovered that robots possessing human gray matter would inevitably lust after blonde floozies and spend all their money on flocking and novelty headgear. And *Bicentennial Man* showed us that robots lacking penises would just buy them on the street and then marry your daughter anyway.

But enough about the robots, what about us? What do these films teach us about how our own society's view of technology has evolved?

In the Fifties, robots lacked souls. Consequently, they were prone to fratricide, megalomania, and violent killing sprees (although they were good with kids). In the Seventies, human/robot hybrids wanted to share in the free love move-ment—and to kill a few people, just for old time's sake. In the late Nineties, robots had ditched the brain tissue and were now actually better human beings than people were. You've come a long way, baby! But *plus ca change, plus c'est la meme chose*—because even with no meat in the can, the modern Hollywood robot still has a bad case of Jungle Fever. So although you may enjoy doing housework in the nude, we'd advise you to wear some clothes around your Roomba, or you might find your husband's severed head riding around the house on your vacuum cleaner.

Weird Sex
or:
Making the Beast with Two Backs with the Beast with Two Backs

Sexuality is a natural and healthy part of life—unless you happen to be watching Marilyn Chambers in *Older Women, Hotter Sex* at two in the morning, in which case just change your sheets and call us when you've sobered up. But as a society, we do a mighty poor job of imparting the facts about human sexuality to our young, and this is probably why so many of them thought The Back Street Boys were heterosexual (you'd think the *name alone...*).

Some children who pose innocent questions about where babies come from are told by flustered parents that when a couple loves each other very much, the daddy plants a seed inside the mommy and a baby grows in her tummy. As well-intentioned as this explanation might be, it frequently results in the child's life-long dread of accidentally swallowing watermelon seeds and getting pregnant, as well as the wish that Daddy would plant radishes instead of little-brother seeds this year, and a suspicion that if some sort of modern threshing equipment were used during harvesting, Mommy's per-hectare yield would increase exponentially.

Other children learn the facts of life on the playground, thus ensuring that alpha male Trevor, who relentlessly beats all challengers to the top of the monkey bars, will successfully pass on his genes, once his testicles drop. But a lot of misinformation is passed along too, like that you can't get pregnant your first time, that excessive masturbation can cause blindness, and that mixing Pop Rocks and Coke can blow your head off. So, if we want to avoid unwanted pregnancies, unwarranted fears, and tragic head explosions, we need to provide kids with accurate, readily available information about sex.

And that's where movies come in. Hollywood has traditionally offered our eager youth detailed instruction in sexual activities such as French kissing, orgasm-faking, and how to carry on long conversations with a sheet stuck to your breasts like a mustard plaster.

But movies also teach about the *perils* of sex. *A Summer Place* shows that teen-age intercourse can lead to unplanned pregnancies. It also informs us that the State of Maine penal code makes deflowering Sandra Dee a Class B Felony. The *Friday the 13th* series depicts young couples engaging in illicit sex while a maniac watches through a crack in the blinds and then kills them in various gruesome ways, thus reinforcing traditional values like chastity and the need for good window treatments. *Goldfinger* warns that sexy women are always wicked (but really, who can blame them—imagine the teasing an 8-year-old Pussy Galore must have undergone at recess).

So, instead of sending the girls to the Home Ec room to watch "Growing Up and Getting Your Monthly Curse" while the boys troop off to the gym to watch "Wet Dreams: Nature's Way of Telling You You're Evil," we think that a good sex education program should involve showing adolescents old B-movies. Because that's how *we* learned about sex, and we turned out just fine, as far as you know!

But there are some movies that we don't recommend as replacements for Dr. Ruth or Masters and Johnson. These are the movies about *weird* sex. No, we're not talking about Penthouse Forum here; we're talking about interplanetary sex. Undead sex. Sex with Doug McClure. Outré, debauched, and anatomically impossible stuff that could easily warp a child's tender sensibilities. Of course, that doesn't mean that *we* can't wallow in it like pigs oinking around in their own filth. Let's face it, even the most loving of partners can grow bored with a steady diet of vanilla sex, and may need to rekindle passion by occasionally trying something wild and nasty, like French vanilla. So get set for a tour of Hollywood's Red Light District. First stop: *The Deadly and the Beautiful*, which illustrates that the brain is the most important sex organ. And that, unfortunately, Viagra doesn't work on it.

Please, kids, don't try this stuff at home.

The Deadly and the Beautiful (1973)
(a.k.a. *Wonder Women*)
Directed by: Robert Vincent O'Neill
Written by: Robert Vincent O'Neill, Lou Whitehill

There have been several great baseball movies and a handful of memorable football films over the years. Even track and field has inspired pictures like *Personal Best* and *Chariots of Fire*. But one sport above all is indisputably *made* for the big screen: Jai alai. Just imagine the thrill of plunking down $8.50 to watch two guys play catch with raisin scoops, and you can understand the excitement with which we viewed *The Deadly and the Beautiful*. Alas, the jai alai match that opens this film is a classic piece of bait-and-switch, and before long we find ourselves knee-deep in a Ross Hagen movie.

A jai alai player emerges from the championships in Manila, and is promptly shot by a tranquilizer dart. The audience expects him to be radio-tagged and released to continue his migration; instead, he's abducted by two hot babes disguised as Joey Bishop.

The twin Joeys rendezvous with two sinister confederates—a blonde dressed like Heidi and a black woman whose Afro was apparently designed by R. Buckminster Fuller. In a hideous scene reminiscent of *The Premature Burial*, the victim is sealed inside a coffin while peppy calliope music plays on the soundtrack. The coffin is shoved into a hearse, and the kidnappers roar off at high speed. Random shots of a Ferris wheel increase the tension.

Meanwhile, at Super Villain World Headquarters and Community College, mad doctor Nancy Kwan is performing surgery while dressed in John Travolta's Saran Wrap suit from *The Boy in the Plastic Bubble*. Back at the kidnapping, the Gal Joeys perform a striptease in the back seat of the hearse to the accompaniment of the song "Wonder Women." Random shots of bra straps and breathable cotton panels increase the tension.

The coffin arrives, and Dr. Nancy, who has changed into a nun's habit from *The Sound of Music*, examines the victim. She is seeking immortality, and has developed a serum that will startle the scientific world by allowing her to transplant the brain of a jai alai player into the body of a snooker champion.

Meanwhile, ex-CIA agent, ex-LAPD detective, and all-around tough guy Ross Hagen arrives at the airport and immediately acquaints himself with the gaily-festooned jitneys of Manila. Lloyds of London hires Ross to find the missing jai alai champ, who was insured for millions of dollars against fire, theft, collision, and unwanted brain transplants.

Nancy meets with a dirty old man in a wheelchair. For an exorbitant price, she will transplant his brain into the body of the kidnapping victim, thereby creating a dirty old jai alai player.

Back at the dorms, the Gal Joeys are debating whether Dr. Nancy's "brain sex" is superior to intercourse, since it eradicates both emotional dependencies and the wet spot. The discussion becomes heated, and the girls nearly come to blows. Random shots of chess pieces, bikini bottoms, and maple syrup increase the confusion.

To settle the issue, they go Nancy's storehouse of previous abductees, defrost some men without brains (the popular but stupid Australian pop band), and have sex with them.

Meanwhile, Ross is attacked by Nancy's hired thugs, sparking the most lethargic foot chase since "T.J. Hooker."

Our next stop is a cockfight. While the soundtrack swells with music stolen from a porn movie, the viewer pauses to marvel. Jai alai. Cockfights. Why doesn't ESPN broadcast from the Philippines *24 hours a day?*

Dr. Nancy, who's now dressed like Raquel Welch in *Fathom*, takes a stroll through the frozen Hunk section of her grocer's freezer, and selects one for transplant. But Gal Joey Vera wants to have sex with him before he completely thaws out. It's the third time this week, apparently, but Vera is addicted to the practice, as it allows her to act like a slut while still remaining frigid.

One of the Joeys walks into a bar, and Ross—who has apparently acquired a hot comb, since his hair is now fearlessly exploring the limits of the Dry Look—gives her his foolproof pick-up routine: He hands her a glass of Tang, then seductively eats a maraschino cherry to symbolize his hopes that he'll be losing his virginity tonight.

Soon, Ross is snug beneath the covers while the girl kneels on the bed in her underwear and pecks at his face in a wan effort to arouse him. Meanwhile, the director tries to set a sultry mood by blasting the theme from "Sanford and Son" on the soundtrack.

Naturally, this all culminates in the girl trying to shoot Ross with a tranquilizer gun, but Ross would rather jump on the bed and have a pillow fight. When she kicks his ass, however, our hero tries to shoot her in the back with a sawed-off shotgun. Predictably, he misses and falls down a flight of stairs.

Ross and his jitney-driving sidekick take the captured Joey back to the Island of Dr. Nancy. As they disembark from the canoe, Ross pauses for a boring argument with the sidekick. The girl takes this opportunity to make a break for it and saunter to freedom. When the two men finally look up and discover she's gone, Ross is dumbfounded. The sidekick is moved to observe, "She's very tricky."

Meanwhile, an army of Joeys pour out of Evil Junior College, armed with machine guns and outfitted for jungle warfare in saffron mini-dresses. They race into the bush and proceed to hunt Ross down like a snipe. Ross runs away; stumbles; fires aimlessly into the foliage, and looks perplexed. Random shots of the Rorschach-like sweat stains on Ross's leisure suit increase the queasiness.

The Gal Joeys capture Ross and take him at gunpoint to the Banquet Room of the Route 46 Ramada Inn in Teaneck, New Jersey. Dr. Nancy, who's now dressed like *That Girl*, explains her evil scheme while Ross is forced to eat a party hat.

They tour the facility, and for some reason, Ross begins to sashay, his elbows and wrists bent and fingers splayed, as though waiting for his nail polish to try. Despite this, Nancy slaps an air filter on his head, and the two of them have "brain sex." At last, we're finally able to see what this mysterious erotic technique looks like. Unfortunately, Ross can't get his brain up.

Eventually, the sexual tension reaches a fever pitch as Nancy falls asleep, and Ross squirms obscenely on a vinyl loveseat until he soils himself.

Sticky but undaunted, Ross escapes and corners Dr. Nancy, who destroys herself in a spectacular explosion of Gold Medal flour.

Safely back in Manila, Ross gets a $100,000 check from Lloyds of London, and promptly blows it all on a drunken hooker. Living up to his well-established reputation for virility, Ross spends the rest of the movie playing chess with the well-compensated prostitute, while she stares uncomprehendingly at the board and fondles a pear stem.

Random shots of rooks, bathrobes, and wax fruit increase the tension headache I'm getting. The End.

As this movie has shown us, in the future people will no longer have sex the old-fashioned way, with their bodies. No, they will just link their brains together with Framm Air Filters and *think* each other to ecstasy. The periodic table of the elements will become an aphrodisiac. Women will waste their money on Mark Eden Brain Developers. Stephen Hawking will become the ultimate sex symbol.

In fact, Dr. Nancy was a far-seeing visionary, as well as a mediocre and cut-rate super villain. Her primitive brain sex technology was later perfected, and by 2032, it was in common use, at least according to the 1996 film *Demolition Man* (which also predicted Arnold Schwarzenegger's election as governor of California). The hot cerebellum-on-cerebellum action allowed Sylvester Stallone and

Sandra Bullock to have a sex scene in which they both remained fully clothed, and on opposite sides of the room, an act of mercy for which we still send the filmmakers a yearly gift basket of smoked holiday meats to express our undying gratitude. Unfortunately, we were again cheated out of seeing just how this technology works, since Stallone's synapses fired prematurely, and their brains just decided to cuddle instead.

Still, the course of future events is clear. Eventually, society will rely on technology not just for pleasure, but for procreation too. As foreseen by Zager and Evans, in the year 2525 (if man is still alive) we will find our son, find our daughter too, at the bottom of a long test tube (whoa, whoa). So have some sex today, before it goes out of style, and can only be found at ridiculously marked-up prices on Ebay.

Mars Needs Women (1967)
Directed and written by Larry Buchanan

A girl is playing tennis with a dork—when she vanishes! A pudgy, middle-aged guy goes to get some cigarettes—and his date disappears! A blonde is taking a shower—then suddenly, she's gone! Either aliens have discovered the secret of stop-motion photography or else women have learned how to ditch annoying men and avoid showering on camera. Meanwhile, an Air Force colonel races to NASA's secret decoding and U-Store-it site, where he is briefed on the message from space they have been receiving for the past three days.

"It's just three words," advises the lab-coated extra, in what sounds frighteningly like a song cue. In fact, the message reads: "Mars needs women." The Colonel looks rather dubious about *this* being our first contact with extraterrestrial intelligence, but the movie title confirms it: yes, Mars Needs Women. And Mars apparently felt that NASA would be in a position to understand their situation, seeing as it's staffed mainly by former members of the AV Club.

After being briefed on the terse interplanetary pick-up line, the Secretary of the Hair Club for Men picks up the Hot Line to inform the President about the horny Martians. The President presumably feels the Martians' pain.

The Colonel and NASA's four remaining employees (apparently everybody else quit when they figured out that NASA was unable to get *anyone* women) are loitering in NASA's combination recording studio/lunch room when Tommy Kirk materializes to reaffirm that Mars needs women—and pretty damned quickly, as they are getting really tense and cranky. He states that he and his crew are "medical missionaries" who have come to Earth to pick up chicks. See, the

Martians have been having problems with their DNA, and now the ratio of men to women is 100 to 1, which makes it very hard for an average guy to get a date for New Year's Eve.

Tommy mentions that before the opening credits, his team attempted to seize three women by "transponder", but this was unsuccessful. (Translation: they struck out, and are looking around for some fresh women who aren't lesbians.) All Mars is asking for is five healthy, fertile, female volunteers to help repopulate their planet, or to have lots of sex while trying.

The Colonel is unwilling to part with even five of Earth's women, since Colonels need women too and he hasn't been doing too well at the Officers Club mixers himself. "Your suggestion is insane!" he shouts.

Tommy says fine; they'll just get some girls *without* NASA's help! And he pops out using the Martians' advanced "Bewitched" technology.

After a "Batman" dissolve, we see some USAF stock footage of airplanes. The four NASA employees gaze at the ceiling while this is being run in order to convey the idea that planes fly in the air. We then stare at a speaker for several minutes while a voice informs us that the Martians have jammed our radar and such. It's a FedTro speaker, and it seems to work very well for channeling voices from stock footage. So, when Earth is under attack from Mars and you're in the market for speakers, choose FedTro!

After crippling Earth's defenses, the aliens are free to land their craft, a copper wok, in an abandoned ice plant in Houston. The Martians, sporting wet suits and earmuffs made from yo-yos and car antennas, make it easy to understand why their own women won't have anything to do with them.

The Martians have less than 24-hours to find and nab suitable women for "Operation Sleep Freeze," their code name for the plan to abduct frigid women who will refuse to sleep with them. And since their only weapon is the power of hypnotism (which they acquired from reading those "How to Seduce Any Woman" books advertised in the back of *Swank*), their mission seems hopeless. But they vow to give it their best shot, on behalf of losers everywhere.

Tommy starts his girl hunt at the Holiday Inn. He pretends to be a humorless, gay medical reporter from Seattle, since Martian research has shown this is catnip to women. The first step in his plan to capture a mate is to stay in his hotel room and watch TV. While so engaged, he catches a story about Dr. Yvonne Craig, Ph.D., a "stunning brunette" with a Pulitzer in Space Genetics (her horn-rimmed glasses verify her academic credentials). She has come to Houston to help the government deal with the libidinous Martians. When Tommy sees a poster advertising her upcoming lecture on Space Sex (admittance only to accredited journalists and others willing to pay $4.99 a minute), he decides to attend, in hopes of meeting Adam West.

Yvonne's press conference isn't going as well as she had hoped—the audience consists solely of three doughy guys who make sexist remarks and flirt with each other instead of her. Yvonne takes off her glasses and prissily informs them that unless somebody can ask a pertinent question, the conference is *over*! This was just the opening Tommy was waiting for, and he throws out something about gene mapping, chromosome research, and how occasional impotence can happen to *any* man. Yvonne is very impressed by Tommy's question and tells the other reporters they should all try to be more like him, causing them to give Tommy a wedgie and steal his lunch money as soon as the lecture is over. But Yvonne is smitten by Tommy's total lack of manliness and asks him out. So, Tommy and Yvonne walk to the planetarium, where they watch stock space footage and fall in stock love.

Meanwhile, the other Martians pursue their dream girls. "Fellow Two" knows exactly what kind of women Mars needs and immediately heads for a strip joint. His choice for the mother of the new race is a rather matronly gal in an evening gown whose act consists of poking out her butt and waving her arms in circles. But she seems really smart.

"Fellow Three" grabs a stewardess, since they are almost as genetically superior as strippers.

"Fellow Four" finds his candidate at stock footage of a football game—she's the Homecoming Queen, and so the "ideal woman" of drunken frat boys everywhere.

"Fellow Five" is running out of time, and decides to take any girl who can pass that drawing test from the Art Institute of America. He meets a girl who can sketch a tree, and he's done! So, everybody has a girl stashed in the flying saucer except Tommy, who still isn't quite sure what he'd do with one once he got her home.

The authorities, as represented by the four NASA employees, the Colonel, and space sex expert Yvonne, assemble in the NASA room to discuss the interplanetary situation. They instantaneously deduce that four women are missing, that the women were all "built like goddesses" (although the film can't really back this up), and they were kidnapped by Martians using hypnosis (which is, after all, the most common cause of missing women). Then, by putting pins in a poster of Julie Newmar, Yvonne concludes that the Martians are hiding in the old ice plant!

She also states that the Martians are planning on freezing the stolen women, to keep them fresh and crispy during the journey (she doesn't have horned-rimmed glasses for nothing!) The Colonel announces they'll raid the place that night, and then swears everybody to secrecy.

Of course, Yvonne loses no time in telling Tommy that they've located the Martian base and plan to attack it in about an hour (she needed something to break a lull in the conversation). She and Tommy race to the ice plant, where Tommy warns the Martians of the Earthlings' imminent raid. He says they must take off for Mars immediately, leaving behind the girls, who have only had time to get slushy and so would probably spoil in transit. It's at this point that Ph.D. scientist Yvonne figures out that Tommy isn't *really* a medical reporter from Seattle…although he may actually be humorless and gay.

Anyway, Tommy wants to stay on Earth, but the other Martians say that either he or Yvonne must go with them to Mars, since they are the only two name stars in the film and SAG rules are very strict about things like this. So, Tommy sacrifices himself and returns to Mars, where there are 100 men for every woman…and 99 men for every other man. As she gazes up at the stock footage of the Milky Way, a tear slides down Yvonne's cheek. Yes, Tommy Kirk *was* the best she could do, and yes, he got away. But not without stealing her heart, and not without giving her space VD. The End.

Who can't empathize with the Martians' predicament? Alone in the darkness, just looking for a little love, a little warmth. Reaching out to Earth for help, only to be rebuffed. But NASA scientists were hardly the right people to contact if Mars needed women. No, the Martians should have approached a group with a long history of helping the unfortunates of this world, men with big hearts, big bucks, and plenty of chicks to spare: Hollywood celebrities. We like to think that stars like Russell Crowe and Tom Cruise would have immediately donated their slightly used women (Tom's would have been just like new).

Or how about *Mars Needs Women: The Musical!* It could help revitalize Broadway while also generating enough box office and cross-promotional merchandising to just buy each of the Martians a hooker.

Here's the number sung by the Martians as they leave the space ship and head out to grab some girls:

> **All**: We're young Martians, and we must procreate!
> With girls who will mate on the very first date!
> **Tommy**: We'll each find the best girl that Earth has to offer
> **Fellow3**: We'll surprise her!

Fellow4: Hypnotize her!
Fellow5: And then we'll boff her!

All: We're young Martians, searching for dames.
They must have good bodies—we can do without brains.
Fellow2: I want a girl with refinement and class.
So I'll head to "Boobs 'n' Butts" to look for my lass.

All: We're young Martians, ready to breed.
We're young Martians, and we're bursting with seed!
Fellow3: I want a smart girl who can serve coffee in space.
We can join the mile-high club as we found a new race.

All: We're young Martians, manly and brave.
And despite all appearances, it's *women* we crave!
Fellow4: A beauty queen of some sort will be my sweet honey.
Fellow5: I just want a girl who can draw Bugs Bunny.

All: We're young Martians, needin' to score,
And without Earthly babes our chances are poor.
Tommy: I'm seeking a girl who's not bossy or vain,
And if she looks like Burt Ward, well I won't complain.

All: We're young Martians, do you like what you see?
We're young Martians, we're HIV-free!
We're young Martians, desperate for sex
We've got lousier love lives than Oedipus Rex!

And here's Tommy's big second act showstopper:

It's sad-making, *mad*-making,
It's crummy an' harsh an',
Worse, leading the life of a Single White Martian.

I've tried every bar
On our rouge-colored planet,
But we've got all of five girls,
And they all told me to cram it.

They've got girls on earth, and it gives me a yen.
Sadly, however, that yen is for men.
But I am First Fellow, and I've got a duty,
To tap me a piece of terrestrial booty.

I *must* do the girl,
Not Third Fellow's arse,
I'll just close my eyes,
And think hard of Mars.

Mars Needs Women: The Musical. Now and Forever.

The lessons one can draw from this movie seem to be that hypnotism and hypothermia are effective seduction techniques, but NASA will charge you with a Mann Act violation if you attempt to transport women across interplanetary lines for immoral purposes. Sadly, this rules out kidnapping (despite the fact that certain peoples' best hope for true love is probably the Stockholm Syndrome); and Brain Sex, as we have seen, is a reproductive cul-de-sac. So what's left? Well, at this point Hollywood recommends the Home Depot approach to Love.

Do you find that every time you get close to a woman, she transplants your brain? Are you having little success meeting girls using conventional methods (abduction, cryogenics)? If so, then do what Sting does! (Well, don't do everything Sting does. Don't, for instance, wear a tiny leather Speedo and shriek like a demented macaw the way he did in *Dune*). Build your own girlfriend! Yes, our next lesson comes courtesy of The Bride, which shows us what happens when a rock star loves a cadaver very, very much.

The Bride (1985)
Directed by: Franc Roddam
Written by: Lloyd Fonvielle

Tagline: "A woman born of electricity...a man driven by passion!"

This film stars Sting, and is probably the best example you'll ever find of *Police* brutality.

It's a dark and stormy night. Baron von Frankensting is sitting around his ancestral home, Schloss Kardboard Kutout, playing "Mousetrap!" with Quentin Crisp and a crash test dummy. For some reason, the game causes Frankensting's Monster to experience nocturnal emissions, so they pack it in and decide to electrocute Jennifer Beals instead. True to the genre, a bolt of lightning succeeds in reanimating her corpse, but it frizzes out her hair something awful. The newly animated Jennifer promptly loses a game of "Mystery Date," and the Monster arrives at the lab door to pick her up. It seems that Frankensting is a sort of necrophiliac's Chuck Woolery, but his matchmaking doesn't go very well. Emasculated, the Monster stumbles blindly into the forest, where he attends a John Bly workshop and attempts to get in touch with his inner corpse.

The Baron, we now learn, is a radical feminist who hopes to use Jennifer to create "the New Woman." Equal and assertive. Fearless as a man. Able to bring home the bacon and fry it up in a pan.

Frankensting sits by the fire, contemplating his utopia of sexual equality, when Jennifer toddles in stark naked, squats at his feet, and begins sucking her fingers. The Baron reassesses his priorities.

Meanwhile, in a cave somewhere in the Alps, the Monster is receiving relationship counseling from a dwarf.

Frankensting gives Jennifer the Eliza Doolittle treatment, and her education progresses swiftly. Soon she has learned to wear a hoop skirt and spin rapidly in a circle until she projectile vomits. Meanwhile, somewhere in Bavaria, the Monster becomes queasy, thus proving that there is either a psychic link between Jennifer and the Monster, or that the curried wurst he had at Oktoberfest isn't agreeing with him.

Frankensting takes Jennifer on a field trip to a mausoleum. A pleasant time is had by all, picking through the loose femurs and ulnas, but the Baron becomes insanely jealous over Jennifer's infatuation with a rotting skull, and refuses to show her *his* bone.

By this point, Jennifer has become sufficiently refined that Frankensting and Colonel Pickering decide to take her to the Embassy Ball, after which she belts out the show-stopping number, "I Could Have Danced All Night (If I Wasn't a Corpse)."

During the ball, she meets the extremely blonde Cary Elwes, who is dressed in a Prussian Hussar's uniform and looking slightly more Aryan than Beowulf. Predictably, Frankensting becomes jealous of Cary's skull, and runs off to hide in his secret fort and smoke crack.

Later, in an astonishing scientific breakthrough, the Baron invents glitter, and throws a party to celebrate. But when he peeks into the master suite and finds Jennifer and Cary making out, he goes ballistic, because his parents are coming home soon and he told everyone to stay out of their bedroom.

Even later, Jennifer goes to Cary's house, and in a tender, erotic scene, they strip down to see which of them has the frilliest underwear. Through their psychic link, the Monster, who is now rotting in prison somewhere, finds his nipples strangely engorged.

Meanwhile, all this talk of engorged nipples proves too much for the Baron, and he suddenly turns into Bob Packwood. The Monster bursts into the room to rescue Jennifer, then turns and runs away as Frankensting chases him with a torch, shouting, "Have a little *fire*, Scarecrow!" They race all over the castle in a weird, pyromaniacal "Benny Hill" sketch, until Frankensting, after trying several times, finally succeeds in falling off the tower. And while the Baron's death doesn't exactly come as a surprise, it does answer a question the audience has been asking with increasing exasperation for the last 90 minutes: Sting, where is thy Death?

As the superimposed face of a dwarf looks on and recites weird platitudes like Obi-Wan Kenobi, the two reanimated lovers go to Venice, where their rotting bodies cause a cholera epidemic that winds up killing Gustav von Aschenbach. The End.

So, if you're a picky guy or gal who just can't find anybody good enough for you, why not make your own partner, using ordinary items found around the house? (And this really isn't necrophilia, since Jennifer Beales is alive, ALIVE—it's just her performance that reeks of carrion). Now you *can* have a woman with the legs, hips, butt, and breasts of your choice—although she may also have a bad case of the frizzies and a yen for your jumper cables. Just don't choose a Flashdancer's brain and you'll have the ideal woman, at least until she gets PMS and starts terrorizing the villagers.

However, some say that celebrities shouldn't be allowed to build their own people since they give them such stupid names. I mean, it's one thing to be born "Rumer" or "Scout" or "Apple"—you get time to adjust to it, and plan your vengeance on Mom and Dad. (It's a little known fact that Trent Lott was born "Starshine Mushroom Zappa," but took a new appellation and joined the Republican Party when he turned 18.) But if you're brought back from the dead by Richard Gere and told that you're called "Free Tibet Now Frankenstein," you will have no choice but to go on murderous rampages, throw little girls into lakes, and generally act out. So, we feel that perhaps everyone is better off just buying pre-fab sexual partners, because while they might not come in as many options as do-it-yourself models, they do have better warranties and aren't as likely to cuckold you with a chorus boy from "Naughty Marietta."

Now, on to a movie that explains why "sleeping with the fishes" is such a potent Mafia threat.

Humanoids From the Deep (1980)
Directed by Barbara Peeters (the extra "E" is for extra Excrescence)
Written by Frank Arnold (story), Martin B. Cohen, Frederick James

Our film opens in a picturesque seaside village, where fishing boat captains Vic Morrow and Doug McClure are locked in a bitter rivalry over their hair. Vic sports a Mike Brady-style perm, while Doug models the loose, grayish, combover hairstyle that would later be made famous by Clint Eastwood.

The village seems to be near Monterey, along California's Central Coast. Nevertheless, the first fishermen we glimpse at work are a group of sea-going Okies (I must have missed that *Grapes of Wrath* sequel, *Ma and Pa Joad Join the Tuna Fleet*), under the command of Hoke Howell, who made a career of playing sub-*Deliverance*-style crackers, and who is best remembered for the dignity and gravitas he brought to *Bikini Hoe-Down*. The Okies catch a Humanoid From the Deep in their net, and in a rapid series of rib-tickling misadventures, Cap'n Hoke accidentally feeds his plump and tender 12-year old son to the Humanoid, sets the deck on fire with a flaregun, blows up the boat, and incinerates his entire crew. This may help to explain why we don't see more jug-sippin', Appalachian hicks trawling for albacore in their bib overalls. If God had intended for hillbillies to deep-sea fish, he would have made them less flammable. And more buoyant. And he wouldn't have stuck them out in the Ozarks where they're less likely to scare the fish when they inevitably blow themselves up. But I digress.

Back on land, Doug's dog "Baron" is attacked by a Humanoid while rooting through the garbage. Thankfully, Doug's cat "The Dauphin," his parakeet, the "Duke of Tuscany," and his gerbil, the "Holy Roman Emperor" are unharmed.

Doug and his wife wander down to the beach, calling piteously for their dog, when they suddenly come upon its gruesome remains. Our horror is tempered by the fact that Baron's remains are being played by a Rolf the Dog puppet, mixed with kelp for a refreshing seaweed salad.

Later, Vic returns from fishing to find that his dogs have also been replaced by eviscerated plush toys. Only the Indians' dog, Vic notes ominously, hasn't been turned into a gutted Muppet.

Now the camera crew pauses to stalk a blonde with a Farrah Fawcet hairdo and a cheap burgundy teddy, and we watch as she wanders through the house and repeatedly startles herself by bumping into the laundry and brushing against a dish. Then the phone rings, causing her to shriek like a demented banshee. At this point, we can only hope her alarm clock doesn't go off, or we might have to watch her lose control of her bladder.

Dr. Ann Turkel shows up at the village's Salmon Festival on behalf of a proposed cannery to explain how adding fish guts and diesel runoff to the water table will be good for the local residents. But one of the Indians appears with his own dead dog, and declares that he will stop the cannery! Vic orders his crew to throw the Indian out, and if the Indian were Billy Jack, this would lead to a really cool scene! But he's not, so it doesn't, and he just gets his ass kicked.

Meanwhile, NotFarrah Fawcett and her boyfriend stroll along the beach, accompanied by music from a tampon commercial. Eventually, they wade into the surf, while the soundtrack switches to the ominous theme from the opening credits of *The Secret Storm*. They jump around and splash each other for awhile, until the Humanoids decide to enforce the "No Horseplay" rule by yanking the boyfriend underwater and pulling his femur out through his ear. Then they grab NotFarrah for a little Afternoon Delight, ripping off her bra, and making the Beast With Two Backs and a Tail. This is our first chance to really see the monsters up close, and they sort of resemble an olive drab Barney with shingles.

Cut to a tent on the beach, where a shapely young woman is flirting with a ventriloquist's dummy. She quickly falls under its thrall, much like Michael Redgrave in *Dead of Night*, and obediently strips naked. Naturally, the sound of a woman being seduced by Mortimer Snerd arouses a passing Humanoid, who rips through the tent. The naked girl flees down the beach, but she's tackled by the safety, another Humanoid who has smartly accessorized his Barney costume by gluing a turban squash to his head. He throws the girl onto her hands and knees, and they do it Humanoid style.

Doug decides to terminate the Humanoids with inept prejudice. Dr. Ann insists on coming along, since she hasn't had a date in awhile, and the Humanoids seem like a sure thing. So we cut to Doug's boat out at sea, where Doug and crew are knocking back a can of suds and fishing for Humanoids. Yes, they're bloodthirsty mutants who do unspeakable things to our women, but they're *good* eatin'.

The Humanoids aren't biting, though, so Doug, Dr. Ann, and NotBilly Jack decide to poke around the tide pools. They discover a herd of Humanoids basking on the sand, and Doug starts blowing them away, while Dr. Ann takes high fashion photos of the carnage. One of the monsters almost gets to third base with NotBilly, but Doug kills it, firing off three shots from a bolt action rifle in less than three seconds, beating Lee Harvey Oswald's old record. Meanwhile, as Dr. Ann snaps away, telling the remains of the slaughtered Humanoids to wet their lips and work with her, Doug finds the nude and ravished NotFarrah languishing in a bed of kelp.

Back at the lab, Dr. Ann shows a junior high school sex hygiene film on the reproductive life of frogs, and explains that the Cannery—like most companies that pack minced tuna in spring water—is heavily involved in genetic engineering and biomedical research. And it seems that in order to make salmon reproduce and grow faster, they seeded the ocean with "DNA-5," or "Chlorinol-3" or something, and it's making the Humanoids whiz their way up the evolutionary ladder. Dr. Ann believes that, in order to further enhance their development, they are driven to mate with human females. Unfortunately for them, the Humanoids have picked some of the stupidest girls in monster movie history to breed with, setting their evolutionary progress back by millions of years. Instead of becoming a super-intelligent hybrid race, they find themselves irresistibly drawn to Wal-Mart, where they stare enviously at the parked recreational vehicles, and snack on Devil Dogs and Hostess Snowballs as they shop for Bermuda shorts and Shania Twain CDs.

That night, the monsters go wilding at the Salmon Festival. Some of the Humanoids set up a Tailhook-like gauntlet, while others rip the flesh off the backs of screaming townsfolk, and one rides the merry-go-round.

Miss Salmon Festival is attacked by a monster, who rips off her top (an early title for the film was *Humanoids From Spring Break*). But she rallies by grabbing a rock and braining the beast (which isn't hard, since their brains are *al fresco*). Flushed with triumph, the bare-bosomed Salmon Queen bounces violently into the camera, as the film momentarily becomes 3-D.

As Vic is sexually assaulted by Humanoids, Doug putters around the harbor in his boat, spreading an enormous slick of gasoline on the water. As the violence reaches a crescendo, he tosses a flare pistol to Dr. Ann and says, "Here. Send them all to hell." But he's so bored with the whole thing that he says it the same way he might say, "Here. Send them a Pick-Me-Up bouquet from FTD."

Later, back at the lab, Dr. Ann is playing midwife to NotFarrah, who's preparing to deliver a bouncing bundle of Humanoid. Unfortunately, NotFarrah has just finished watching *Alien*, and opts for a natural delivery through the sternum. The End.

So, Amalgamated Salmon Canning tries a little illegal bioengineering, just to improve their profit margin, and who pays the price? Busty, rock-stupid women with Farrah hair. As usual.

And while we don't want to seem to be blaming the victims, we must ask: is it possible that the women were leading the Humanoids on? After all, this isn't the first time that slimy monsters have pursued one-sided relationships with human women, and one must ask why. For example, there was the Creature from the Black Lagoon, another romantic just looking for love in all the wrong species. Why did he fall for Julie Adams, when she appears to lack every major quality he looks for in a woman, namely gills, fins, and a zipper? Is it possible that when Richard Carlson wasn't around, Julie made suggestive remarks to the monster about the size of his "fish stick" and wanting to taste his tartar sauce?

Or perhaps the media is to blame for inciting humanoids and gill-men to commit forcible, Salmon-on-girl sex. Maybe the monsters had been profoundly influenced by *Titanic*, another "fish out of water" story in which the working class Leonardo Di Caprio courts an aristocratic Kate Winslet. Is their tragic *mesalliance* really any different than a pair of bipedal trout gang-fertilizing a Denny's waitress? In fact, (according to the supplemental materials on the DVD) when *Humanoids* director Barbara Peeters was temporarily felled by illness—a kidney infection, or possibly a bad conscience—future *auteur* James Cameron was brought in to finish the film, and it's evident that he used the opportunity to touch upon themes he would later explore more fully in *Titanic*. For instance, the dramatic picture hat worn by Kate Winslet in her first appearance, which allowed her beauty to be slowly, breathtakingly revealed, is clearly prefigured by the lead humanoid's fetching turban squash. Likewise, the constraining dinner clothes worn by the condescending First Class passengers—the corsets and bustles, the stiff celluloid collars and starched dickeys—symbolized their inflexible views of social mobility, while the Humanoids' appearance symbolized inflexible rubber costumes that were really cheap and hard to move around in. Lastly, the cuckolding that drives Billy Zane's character into a murderous rage is clearly foreshadowed by the humanoids' frenzied reaction to the girl in the tent sexually taunting a ventriloquist dummy. (If there's one thing they hate, it's a fishstick-tease.)

So, four classic Hollywood films, four visions of aberrant sex. And now you're probably thinking: how can I use some of the perversions presented in these movies to liven up my own stale and unsatisfying sex life? Well, we *knew* you'd think that, so here are a few ideas:

1. Be like the white insurance investigator who's a sex machine with all the chicks (just talking 'bout Ross Hagen): go to singles bars and lasciviously eat the maraschino cherry out of your Shirley Temple. Research done by Masters and Johnson shows this is almost as effective as Hai Karate after-shave.

2. Want a man, but in a hurry? Try Pillsbury Thaw and Serve Stud-Muffins, in your frozen food case.

3. If you too need women, do like the Martians and go where the girls hang out: the third planet from the sun. And if you get there between 5 and 7, they've got a two-for-one deal on watermelon shooters.

4. And don't overlook press conferences as way to meet women. Look for subjects that are bound to make attendees hot, like "Space Sex" or "The Economy."

5. Tired of consistently spending Saturday nights alone (always the bridesmaid, never the Bride of Frankenstein)? Then ask your mad scientist buddies to start making dates for you (and we mean that literally). The next story you tell around the water cooler come Monday morning could be, "I Slept With a Zombie"!

6. Is your relationship lacking electricity? Try doing it during a thunderstorm with a large conduction device on the roof. Or, if that sounds too elaborate for you, just rub your feet on the carpet before you touch each other.

7. Eat salmon (you'll be amazed how much more action you'll get if you make sure the salmon is satisfied first.)

8. Ventriloquist sex. 'Nuff said.

9. Do some role-playing. Once you tire of "Horny Humanoid and White Trash Bimbo," get out your rain slicker and play "The Gorton Fisherman and the Little Mermaid," or "I Know Who You Did Last Summer."

Well, that concludes our walk on the wild side of cinematic sex. We hope it has proved enlightening for those of you who are seeking a deeper understanding of the diverse ways in which humanity expresses its essential nature, and sufficiently perverted for those of you who are still depressed because they tore down the drive-in.

It's a Mad, Mad, Mad, Mad, Scientist

Like Hollywood filmmaking, scientific research has grown prohibitively expensive over recent years; and *mad* science, once a quaint cottage industry, is now the sole province of evil multinational conglomerates or shadowy government agencies. This means that without grants or corporate sponsorship, the criminal misuse of basic and applied research is now beyond the reach of the average small businessman.

As a result, today's mad scientist is no longer an outcast visionary, no longer a demented genius laboring in secret to avenge himself upon the world. Now he's just an employee with a 401k. But there was a time, not so long ago, when the typical mad doctor worked out of a one-man laboratory; occasionally assisted by an unpaid university student from Wittenburg or a hunchback on flex time. In that far simpler era, it wasn't necessary for the fledgling mad scientist to labor in a high-tech facility a hundred feet below Area 51. All he needed was a finished basement, a 220-volt outlet, and the aspiring madman was ready to jump in and start reanimating corpses.

Sadly, those entrepreneurial days are over. In 1940's *The Devil Bat*, Bela Lugosi had only to clear the snow shovels and the old *Highlights* magazines out of the garage, and he was free to start mutating rodents. But by the year 2000, in *Hollow Man*, demented physicist Kevin Bacon required a Pentagon appropriation and a high security subterranean laboratory complex before he could even *think* about tampering in God's domain.

In this chapter we will chart the evolution of Mad Science from the Golden Age of rugged individualism, when any broken-down old Magyar with a death ray and a dream could conquer the earth, to today's world, where the military-industrial complex spends billions of dollars to protect our national security with transparent Kevin Bacons.

The Ape Man (1943)
Directed by: William Beaudine
Written by: Karl Brown, Barney A. Sarecky

Tagline: *"No one is safe from the cruel desires of this inhuman fiend!"*

Agatha Brewster, world famous ghostbuster, arrives in New York after winning the Whistler's Mother Look-Alike Contest, and is met by the winner of the annual Neville Chamberlain Separated-At-Birth Competition. Neville reports that her brother, James Brewster (Bela Lugosi) has conducted weird experiments upon himself, and warns Agatha (who apparently wandered away from Budapest at an early age and was raised in the wild by a pack of Margaret Dumonts) to prepare herself for a shock: Bela has transformed himself into a monster!

Meanwhile, a mysterious figure lurks in the shadows. Tall, skeletal, with a pencil-thin mustache and a porkpie hat, he combines the sinister aspect of the Insidious Doctor Fu Manchu with the fashion sense of Eb from "Green Acres."

Arriving at Brewster Manor, Neville slides back a secret panel in the laboratory and reveals Bela, asleep in a cage, his limbs tenderly entwined around a gorilla. Noticing the sister's horrified expression, the great ape coughs discreetly and nudges Bela, his hurt, plaintive eyes seeming to say, "I thought you *told* your family about us."

As he turns toward the camera, we see that Bela has hideously transformed himself into an Amish farmer! With a bushy beard, but no mustache, and a hairpiece shaped like a bike helmet, Bela's appearance suggests the results of cold fusion between Abraham Lincoln and Curious George.

The only thing that can return him to normal is an Epi-Lady, but they haven't been invented yet. So Bela falls back on an old Mad Science favorite, and starts coveting spinal fluid. Unfortunately, none of his selfish friends will let him drain their spines, and Bela, in a fit of animalistic rage, flings beakers and test tubes at the wall, then flings his own feces at a family of Canadian tourists when they try to snap his picture.

Whistler's Sister gasps, "James, are you *mad?*" Considering he's spent the last three months injecting himself with "ape fluid," Bela sensibly regards this question as rhetorical.

Later, giggling like a pair of 12-year olds, Bela and his gorilla sneak over to Neville's house to soap his windows, TP his shrubs, and steal his butler's spinal fluid. The injection proves a success: Bela still looks like C. Everett Koop wearing Ted Danson's toupee from "Cheers," but he can now straighten his back. Alas, the effect is only temporary, and Bela takes to the needle like Kurt Cobain; within days he's hooked. Strung out. Got a monkey on his back.

He and the gorilla go on a killing spree, tapping the townsfolk for their spinal fluid like it's maple syrup season in Vermont.

Meanwhile, the mysterious specter from the first scene has returned, and is peering through the laboratory window. His wraith-like form and delicate, spidery hands strike fear in our hearts. His luminous, hypnotic eyes recall the evil mesmerist in *The Cabinet of Doctor Caligari*, while his turned-up hat-brim and chuckle-headed drawl conjure a chilling image of Goober from "The Andy Griffith Show."

Bela prepares to visit Neville Chamberlain again, perhaps hoping to siphon his pool boy for a quart, but Whistler's Sister won't let him leave the house until he's been groomed for nits. In a rage, Bela strangles his sister, crushing her windpipe and letting her lifeless body slip to the cold dungeon floor before fleeing into the night.

But like a defiant kid who refuses to fall down when he's killed fair and square in a game of Cowboys and Indians, Whistler's Sister leaps to her feet the instant Bela leaves and starts performing step aerobics. Then she runs a 10K over to Neville's house, but is nabbed by the cops before she can finish the biking and swimming legs of the Ironman Triathlon.

Meanwhile, Bela has called upon his old colleague with a request that he shoot him up. But Neville refuses, unwilling to implicate himself in murder, and because the needle-tracks around Bela's hairy coccyx are really starting to gross him out. So Bela strangles Neville too, but lacking the manic athleticism of an elderly spinster, Neville takes the hint and actually dies.

Bela goes home and discovers a fat newspaper reporter and a plucky girl photographer sneaking around his house. Naturally, he starts sneaking around after them, and pretty soon everyone is sneaking around after everyone else, creeping so slowly in and out of doors that it looks like a Feydeau farce performed by a cast of ground sloths.

Suddenly, Bela realizes the girl is blonde, and he's dressed like an ape. He picks her up and carries her off, struggling mightily not to drop her or smack her head against a piece of furniture as he lopes awkwardly around the tiny set. At this point, the audience's sympathy shifts decisively to the hideously deformed and half-demented Dr. Brewster. True, he's a serial killer, and he's involved in an unsavory domestic partnership with a primate. But at least—unlike the director—he's never forced an elderly morphine addict to risk a hernia.

Bela and the blonde perform the Forbidden Dance. The gorilla, in a jealous rage, breaks free and basically does to Bela what Eric Roberts did to Mariel Hemingway at the end of *Star 80*.

Think the movie's over? You wish. In a touch worthy of Pirandello, the skinny lurker pops up and finally introduces himself. "I'm the author of the story," he says. Then he leaves us with an insoluble existential riddle by asking: "Screwy, wasn't it?"

Well…yes. With an aging Hungarian ham made up to resemble a Mennonite and loping around a sound stage like Lancelot Link, Secret Chimp, this does appear to reach the generally accepted threshold of "screwy."

As we see from this example, in the first part of the 20th century, mad scientists were much like modern day bloggers—they worked from home, which allowed them to set their own hours, avoid long commutes, and sleep with large, muscular, hairy beasts (a tradition kept alive today by internet sensations Matt Drudge and Andrew Sullivan). Back in the day, all scientific equipment, no matter how complex, dangerous, or world-shattering, could easily fit into your basement, and still leave room for the washer and dryer, the ping-pong table, and your Nordic Track.

But what happens when your schemes for global hegemony exceed not only the limited grasp of your mental inferiors, but also the square footage of your bonus room? Well, if you're a deranged entomologist bent on conquering the world with a race of monsters made from Mexican Tarantulas and Hooter Girls, then you relocate to the…

Mesa of Lost Women (1953)
Director: Ron Ormond
Written by: Herbert Tevos

The story of a homicidal simpleton who saves the world from evil Jazzercize instructors, *Mesa of Lost Women* features a more stellar cast of has-beens and never-weres than usual. Headlined by Jackie Coogan, the supporting players include George Barrows, who played "Ro-Man the Ro-Man" in *Robot Monster*, Dolores Fuller, who played Ed Wood's angora donor in *Glen or Glenda?* and "Introducing Tanda Quinn," who observes an old Hollywood tradition by immediately returning to the obscurity from which she was introduced, never to be heard from again.

Our movie begins in the "Muerto Desert"—which narrator Lyle Talbot, another Ed Wood alumnus, calls the "MOO-ee-AIR-toe" desert, setting an unfortunate precedent for the rest of the cast. We've caught Lyle on a bad day, and he spends the first ten minutes of the film sneering at the audience because we're not nearly as fecund as spiders. "In the continuing war for survival between Man and the hexapods," Lyle says with undisguised contempt, "only an utter *fool* would bet against the insects." Hmmm. I was about to take some of that action when it dawned on me that Lyle was laying it on pretty thick, and might have bribed the insects to throw the fight.

Meanwhile, two ragged figures are seen wandering the desert: Captain Grant Chincleft and Sharon Stone. On the verge of collapse, they are rescued by sombrero supermodel Pepe, who notes their near-fatal state of exposure and takes them to an oil company office for first aid, since their HMO won't pay for a hospital visit.

Once he regains consciousness, Grant reveals that they were prisoners of "Dr. Aranya."

"Dr. Aranya!" Pepe exclaims. "Ay caramba!"

Captain Chincleft starts to recount the tale, and the camera slowly zooms in as we prepare for a flashback. Then Lyle barges back in and sneers, "That's quite a story he's telling. *Isn't it*, Pepe?" Pepe looks pensive, and the screen goes fuzzy as he and Captain Chincleft race to flash back first. They're neck and neck, until Lyle suddenly announces, "Actually, it all *really* started over a *year* ago." And then *he* flashes back...

Phil Harris is dropped off in the middle of the desert by Vampira, and greeted by Bozo the dwarf. Inside the Mesa, Dr. Aranya (Uncle Fester) introduces Phil to Tanda, who's playing a half-human/half-tarantula with really big fun bags. He mentions in passing that he wants to use his homo-hexapod hybrids to rule the world, then tries to freak out Phil by pulling back a curtain and showing him a giant tarantula puppet wearing a diaper.

Phil objects to Uncle Fester tampering with nature. Fester takes a cue from Lyle, and contemptuously mispronounces the word "gibberish." Tanda shoots up Phil with a speedball, which causes him to montage badly, and a spinning headline informs us that Phil has been confined to the MOO-ee-AIR-toe State Hospital for the Criminally Dull. But he's escaped!

Cut to a coffeehouse full of Mexican beatniks. Phil Harris appears, and now we see what the newspaper *didn't* say: That the injection produced a hideous metamorphosis, causing Phil to dress like W. Averell Harriman and talk like Wimpy from the old "Popeye" cartoons. Tanda, who still hasn't had a line, is sitting at a corner table, smoking a cigarette and waiting for someone to come into her parlor.

Suddenly, Sharon Stone arrives, accompanied by Mr. Mooney. After some snappy patter stolen from other movies (Sharon looks around and says, "*What* a *dump.*" Really. She does), we get to the boring exposition: It seems that Sharon and Mr. Mooney were en route to be married in Mexico when their plane broke down.

Wimpy comes over to compliment Sharon on her Bette Davis impression and ask if she'd do that leg-crossing thing, but he's interrupted by Tanda, who has succumbed to the tarantula's deeply ingrained instinct to perform modern dance. She proceeds to wow the crowd with her act, which consists of standing barefoot on peanut shells while cupping her left breast, then reaching up to massage a crick in her neck.

Wimpy pans Tanda's performance by pulling a gun and putting a bullet in her bullet bra. Then Wimpy hijacks Mr. Mooney's plane and demands to be taken to Havana, which is a pretty bad movie, but still not as crappy as this one. Captain Chincleft is afraid to take off, because he just finished putting the plane together and the glue isn't dry. But Wimpy insists, and the whole gang takes to the sky in Mr. Mooney's Cox Mustang. Within seconds the control string gets tangled up in some telephone wires, and they crash-land atop the Mesa of Lost Women. Or onto a Ping-Pong table trimmed with sphagnum moss. You make the call.

Now the action really heats up. Wimpy's male nurse Ro-Man wanders into the jungle and is mauled to death by a giant pipe cleaner. Captain Chincleft grabs the flare gun and tries to summon help by firing a slide whistle into the air, then we get to watch the opening credits of "Love, American Style." He salvages a bottle of brandy and passes it between Sharon Stone and Mr. Mooney. Then he turns to Wimpy and says, "What about you?" The music reaches a sudden, ominous crescendo, and Wimpy's response is symbolized by a cutaway to Uncle Fester, who is glumly contemplating urine specimens.

Wimpy and Mr. Mooney fall asleep. Sharon Stone and Captain Chincleft share a tender moment, as they quietly confess their deepest desires to one another. Sharon's dream is to take Mr. Mooney for everything he's worth, while the Captain wants a woman who is "real," having tired of the inflatable kind.

Mr. Mooney obligingly runs off and gets killed by the giant tarantula puppet, which is larger and more fearsome-looking now that it has outgrown diapers and graduated to pull-ups. Meanwhile, Captain Chincleft, Sharon Stone, and Wimpy are captured by the Bangles.

Back in the lab, Uncle Fester gives Wimpy another speedball, which transforms him back into Phil Harris. Oh, and it turns out that Tanda was only *mostly* dead, and now feels well enough to have a Roller Derby-style cat-fight with Sharon. Phil takes advantage of the confusion, and makes a bomb by dropping a piece of dry ice into a glass of Country Time Lemonade. He tells Chincleft and Sharon to leave, because "You belong living. We belong *deaaaaaad.*" Then he detonates his lemonade, starting a fire that kills Fester, Tanda, Bozo the dwarf, the Bangles, and for some unexplained reason, Sigmund the Sea-Monster.

Now we're back at the oil company office, where Captain Chincleft is wrapping up his recitation. Which finally answers the *biggest* question posed by the film: Exactly whose flashback were we watching, anyway? Meanwhile, Pepe is sitting beside Sharon Stone's cot, telling her *his* story, and asking if she'd do that leg-crossing thing. Then Lyle returns once more to tell us that we're all scum, and that he scorns our infertility; but I think it's just sour grapes, because nobody wanted to watch *his* flashback.

Even though Dr. Aranya's scheme of genetically splicing a tarantula with Martha Graham didn't really pan out, he was still a visionary, being among the first to join the great postwar migration of mad scientists from the cities to the suburbs. But unlike so many of his colleagues who were content to conquer the world from a three-bedroom rambler in Levittown, Fester went even further, pioneering the use of topographical features as secret lairs, a trend that reached its zenith with the headquarters-cum-spaceship-hanger-in-a-volcano in *You Only Live Twice.* Unfortunately, Uncle Fester was on a budget, and even with double coupons and a loan from his brother-in-law, he could only afford a two-room mesa. Conditions were cramped (the giant spider didn't have a room of his own, just an alcove, despite the fact that he had begun wearing Huggies training pants and was becoming more body conscious) and the plumbing and wiring were below code, with the result that the blaze touched off by Wimpy resulted in a death toll unmatched since the Triangle Shirtwaist Factory fire. The subsequent public outrage spurred legislation requiring all secret laboratories to install smoke detectors and sprinklers; and many lives were saved as a result, although the pace of certain movies has suffered, since super villains are periodically required to interrupt their lasering of Washington D.C. or their lowering of James Bond into a pool of piranha in order to conduct a fire drill.

But while Americans were quick to embrace the latest fads in mad science, not every man with a psychosis and a Ph.D was so eager to abandon tradition. For just as there shall always be an England, there shall also always be the stately homes of England. And the greenhouses behind the stately homes of England where deeply weird men labor to shock the world by setting up a play date between a chimp and a shrubbery.

Konga (1961)
Director: John Lemont
Written by: Herman Cohen, Aben Kandel

Our movie opens with an airplane crash in the jungle. We soon learn (thanks to the ever-helpful newspaper vendors) that a Famous Botanist was on board. A year later, a newsie informs us that the Famous Botanist has been found alive, and proves this by pointing to a paper with the headline "Famous Botanist Found Alive" (it was either a slow news day or botanists were the Spice Girls of the early '60s).

Soon Famous Botanist Charles Decker (Michael Gough), accompanied by a baby chimp that he fondles incessantly, returns home to Margaret (Margo Johns), his "housekeeper, secretary, assistant, and good friend." Margaret quickly picks up on the peculiar closeness between Decker and the chimp, and gets jealous. Decker tells her that little Konga is very important to his plans, and implies that in a showdown between Margaret and Konga, Margaret would be the one donated to the petting zoo. He also explains that while he was lost in Africa, he discovered "the link in evolution between animal and plant life," which turns out to be the Venus Flytrap. Soon Decker has a whole greenhouse full of giant Venus Flytraps, and is now ready for the next phase of his experiment—injecting his good buddy Konga with flytrap juice. The results are astounding, transforming Konga from a baby chimp into…an adult chimp!

Back at the university, Decker attempts to sexually harass a blonde and busty co-ed named Sandra, but he's interrupted by a summons from the Dean, who objects to Decker's wild evolutionary theories. Decker protests that they are perfectly good theories, and that "Ultimately, I will be able to change the shape of human beings!" (Just like Jenny Craig!) The Dean exclaims, "Charles, you're *mad!*"

Decker goes home to whine to Margaret about the mean dean, then suddenly cries out, "Please leave; I want to be alone with Konga." Margaret looks troubled as she departs, possibly to seek expert advice. ("Dear Abby, my relationship is being threatened by a chimp…")

Alone at last, Decker shoots up Konga with more flytrap juice. The picture wavers, and Konga becomes…a man in a bad gorilla costume! Decker reminds

Konga that "We know each other much better than the world suspects," (um, okay), and has Konga seal their love by strangling the Dean.

Later, in an attempt to prove that she's more fun than a whole *barrel* of mutated chimps, Margaret throws a party at Decker's place. In attendance is Professor Tagore, who, in the *strangest coincidence ever*, is *also* doing research into Venus Flytrap juice. Decker realizes that Tagore will soon be able to produce his *own* killer chimp, so he pays a call on Tagore, taking Konga along for the ride. Each scientist tries to one-up the other with stories about how well their mutations are proceeding, until finally a pair of ape arms burst through the shelving behind Tagore and strangle him.

The next day Decker takes his botany class on a field trip. He loads the students into the ape-mobile, but tells Sandra he needs her to ride in the cab with him. Bob, Sandra's boyfriend, asks if he can sit up front too, but is quickly put in his place, which is the back of the van with the other *To Sir with Love* rejects. Bob's friends try to cheer him up by making ribald comments about what Sandra and Decker are probably doing.

A sudden downpour puts an end to the excursion, but Bob stays behind to confront Decker. He tells Decker to leave Sandra alone, "or else!" Decker takes this as a threat, and slaps Bob. Bob punches Decker and sneers, "You'll probably have me expelled for this."

Uh, no, Bob, he'll just have his gorilla strangle you.

While Decker is trying to read his morning paper, Margaret flounces around, perturbed about *something* (I know you men can relate to this). "What are you having with your poached egg?" she demands. "*Murder?*" Decker tries to play the old game of denying that he, personally, murdered Bob, and makes her define "murder" and "Bob," but you can tell his heart isn't in it. Decker admits that he did have Bob whacked, but purely in the interest of science. And to allay suspicion, he has invited his murder victim's girlfriend to dinner.

After dessert, Decker offers to show Sandra his greenhouse. Sandra is clearly in mourning, as evidenced by her short, extremely tight skirt and her clingy, low-cut orange sweater. Decker says he wants her to assist him with his "greatest discovery." Sweet, innocent, stupid Sandra says, "But you already have a very capable assistant!" Decker replies, "I require more that just a laboratory assistant. I need *you*! To *be* with me!"

Margaret, who has been eavesdropping from the bushes, is none too thrilled to hear this, and runs off.

Decker is pawing Sandra in earnest now, as she bleats something about feeling faint and wanting to leave. Decker says she can't until she promises to "work" with him. She says no. He says she *must*, since he is her teacher and it's part of his benefits package.

Margaret gives Konga a Sid Vicious-style overdose of flytrap juice, and suddenly Konga is 20 feet tall! He reaches down towards Margaret and picks up a red-headed doll (possibly Barbie's friend, Midge).

Meanwhile, Sandra is *still* fighting for her honor. Konga watches all this and decides to make the point that *no means no*, so he bursts through the glass, reaches an enormous paw down towards Decker, and picks up a Ken doll.

The people of London seem quite calm at the sight of a 50-foot ape strolling down the street, no doubt because making a fuss would be rude. Eventually Konga gets annoyed at their typical British understatement and swats at them, causing the bystanders to run and scream (but quite politely).

Konga reaches Big Ben, London's answer to the Empire State Building, and stops. ("Hey, look—he's stopped," the exposition extra exclaims.) Everybody stands and stares at Konga. Konga stares back. Everyone looks at their watches and waits for something to happen so the movie can end.

At last, we have some action—a few soldiers climb out of a truck. They fire rifles, machine guns, and mortars, but apparently not at Konga. By this time, however, Konga is fed up, so he throws Decker at them and falls down dead. Then, in an unexpected twist, Konga's body suddenly becomes…a toy chimpanzee! In a tableau evoking the tragic final scene of *Romeo and Juliet*, the dead sock monkey lays beside the bloody corpse of Decker, making us realize how sad it is that the love of a man and his chimp has to end this way.

Although the message is subtle (typical British understatement), this is the cinema's most eloquent evocation of that old aphorism, "People who mutate chimps shouldn't molest co-eds in glass houses." Something like that. The point is, *Konga* represents the last gasp of the Toni Home Perm School of Science. Now, in the interest of full disclosure, it should be pointed out that we ourselves work from home, but if one of our assignments goes awry, we can just hit the Delete key, and no one's the wiser. However, if there was a good chance that a failed movie summary would abduct and carry us to a major tourist attraction, where it would roar and shake us violently like a rag doll while the army fired bazookas and flamethrowers at us and tourists took snapshots and home videos as TV station helicopters hovered overhead, beaming live images of the fracas coast-to-coast, then we'd probably put some pants on before settling down to work.

We'd also consider moving out of the downtown area. Because after all, if Konga had gone on a rampage in the village of Grommet-on-Treacle instead of near Big Ben, then he might have upset a costermonger's cart, maybe bruised a few cabbages, but the Army certainly wouldn't have gotten involved, and Charles would have been free to chalk the whole thing up to experience, and return to his research into co-ed molestation.

Fortunately, mad movie scientists have finally copped a clue, and now confine their experiments to secret, subterranean redoubts where it's easier to isolate their victims while avoiding inadvertent appearances on *Good Morning America*, or *Live at Five!*

Hollow Man (2000)
Directed by Paul Verhoeven
Written by Gary Scott Thompson (story)
and Andrew W. Marlowe (story and screenplay)

Hollow Man, while boasting some astonishing special effects, is not a very faithful adaptation of the poem by T.S. Eliot. Nevertheless, even when the story bogs down, the presence of star Kevin Bacon allows the audience to while away the time with that popular parlor game, Six Degrees of Crap.

As our story opens, a brown Norway rat is twisted in half like a balloon animal, then its head is bitten off and eaten by an invisible...rat head-eating thing. Cut to Kevin Bacon, who is attempting to use recombinant DNA technology on Scrubbing Bubbles. When his efforts fail, he pauses to peep at his neighbor as she strips down to her underwear. His scientific genius rekindled by voyeurism, Kevin returns to his computer, and with a few keystrokes, creates a perfect three dimensional model of an Everlasting Gob-Stopper.

Next day at the lab, Josh Brolin gets lightly mauled by an invisible gorilla. Kevin and Josh join forces, and hunt down the diaphanous primate with infrared goggles in a sequence that's sort of a cross between *Predator* and *Donkey Kong*.

Having tranquilized the ape, they inject it with Orange Crush, which causes the invisible beast to slowly reappear, organ by organ—first the circulatory system, then the viscera, and eventually—after we're all mildly nauseated—the flesh and pelt. Kevin's team is ecstatic. He's *done* it, he's finally realized one of man's oldest dreams—showing a gorilla its own guts.

To celebrate, Kevin tries to seduce Elizabeth Shue, his research partner and former girlfriend, but having just seen an ape's endocrine system, she's not feeling aroused.

Against the advice of his colleagues, Kevin decides to test the invisibility process on himself, since this will allow him to avoid appearing in the rest of the movie. He shoots himself up with a vial of Windex (don't try this at home), then screams and flops around nude on an operating table, terrifying his team with the possibility they might glimpse his scrotum.

The formula works, and Kevin disappears—skin first, then nerves, organs, and finally bones. It's a historic moment; Kevin has achieved a quantum shift out of the visible spectrum, and immediately realizes the scientific potential of this breakthrough technology by molesting a veterinarian.

Alas, the Orange Crush fails to reverse the process and return him to visibility. Elizabeth creates a mask for Kevin by pouring flesh-colored pudding over his head, which makes him look like Mr. Clean after an industrial accident.

Kevin goes insane, in the time-honored manner of invisible men, giving the old You-can't-imagine-the-FREEDOM-and-POWER speech, and then decides to kill off the rest of the cast before the critics do. After trapping them down in his secret underground laboratory complex, he deals out a succession of head wounds to the supporting players, then stabs Josh with a crowbar, and locks Elizabeth in a walk-in freezer. But, as Nietzsche said, Whatever doesn't kill you, makes you into McGyver, and she promptly concocts an elaborate escape utilizing a defibrillator, a length of heavy gauge plastic tubing, the handle from a file cabinet, and a Hostess Ding Dong. Not to be outdone, Kevin crafts a powerful bomb out of duct tape, some orange juice, and a snowglobe.

Inspired by her success, Elizabeth whips up a flamethrower out of ordinary items you'd find around the house, and roasts Kevin at close range. But, as Nietzsche said, Whatever makes you invisible, apparently makes you flame-retardant too, because after screaming in agony and burning to a crisp, he shakes it off and resumes killing her.

Josh, inexplicably back from his near-death experience, caves in Kevin's skull with the crowbar. But, as Nietzsche said, whatever makes your screenplay stupid and implausible makes your climax laugh-out-loud goofy, and Kevin bounces back from his subdural hematoma and takes a swing at Josh with the crowbar. Missing, he hits a high voltage…something on the wall. Fuse box, I guess, and is electrocuted. As a bonus, death renders him partially visible, so we get to ponder his lymph nodes again.

Fleeing Kevin's homemade bomb, Elizabeth and Josh climb up the ladder inside the elevator shaft. They're nearly to the top, when we learn anew the truth of Nietzsche's dictum that Whatever doesn't kill you makes you incredibly anti-climactic, because Kevin appears out of nowhere, and suddenly Elizabeth is locked in a life and death struggle with the Transparent Man from high school biology class.

Eventually, Kevin dies as he lived—hamming it up with his skin off. Back on the surface, there's a bunch of fire trucks, and an ambulance pulls away as the credits roll, giving you the odd feeling that you've just watched a really perverted episode of "Emergency!"

I don't know what kind of weed they're smoking in those Amsterdam hash cafes, but in my opinion, it's time that director Paul Verhoeven learns when to say when.

A grim tale, but one that offers several important lessons. For instance, while the medicinal properties of Orange Crush has been known since the Middle Ages, it does not have a 100% success rate in curing quantum shifts out of the visible spectrum. (Although we shouldn't discount the possibility that the government, in attempting to save tax dollars, might have scrimped and used Orange Nehi, or even Fanta.) Also, if you're a middling actor who got the part because your dad is a former TV star and transmission-repair spokesmodel, you *might* get the girl, but you're more likely to get your colon pierced with a crowbar. And finally, if you're going to have Kevin Bacon naked in your movie, it's best to also have him invisible, and as far underground as possible.

But what's the broader lesson we can draw from these films spanning the latter half of the 20th century. In short, to be a successful mad scientist, you must always remember these three words: Location, location, location. Find a secluded, preferably subterranean spot with plenty of closet space and fresh batteries in the smoke detector. Otherwise, after tampering in God's domain, you might find your unholy, misbegotten creature giving you a wedgie in front of Westminster Abbey. And let's face it—that's *gotta* come up at your next class reunion.

Bats Entertainment!

Like every other field of science, Mad Doctoring has its areas of specialization—atomic robots, genetically engineered plagues, giant death rays, and advanced henchman-whipping. But year in, and year out, one of the most popular courses of post-graduate study for the aspiring movie madman is freestyle Bat Mutation.

Let's take a look at two famous examples from the Killer Bat canon, one from the Golden Age, and another of more recent vintage, and see if we can determine why schemes for enlarging these ecologically helpful mammals to monstrous proportions and imbuing them with a lust for human blood continues to generate so many grant applications each year.

The Devil Bat (1940)
Directed by: Jean Yarborough
Screenplay by: John Thomas Neville, which seems like a pretty snooty moniker for a guy who's written something called *Devil Bat*.

Our story opens in the quiet village of Heathsville—a town apparently founded on the candy bar industry, and controlled by two powerful families, the Heaths and the Zagnuts. A title card appears, saving many minutes of expensive exposition, informing us that kindly village doctor Paul Carruthers (Bela Lugosi) is conducting "weird, terrifying experiments." Bela is embittered that, despite his obvious *mitteleuropean* origins, he's been stuck with a name like Paul Carruthers, and seeks revenge by speaking in an accent so impenetrable that he makes Eva Gabor sound like Alistair Cooke.

Bela walks into an attic full of bats and explains his theory of "glandular stimulation through electrical impulses," leading the viewer to conclude that Bela has just invented a vibrating novelty item. Instead, the good doctor takes one of the bats—now dangling upside down from a coat hanger—puts him in a closet, and turns on some humming electrical equipment, causing the bat to grow to horrifying proportions. The viewer's worst fears are confirmed: Bela has learned the secret of creating hideous monsters with One-Hour Martinizing.

170

Meanwhile, Mr. Zagnut sends his dim-witted son Roy over to Bela's lab to present him with a $5,000 bonus check on behalf of the firm. Naturally, this makes Bela want to kill everybody, so he asks Roy to try the new shaving lotion he's just invented. The deeply stupid young man sees nothing sinister in Bela's request that he "rub some on the tender part of the neck," and happily complies.

After the reeking Roy departs, Bela takes center stage with a dramatic, *Dune*-style voice over, telling us that he feels ill-used by his employers and will make them all pay. We also learn that "the worm *is* the spice! The spice *is* the worm!"

Bela releases the Devil Bat, which promptly follows the stink of the shaving lotion to Zagnut Manor. It dives out of the night sky and murders Roy, all the while shrieking "Yeeeeee-HAAAAAAA" like Slim Pickens at the end of *Dr. Strangelove*.

Later, at a big city newspaper, managing editor Perry White gets ace reporter Johnny Layton on the case. Something of a science whiz himself, Johnny has been conducting secret experiments to enlarge the brim of his hat, and makes his first appearance wearing a fedora the size of the Flushing Meadows Unisphere.

Johnny heads for Heathsville in the company of his incredibly abrasive photographer-sidekick "One Shot McGuire." The less said about this character the better, but if Jimmy Olsen had been *half* this irritating, Superman would long ago have popped his skull like a zit.

Johnny visits the local Chief of Police, who is impressed by the awning-like brim of Johnny's hat, and instantly agrees to let this total stranger conduct the homicide investigation himself. He also allows Johnny to carry a gun, declare martial law, and suspend the Constitution at will.

The following night, Roy's brother Tommy permits Bela to shave his butt and apply the untested shaving lotion. Predictably, the monster drains Tommy's blood and leaves nothing behind but the great smell of Brut, leading Johnny to believe that the murders and the after-shave lotion are connected. The chief scoffs at Johnny's theory, even though Bela has just given them each a sample of the lotion in a bottle labeled "Big Bat Bait."

Johnny, being no smarter than anyone else in this film, slaps on the shaving lotion, causing the Devil Bat to attack Jimmy Olsen. Johnny pulls his gun and fires five times, idiotically missing Jimmy and killing the star.

Undaunted, Bela One-Hour Martinizes up another monster, then goes into the closet and gives the bat a hernia examination ("Turn your head and echo-locate").

Bela then visits the head of the Heath family, Oh Henry, to dab him with the scented lotion and remind him that "Your brain is too *feeble* to grasp what I have achieved!" Bela works himself into a Hungarian tizzy, and gloats aloud about killing half the Heath and Zagnut clans with his perfume and bats. The truth dawns on Oh Henry, who finally realizes that between love and madness lies Obsession. He's on the verge of discovering that nothing comes between Bela and his Calvins when we cut back to Johnny, who is searching the laboratory. He has finally found ironclad evidence that will send Bela to the gallows: Bat guano and dry-cleaning fluid.

Meanwhile, Bela drives off to kill Mr. Zagnut. He has the new bat in his trunk, but he has to release it just outside Zagnut Manor, since it's a spare bat, and is only good for 25 miles at 50 miles per hour.

Johnny splashes Bela with the lotion, and then, while they wait to see which one of them the bat will kill first, Johnny asks Bela how he managed to develop the monster. Bela gives the "your brain is too feeble" speech again, then he and the reporter Apache dance until the giant bat arrives to kill Bela with a hearty "Yee-Ha!"

The movie comes to an abrupt end, and we are left not so much with a moral as with a motto. "One-Hour Martinizing: Gets Clothes Clean. Makes Bats Big."

Poor Dr Carruthers. Despite his murders and his hammy theatrics, one can almost feel sorry for him. After all, we've all been there: not appreciated by the candy bar industry despite our cutting-edge work in the field of rodent-attracting shaving lotion; forced to go by the slave name of "Paul Carruthers"; and hungering to get bat-related revenge on those who gave us bonus checks. And Carruthers would have got away with it too, if it hadn't been for his big mouth!

The lesson to aspiring mad scientists is obvious: a successful killing spree requires you to refrain from bragging to everyone in town about how you used giant bats to knock off those who wronged you. Hey, you don't need validation from people whose minds are too feeble to grasp what you have accomplished—their gory death should be its own reward. If you want to explain how you managed to enlarge flying mammals via a secret dry cleaning technique, and made them attack the Old Spice man, then do it at Batty Scientists Anonymous meeting, since there at least you'd have a slight expectation of confidentiality.

And speaking of BSA, let's meet Dr. Bob Gunton ("Hi, Dr. Bob!"). He too has an acknowledged addiction to bats—hopefully, the Twelve Steps will work for him.

Bats (1998)
Directed by Louis Murneau
Written by John Logan

Gallup, Texas: A hunky teen parks with a girl in lovers' lane and proceeds to strike out, despite his wearing a fetching shirt from the Roy Rogers collection. Suddenly, we hear squealing, and an ominous flapping sound. "Something touched my hand," he remarks, uneasily. Then he gets out of the car so it can touch other parts of his body, since random contact with night-flying pests seems like the only action he's going to get tonight.

When even *that* doesn't work, he rejoins the girl, who has agreed to neck with him in exchange for a lukewarm Coors. Suddenly, and all at once, the ardent couple is struck by a freight train, hit by a swarm of bats, and rammed by the camera dolly.

A representative from the Centers for Disease Control whisks Dr. Dina Meyer away to Texas, where she's met by Sheriff Lou Diamond Phillips. Sheriff Lou drawls "Uh-HUH" in response to everything Dr. Dina says, but with a heavy ironic stress on the last syllable, so the audience will know that while he's Walking Tall, he's doing it in a post-modern kind of way.

He shows Dina a mannequin saturated with Beef-A-Roni, and she digs a bat fang out of its jugular vein. Nevertheless, she insists that "bats do not kill people!" and suggests that the fang was planted by Detective Mark Furhman. But at the autopsy, they are joined by Dr. Bob Gunton, who instantly strikes the audience as creepy, due to his shifty-eyed, evasive manner, and his history of appearing in Andrew Lloyd Webber musicals. Dr. Bob has been performing "virus-based" experiments on two Indonesian Flying Foxes, which subsequently escaped, and now it seems that bats *do* kill people, requiring the National Bat Association to coin a new slogan.

Later, they find another mutilated corpse. The crusty female mayor of the town arrives—judging by her apparel, she was interrupted in mid-square dance—and demands to know what's going on. "Well," says Sheriff Lou, "We think this was done by some sort of...*bats*." But he can't quite keep a straight face, and you get that feeling that for Lou, he might as well have been saying, "We think the victim was mauled by Smurfs." Regardless, the Sheriff goes on to insist that they have to alert the public and close the square dances! But the mayor is reluctant, knowing the local merchants rely on the vital square dancing economy for the majority of their sales of ugly shirts and huge belt buckles.

Dr. Dina quizzes Dr. Bob about just what he did to the bats, deducing that his virus increased their intelligence and capacity to work together communally, giving bats, for the first time in their evolutionary history, the ability to compete on "Family Feud."

And why did he do this? "Because," he says, "I'm a scientist. That's what we do. We make everything a little better." Well, he does have a point. From drought-resistant strains of corn, to bats that can kill Texans, the history of science is the story of small, but necessary improvements in our quality of life.

Unfortunately, the virus begins to infect the local bats, making them all dangerously smart. Even worse, the virus is limited to bats, and so can't be spread to Texans. Dr. Dina and her plucky crew must now annihilate the colony before it migrates, spreading the contagion and eliminating square dancing all over the hemisphere.

Dr. Dina and Sheriff Lou wander around outside at night so they can be attacked by computer-generated effects. They make it to his truck, but the super-intelligent bats keep smacking into the windows and sticking there, like so many suction-cupped Garfield dolls. Realizing they look ridiculous, the bats take off, but leave behind an ugly hand puppet.

Dr. Dina cleverly radio-tags the puppet and releases it so they can follow it back to the roost. But Dr. Bob's original two Superbats realize he's wearing a wire, and they kill him before he can squeal.

The CDC contacts the inhabitants of Gallup, and orders an immediate evacuation. Unfortunately, the townsfolk think this means they're supposed to eat plenty of roughage and prunes, and they just keep hanging around. Suddenly, Junior Samples gets into a wrestling match with a giant bat over a Ham and Swiss Bowl at Dennys, while other bats swarm and attack the Village People.

As the flock begins to kill and feast on everyone in sight, Dr. Dina drives the surviving people into the safety of the local movie house. Unfortunately, it's showing *Patch Adams*, and they all come rushing back out into the street.

Dina grabs a gun and corners one of the giant Superbats in a convenience store. She takes frantic shots at the creature while it leisurely shops for Moon Pies and motor oil, but only manages to blow out the windows and destroy a point-of-purchase display for Saltine crackers.

Suddenly, the entire flock of killer bats turn as one and flap away into the night, because they realize that it's 8:50 PM. *The West Wing* will be on in ten minutes, and as super-intelligent mammals, they're naturally swayed by its impressive showing at the Golden Globes.

Daylight arrives, and with it comes the Texas National Guard, giving this movie something most cheesy horror films lack: a whole bunch of future presidential candidates. As they haul away the corpses, Sheriff Lou pulls out a bottle and takes a swig. "Old Texas custom," he explains. Whenever a town full of rednecks gets slaughtered by mutated bats, local law enforcement is supposed to celebrate with a snort of Old Granddad.

They barricade themselves in the schoolhouse and cover the windows with chain-link, while Sheriff Lou puts on Montserrat's recording of Donizetti's "Lucia," on the theory that opera will repel bats the same way it keeps teenagers from hanging around the parking lot of the 7-11.

Realizing that Dr. Bob isn't cutting it as a villain, the filmmakers suddenly lob in an Evil Government Guy, who explains to no one in particular that Dr. Bob works in the weapons division, and the Pentagon has been developing killer bats for over a decade. "Yes," he declares. "It was *us!*"

But Dr. Bob isn't about to be out-evilled that easily, and pulls a gun. He calls his creations to his side, and the director makes another stab at horrifying us, but with the bat puppets taped over the windows, it just looks like a school-sponsored haunted house. (Which, we should note, did raise considerably more money for the marching band than last year's Murderous Bat-themed car wash.)

Dr. Bob goes outside so he and the bats can rip off the end of *Willard* and he can go back to playing Juan Peron in the Long Beach Civic Light Opera production of "Evita!"

Dr. Dina decides to enter the mine where the bats are roosting, and turn on a big air conditioner that will freeze them all to death. Unfortunately, an air strike has been ordered, and they only have an hour before the bombs start to fall. On the bright side, the mission has been entrusted to the Texas Air National Guard, so they'll probably wind up bombing the Mall of America by mistake.

Dr. Dina and Sheriff Lou put on space suits and descend into the mine. They switch on the cooler, but one of the Superbats knocks Lou down, rubs his face in guano, and makes him say "Chiroptera."

Eventually, he and Dina wind up running frantically from an onrushing swarm of computer generated bats, and their own stink. They reach the surface and blow up the entrance to the mine, just as the fighter craft release their payloads, and score a direct hit on the Arrowhead Motor Lodge in Fond du Lac, Wisconsin. The End.

You will have noticed that like other fields of mad science, Bat Mutation has followed the familiar arc, from Bob Vila-like mad doctors who crank out their

Do-It-Yourself abominations in basement workshops, to multi-billion dollar bio warfare programs using the latest in genetically engineered viral pathogens and actors who can panic in front of a blue screen.

But more importantly, these films demonstrate that Bat Mutation is a fine art, like winemaking or glassblowing, steeped in tradition and passed down from generation to generation. Oh sure, Dr. Bob employed state-of-the-art gene-splicing techniques to create a more intelligent and aggressive breed, whereas Bela relied upon dry cleaning technology to produce an abnormally large bat with a fierce distaste for imposter fragrances, but their goals were the same. In fact, throughout the entire history of cinematic mad science, from Edison's *Frankenstein* in 1910, to *Bats, Hollow Man* and beyond, nearly every mad doctor has pursued the same unchanging ambition: to create, with his own hands, a startling, undreamt-of thing that will cause a tremendous amount of inconvenience and property damage before eventually coming back and killing him.

Today, critics bemoan the dearth of students pursuing higher degrees in math or science, but we believe they err in blaming the nation's schools. Instead, we say blame Hollywood. After all, would you rather take a marketing job with room for advancement, or spend many years and hundreds of thousands of dollars on post-graduate studies that will inevitably culminate with your getting squished by a giant tarantula?

Anyway. Just something to think about while you browse those brochures at the Junior College Job Fair.

Teenage Wasteland

Teenagers have posed a problem since the dawn of history. Aristophanes' play, *White Punks on Mead* tells the story of a disaffected youth who refuses to follow in his father's footsteps by having man-on-boy sex with a middle-aged amphora merchant from Lemnos, and instead gets involved in extreme sports like bull-dancing and minotaur-tipping.

Nowadays, of course, teenagers face many more dangerous temptations than simply getting hammered on restina and sleeping with their moms. Today's teens are exposed to a multitude of mind-altering influences, from violent video games to internet porn to Mentos, and according to our extensive research on American youth (which basically consisted of watching the opening credits to *The Patty Duke Show*), "a hotdog makes [them] lose control." So how can we, as a society, possibly cope with an entire generation hopped up on swine rectums and sauerkraut?

Simple. It's a well-known fact that teens compose the target demographic of most movies, since young people have plenty of spending money, lots of free time, and lack the critical awareness to realize that *Dude, Where's My Car?* is really a rhetorical question. So, since movies are geared towards teens, we think it's only fair to make movies be responsible for them. Based on this idea, we've taken three films about teens from the past 50 years, and have examined them for tips on handling today's troubled youth. 1952's *Teenage Devil Dolls* suggests that extensive overdubbing is one solution, since it saves you from having to hear Eddie Fisher sing "Dungaree Doll." 1960's *Because They're Young* proposes honest dialogue, mutual respect, and a savage ass-kicking by Dick Clark, while 1998's *Disturbing Behavior* advocates dealing with lawlessness through bralessness, backed up by *A Clockwork Orange*-style mind control experiments sponsored by K-Mart. Let's begin, shall we?

Teenage Devil Dolls (1952)
Directed by Bamlet Lawrence Price, Jr.
Written by Bamlet Lawrence Price, Jr.
Produced by Bamlet Lawrence Price, Jr.

Okay, I think you already see what the problem here is—somebody told young Bamlet that he was another Orson Welles. As this movie demonstrates, however, he's not even another Orson Bean. And what do we learn from all this? Well, that when mixed-up kids who have no other outlets for their angst are subjected to peer pressure, they turn to filmmaking, and it's society as a whole that suffers.

Anyway, *Teenage Devil Dolls* presents the horrifying story of a young auteur who didn't have enough money to shoot a sound track and had to rely on over-dubbed narration to tell his story. It's also about heroin.

Let's join our movie, already in progress. It's the morning of September the 11th, 1952. We know this because the narrator has a compulsion about giving the exact time that everything happens—I hear there are now drugs to treat this kind of thing. Our main characters are assembled at the train station: Martinez (Bamlet Lawrence Price Jr. yet again), a really wimpy drug lord; Cassandra, a perky, pony-tailed miss who looks just like Barbie, the "teenage devil doll" of the title; and Lt. Jason, a square-jawed police officer who claims to be our narrator's onscreen persona.

Cassandra is being sent to a Federal Narcotics Hospital, which is a proud day in every young girl's life. Martinez, Cassandra's pusher/boyfriend has come to try to renew their love. Lt. Jason confides that addicts have a strange code of ethics, so he is staying close to Cassandra, "even though she now has sufficient reason to hate my penis." (Okay, he may have really said something about her having cause to hate *Martinez*, but that's not what it sounded like.)

The rumble of motorcycles causes Lt. Jason to dreamily recall that "Motorcycles were a part of Cassandra's turbulent past," and then suddenly it's 1949. Cassandra stares blankly at the camera to convey teen-age angst, and her mother glares at her to indicate oppression (this is basically the all-mime version of *Rebel Without a Cause*).

When some kids on choppers pull up at the sweatshop where Cassandra works, she rides off with them. Poor, weak Cassandra is unable to resist the terrible peer pressure they exert on her by handing her a reefer, and soon she is laughing maniacally, which can't be good.

Now that she's an addict, Cassandra's old friends start avoiding her. Everyone but Johnny, the poor lunkhead who waits outside the school to walk her home every afternoon. Thanks to this process of elimination, it's a quickie wedding to the lunkhead, then Cassandra steps into the exciting world housewifedom! The lesson here is as obvious as it is chilling: Marijuana leads to marriage.

The "emotionally immature and badly adjusted" Cassandra can't cope with the taunting cries of "ring-around-the-collar" that come from the laundry, and begins crying hysterically while hanging up clothes. Johnny knows that most young brides do this in the bedroom, not the back yard, and concludes she has a problem. The doctor diagnoses it as "post-marital depression," and gives her some sleeping pills, reasoning that the cure for marriage is more sleep. Alas, the mother's little helpers don't help, and soon Cassandra is back with the Heck's Angels. Yes, "Cassandra had kicked over the traces and pulled out the stops," Lt. Jason tells us. She has "Started the long road the junkies call 'the route.'" Ah, the junkies have such a colorful patois, so rich and expressive!

One day Johnny comes home to find Cassandra rolling around in the back yard in apparent homage to the Three Stooges, and finally makes that call to Hazleton. But Cassandra, who thought it was a General Foods International Coffee flavor, doesn't like the program and runs away.

She gets a carhop job at "Hamburger Hotdogs," where her duties consist of delivering marijuana under the food trays. And you should try their Quarter Pounders With Weed! Eventually, Cassandra becomes involved with Sven Bergman, a heroin dealer and director of gloomy art films about playing chess with death. Suddenly, there's a high-pitched shrieking tone, signaling that Cassandra is now addicted to smack, or else the movie is airing a test of the Emergency Broadcast System.

The highly efficient Lt. Jason arrests all the dealers in town with the exception of Martinez, the sleazy director/writer/actor we met at the beginning of the movie. Cassandra immediately signs up to be his bitch, since her tenure with the Swedish heroin cartel didn't work out that well.

When Cassandra and Martinez stop at a service station, Lt. Jason scares her by strolling over to say hello. Cassie pantomimes dismay and horror (she apparently *does* hate his penis), and she and Martinez drive into the desert and hide in a cave. The cops spot their abandoned car, and, with a cry of "finder's keepers!" also discover the couple's heroin stash in the glove compartment. See, the runaways had forgotten they were "slaves to a needle." One would think this is something a junkie would remember.

Soon the 107-degree heat and the lack of water and heroin cause our two druggies to writhe on the ground, foam at the mouth, and get tattoos. Cassandra eventually crawls out of the cave to lie in the direct sunlight, apparently hoping to get rid of her junkie pallor. Lt. Jason finds her and carries her lifeless body out of the shot.

Now, back in 1952, Cassandra is off to Betty Ford Memorial Penitentiary, apparently none the worse for having died. Martinez is also looking well, having survived the withdrawal, the heat, the dehydration, as well as the long walk back to L.A. And he owes it all to drugs! Anyway, Cassandra gets on the train. The cops arrest Martinez. Our narrator informs us that the Cassandra will probably never be cured, and will only come to a degrading end in some other movie. As if *that* wasn't depressing enough, we are then given a screen full of statistics—for instance, there has been a 2000% increase in the number of juvenile addicts over the past ten years. Extrapolating from this data, it means that by 1964, the entire country will be addicted to narcotics, which explains how they got away with that bizarre color scheme on *Shindig!* It also explains why the set of the *Mike Douglas Show*, a program directed at middle-aged, Lark-smoking Midwestern ladies in hairnets, was bedecked with psychedelic Flower Power daisies. Now you know. Even though your Aunt Ruth from Fergus Falls favored quilted housecoats, adored Lawrence Welk, and faithfully brought her delightful lima bean-and-Velveeta hotdish to Casserole Night at the Lutheran Church, behind your back she was mainlining horse.

So what does this movie teach us about handling the problems of today's teens? Well, *Teenage Devil Doll*, much like the U.S. Justice Department, propounds the "gateway" theory of narcotics addiction. This hypothesis holds that the use of a relatively mild mood-altering substance such as nicotine or marijuana inevitably leads to a craving for more powerful mind-warping agents such as matrimony. According to a recent DEA-funded study by the Harvard School of Medicine, motorcycles lead directly to the use of cannabis, with potentially serious side effects such as fake laughter, flashbacks, and excessive narration. Laundry, experts warn, can lead to involuntary Curly Howard impressions, while employment in the fast food industry leads to fornication with Swedes, death by exposure, and, uh…a train ride.

Therefore, the lessons troubled teens should take from this shocking exposé are twofold: 1) Drugs are bad, and will kill you, and then bring you back to life, and 2) The policeman is your friend, and you should trust him, no matter how much you may hate his penis.

But drugs are not the only route to juvenile delinquency. Sometimes the path to perdition is paved with Tuesday Weld and Doug McClure, while the road to salvation leads to Dick Clark. Sometimes, as we see in our next film, you've got to just say No to Sex, but Yes to Dick.

Because They're Young (1960)
Directed by Paul Wendkos
Written by James Gunn, based on a novel by John Farris.

Tagline: *"Whoever you are, you're in this picture! Because this tells of youth's challenge to grown-ups who can't understand!"*

Yes, this movie is about *all* teens: hoody ones, trampy ones, horny ones, dorky ones, and especially, really old ones. Maybe this movie should have been called *Because They're Not Quite Liver-Spotted*. Anyway, it's a safe bet that if this film were made today, the porn parody would be entitled, *Because They're Hung*.

But let's meet our cast of characters:

Dick Clark is a new history teacher, a "firebrand" who believes in really talking to teens, asking them meaningful questions like what they think of the new single by The 1910 Fruitgum Company. But *this* school doesn't allow gum, so Dick is in for trouble.

Joanne, the principal's secretary, is an uptight, sexless spinster known around campus as "The Snow Queen." She'll be Dick's love interest.

Shy, awkward Buddy. He worships his mother, who, unbeknownst to him, is a blowsy drunk who "dates" guys for a bottle of tequila. Buddy will be having some emotional problems in this movie.

Ricky is a cute, wholesome cheerleader who can't wait to get married to boyfriend Doug McClure, while Doug is a red blooded, boneheaded football player who can't wait to get into Ricky's pants. "Don't give me that malarkey about cold showers," he says. Doug will be learning a few things about sex in this movie.

Tuesday Weld has already learned a few things about sex. Her shrewish mom thinks she's a slut, but Tuesday avers, "I am not going to be a scarlet woman! I made a mistake! It won't happen again!" Or *will* it?

Griff has a bad reputation, a worse attitude, and a history with Tuesday (she used to be his regular Tuesday night thing). He's your typical suburban JD, a rebel without a brain.

So, let's begin our movie. It's the first day of school and already Dick has been called to Principal Woodman's office because he doesn't like Dick's casual way of dealing with the Sweathogs. Secretary Joanne begs Dick to do things by the book, that book presumably being "Blackboard Jungle." While it looks like something is brewing between Dick and Joanne, the kids give the romance a "3," saying that it doesn't have a good beat, you can't dance to it, and Joanne is frigid.

Dick shows his heroic idealism at the big event of the year, the Honor Society Dance. First, he makes them admit all the students, not just the ones with honor. Then, when some young toughs from Hoodlum High try to crash it, Dick won't let the football players trounce them. Joanne offers to call the police, but Dick nixes that too—*he* will handle it. And he does, by telling the hoods to leave. They sneer "Says who?"

"I do," Dick answers firmly. So, the gang departs, intimidated by the stern dance-show host. Or maybe they knew that James Darren was going to sing the title song now and wanted to escape before they were overcome by the stench of Brylcream.

Later than night, Doug McClure gives Ricky his school ring, and then kisses her. Ricky pushes him away and flounces off—she is *not* the kind of girl who goes to first base, and especially not when it's a base on balls. When Doug returns to the gym, Dick can see something is wrong—but he tactfully averts his eyes from Doug's groin. Doug whines that Ricky is supposed to love him, but she won't, and stuff. Dick tells him to think about it from her perspective—and to take a cold shower.

Joanne is jealous of all the attention Dick is paying to Doug's...problem, and warns Dick that he can't give so much of himself to his students. At least not with the authorities pressing charges. But Dick says he can't change, because being a teen messiah is just who he is.

Now it's report card time. Griff got good grades, and it's the talk of the school! Doug and all the cool kids are really impressed with how nicely Griff's conforming these days. We learn why when he tells Tuesday he modeled himself on Eddie Haskell just for her. He turns off the lights, throws her on the couch, and kisses her passionately. Sleazy music plays and he says hungrily, "Let's take that ride now!" But Tuesday doesn't want to ride Griff's Wild Mouse, since it's cheap, tawdry, over in two minutes, and leaves her feeling nauseous. She pushes him off and orders him out. Griff is furious to have fake-changed his life for her. He immediately goes to Chris, the butcher at Safeway, and the town's criminal mastermind and signs up for a life of crime.

Chris invites Griff to a felony scheduled for that weekend. Chris and teen henchman Patcher have a big heist planned, and Griff can be the getaway driver. But when Chris sets off the alarm at the wiener and cold cuts warehouse, Griff gets scared and runs, leaving the ruthless Chris and the homicidal Patcher to trudge home with link sausages draped around their necks.

Meanwhile, Buddy comes home unexpectedly and finds Mom entertaining Otis, the town drunk. Buddy is horrified to learn that any man can have his mother for a bottle of cheap wine, so he runs away from home. He winds up at play rehearsal, where he weepily confides in Tuesday that mom really isn't a saint. She puts a comforting hand on his shoulder, causing him to yell, "Don't touch me! You'll get dirty, just like me! Just like my mother!" Griff, who was hiding in the shadows, pops out to tell Buddy that Tuesday is already as grimy as Buddy's mother, and it's a ground-in grime that leaves her with Ring Around the Hymen. This totally destroys Buddy's faith in virginity, so he pummels Griff, then throws him down the stairs and runs away. Again!

Dick is suspended for having taught Buddy history, which is probably what caused him to go berserk. The FBI initiates a shoot-to-kill search for Buddy, but just then, a student rushes in with vital evidence: it's Tuesday's library book, and it has blood on it! DNA testing reveals that Tuesday went all the way with Griff, and so Buddy was justified in beating the crap out of him. Joanne tries to get Tuesday to come forward and save Buddy, but Tuesday hysterically explains that her mother thinks she's a tart so she *has* to get away to drama school! But if anyone knows she's impure she will never be admitted, since the acting profession has very strict moral standards.

Griff, jealous of Buddy's and Tuesday's bad mothers and the opportunities they provide for big, dramatic scenes, shouts at his father, "You never did care about me!" and storms out of the house.

Dick finds Buddy and tells him sympathetically that it's always a shock to find out that your mother is the town's cheap floozy, but hey, nobody's perfect. Mom and Buddy hug and cry, and Buddy gets a contact high from her breath.

Tuesday resolves to confess and save Buddy from the death penalty, even if it means she'll never get her SAG card. But when she and Dick arrive at the principal's office, they find that Griff has already cleared Buddy. So, Tuesday's reputation is safe and she can play a virgin in "Dobie Gillis" without anyone being the wiser.

Doug and Ricky reflect that they have learned a valuable lesson from all this: never have sex, because it only leads to violence, shame, and overacting. Doug says half-heartedly, "We can still have fun," as he and Ricky sublimate through bake sales or something.

But just when everyone's problems are solved, Patcher shows up and tries to kill Griff. The two boys have a knife fight in the biology lab, considerately avoiding the big aquarium that modern movie teens would feel compelled to break. Patcher stabs Griff, but Dick, who was a football star at Neurasthenic University, tackles Patcher, thus proving that while history is all well and good, it's sports that *really* matter. As the police take Patcher away, Principal Woodman calls an ambulance for Griff, causing him to say in amazement, "What you do you know? You guys give a damn!" Even better, the knife-fight cured Joanne's frigidity, and she symbolically embraces Dick, and all that Dick stands for. The End.

Thanks to *Because They're Young*, we now know that back in the early Sixties teenagers were all in their thirties, so normal adolescent angst was often complicated by erectile dysfunction, or osteoporosis. But perhaps a more eye-opening element is the filmmakers' conviction that the proper way to treat erotophobia is with a shiv-wielding rumble. Our understanding of human sexuality is still incomplete, but it is clear that *Because They're Young* was largely responsible for inspiring the Sexual Revolution. Its influence was apparent the very next year, when *West Side Story* was released, and countless potential spinsters found their career plans to be cold and unresponsive ruined by the musical's climactic knife fight. No longer able to effectively sublimate, America's sour-faced secretaries and purse-lipped librarians found that the merest suggestion of an attempted stabbing rendered them moist and febrile. Before the decade was out, these same prissy, bun-wearing killjoys were doffing their cat-eye spectacles and rolling around naked in the mud at Woodstock. There are even some who claim *Because They're Young* paved the way for the Voting Rights Act of 1964 when its bold therapeutic approach was adopted by *The Black Rebels*, made later that same year, and released with the tagline, "Switchblade fights and civil rights!"

So while *Because They're Young* may not have much to offer in the way of handling teens, it does have much to teach us about curing vaginal dryness and eliminating the poll tax.

And that's all well and good, but what about *today's* teens? How can we pass on the traditional verities and old fashioned values to kids raised with TV, addicted to the internet, and under constant pressure by an omnipresent consumer culture? Well, as our next film shows, one option is to become a really lame super hero, and run around an insane asylum without benefit of proper foundation garments until you sprain a breast.

Disturbing Behavior (1998)
Directed by David Nutter
Written by Scott Rosenberg

The film begins with two teens making out beside a hydroelectric plant. But even as they steam up the car windows, the boy protests that he has a big game on Friday, and "I need my fluids." The girl, who evidently hasn't seen *Dr. Strangelove*, will not be denied his essence, and leans down to siphon him. On the verge of orgasm, the boy's right eye announces a K-Mart Blue Light Special, and he celebrates by snapping her neck. Just then, Sheriff Steve Railsback arrives to chat about the big game, and to check the boy's dipstick for proper fluid levels. But when Sheriff Steve's deputy discovers the dead girl in the car, Dipstick Boy grabs Steve's gun and shoots the deputy (but he did not shoot the Sheriff).

Meanwhile, on the bluff above, we see a lone hooded figure: It is one of the lesser known Teen Titans, Stoner Lad, and his faithful companion, Cannabis Canine. The young crime-fighter silently observes the murder scene as he tokes on a honkin' spleef.

The next day, pointy-cheekboned heartthrob James Marsden arrives in town with his family. James is apparently our hero, even though he's a wuss who is tormented by nightmares about *America's Funniest Home Videos*.

At the High School, James notices friction between the run-of-the-mill slackers and the elite "Blue Ribbons." The latter are a spiffy crew of cheerful, gung-ho boosters who wear cardigans and nice wool-blend slacks, and are prone to sudden fits of bloody violence—sort of like Up With People on angel dust.

On the bright side, James himself acquires a posse at Lunch Period, when he is befriended by Stoner Lad and his sidekick, Albino Boy, and inducted into the Teen Titans.

Later, at home, James' little sister and a classmate are practicing for a spelling bee. But her friend's inability to sound out the word "phlegm" blows the lid off the family's dirty little secret—James has a dead brother! And because of it, their father can no longer trust James to pass him the mashed potatoes.

The next day, James is called to the office to meet Dr. Bruce Greenwood, who will be our Mad Scientist today. Dr. Greenwood points out the restrooms fore and aft, and reminds James that in the event of a sudden loss of plot coherence, his ego will double as a flotation device. Dr. Bruce runs the Blue Ribbon program, and is brilliant, but unhinged, driven mad by his inability to grow a convincing mustache.

After school, James meets Katie Holmes, whose pale skin and black-ringed eyes are supposed to make her look Goth, but instead suggest Marilyn Manson in *The Tammy Faye Bakker Story.*

Stoner Lad takes James to the basement for a smoke, where they meet janitor William Sanderson, who has convinced himself that he's not in a crappy teen horror movie, but in the comparatively dignified position of playing the "Rat Catcher" character at the Renaissance Faire in San Bernardino.

Stoner Lad tells James that all the troublemakers in school are undergoing a terrifying process of Eddie Haskellization. James is skeptical, until Stoner Lad himself is captured by Dr. Bruce, and forced to wear an argyle sweater vest.

The Blue Ribbons beat up James in the cafeteria, and he strikes back by hiding in the basement during lunch period, and gnawing fretfully at an apple. The Rat Catcher is impressed by James' heroic example, and bestows upon him his new super hero identity: "Lunch Boy."

When James gets home that night, he finds the perky and soulless Blue Ribbonette Lorna waiting on the couch for him. He responds by pulling a Coke out of the fridge, and boldy drinking it. Lorna is aroused by the male's display of product placement, and opens her blouse. She kisses James, then smashes a mirror with her face, and tries to slash his carotid artery with a shard of glass. James feels that Lorna is sending him mixed signals, and the encounter ends uncomfortably for both of them.

The next day, Katie goes down into the basement so she can be menaced and pawed by Chuck, one of the Blue Ribbons. Just as he's getting started, however, he's driven insane by a squeal emitted from the Rat Catcher's ultra-sonic pest-repelling boom box.

Hmm. So the evil, conformist Eddie Haskells operate on the same frequency as *rats*! How's *that* for stinging social satire? Eat *Disturbing Behavior's* DUST, Voltaire!

Lunch Boy joins forces with Katie (who keeps uttering the word "razor" in non-tonsorial contexts, so that's apparently *her* superhero name) to investigate Dr. Bruce.

They take the ferry to Sinister Acres, the gothic asylum where Dr. Bruce last worked. On the way over, Lunch Boy reveals that his brother shot himself in the head—so I guess *he* was Superman.

Razor and Lunch Boy use their powers to jump-cut the Security guard in a single bound, and wander freely around the asylum, stopping periodically to tap on the glass and annoy the deformed inmates.

Eventually, they find a girl in a flannel nightgown, sitting in a rocking chair, and waiting to decompose into Norman's mother from *Psycho*. A hospital bracelet identifies her as Dr. Bruce's daughter, which seems like it ought to be a plot point, but really isn't.

"Let's get out of here," Katie says. Yes, let's. But first, let's take a moment to sandwich in a music video; so the director cranks up the Harvey Danger on the soundtrack, while Katie bounces bralessly down the corridor.

Back home, Lunch Boy is jumped by the Blue Ribbons, who strap James into a barber chair and force him to commit plagiarism, by propping his eye open and making him watch images of hackneyed Americana—thereby ripping off both *A Clockwork Orange* and Reagan's old "It's Morning in America" commercials at the same time.

James escapes, and finds Katie strapped into another chair, but she seems groggy, disoriented. Did they manage to seize control of her will, or did he get to her in time?!

Oh, who cares? They escape from school with the aid of Albino Boy, but run into a roadblock of Blue Ribbons. Is this the end for Lunch Boy and Razor?!

Sadly, no. Because suddenly, the Rat Catcher arrives, with dozens of rodent-repelling boom boxes in the back of his El Camino. He switches them on, and the Blue Ribbons scream and writhe with agony. Naturally, they can't get enough of this, and when he drives off, they follow him to the hydroelectric plant.

Rat Catcher, who was shot by Dr. Bruce just before he ran the mad doctor down with his car, now plans to rip off the end of *Thelma and Louise*. He turns to James, and speaks the words that would become the rallying cry of the Teen Titans from that day forward: "Do *good things*, Lunch Boy!"

Okay, that's a pretty lame battle cry, but you have to remember that he had a sucking chest wound. So did the screenwriter, for all we know. It would explain much.

As the berzerker Blue Ribbons climb all over his El Camino, the Rat Catcher tries again for an inspirational epitaph. Pushing the gas pedal to the floor, he shouts, "Hey! Teacher! Leave them kids alone!"

Okay, that's not a big improvement; but as heroic last words go, it's better than plunging into the abyss while screaming, "How can you have any pudding when you don't eat your meat?" Rat Catcher drives off the dam, taking the entire Student Council with him.

Dr. Bruce comes back from the dead so they can rip off the end of *Niagara*. "There'll be other towns, and other troubled teens," he says, adding, "Science is god!"

James retorts, "Be the ball!"

The audience cries, "Where's the exit?"

Brain washing: is it really an effective method to control teens? Research indicates that although it has some unfortunate side effects (violence, sweater vests, overacting), it can be effective in the short term. For instance, there is the Katie Holmes/Tom Cruise engagement. Katie appeared to have been unaffected by Dr. Bruce's conditioning at the time, but when Scientology (and the need to generate publicity for two summer movies) was later added to the mix, she promptly fell in love with the older, weirder, shorter Tom Cruise in a matter of hours, and agreed to marry him in a matter of days. Proof that mind control does work!

However, L. Ron Hubbard isn't the only one who can help you keep your child bride in line with a mixture of science, mysticism, and multi-tiered marketing techniques...

A long time ago in a galaxy far, far away, they went so far as to try using Jedi training on their adolescents, but even it couldn't keep their young people from pouting, sulking, and genocide. So, I don't know what to tell you.

Attack of the Clones (2002)
Directed by George Lucas
Written by George Lucas (story and screenplay) and Jonathan Hales (screenplay)

Tagline: *A Jedi shall not know anger. Nor hatred. Nor love.*

Nor how to act.

In Episode II, visionary filmmaker George Lucas continues his six volume *pensées* on good and evil. In this installment, he examines Man's age-old struggle against the forces of petulance.

The Galactic Republic is on the verge of war. Hundreds of star systems are being urged to secede by the mysterious Count Dooku. A former Jedi Knight, Dooku turned to the Dark Side after his fellow Jedi repeatedly pointed out that his name sounds like the stuff you find in an overloaded pair of Pampers.

Meanwhile, Padme Amidala, who was the teen queen of Naboo in the previous film, is now a member of the Galactic Senate. She arrives for quorum call in a stainless steel B-52 that promptly blows up and she dies. Well. That wasn't as bad as I thought. Let me just grab my coat and we'll—

Oh. Wait. Damn. It was just a day player dressed in a goofy costume—apparently Lucas is still playing 3-Card Padme with the audience. However, the assassination attempt gives the Chancellor (future Emperor Palpatine) the chance to assign Padme two bodyguards: Obi-Wan Kenobi (even more wan than usual), and unstable Tiger Beat coverboy Anakin Skywalker. We sense this is going to work out badly because Yoda is squinting at the Chancellor, and because Jimmy Smits is hovering in the background dressed like Sir Walter Raleigh.

When they get to Padme's hotel suite, Anakin flashes his thong at the Senator, and he and Obi Wan immediately get into one of those tense, loudly muttered public arguments that makes all the other guests stare into their drinks and wonder why this has to happen every New Years Eve. ("I've never been so embarrassed. I don't care if they *are* your friends, we're not inviting the Jedis next year.")

Oh, and besides the news that our hero is a sullen, creepy stalker, guess what? Jar-Jar is back. Which is like being told by your doctor, "We're going to have to amputate your legs. But we thought we'd let the gangrene run its course for awhile just to see what happens. Bill and I have a bet."

Padme's relative acting talent misleads the audience into thinking she's the smart one of the group. This illusion is quickly shattered when she is ordered home, and decides to appoint Jar-Jar as her successor. Yes, the giraffe-necked, fish-faced, crab-eyed scarecrow who sounds like Ziggy Marley sucking the helium from a Mylar Happy Birthday balloon is now a Senator. Which is obviously bad news for us, although it does make Mississippi feel better about its selection of Trent Lott.

They return to Padme's home, Planet Pedophilia, where an even younger prepubescent girl has won the election for queen. Frankly, I still want to know what kind of a world has "elected queens." I guess this means that Leia was only an "elected" princess, and the whole thing is basically as meaningful as prom royalty.

Meanwhile, Obi-Wan goes to a Fifties theme dinner, where he is greeted like the Fonz. He chats with the short-order cook, who has apparently escaped from an X-Box game, and heads off for a distant planet where a race of albino basketball players are cloning an army for the Republic, much to the Republic's surprise.

Time out for a Harlequin Romance interlude, where Anakin again tries to seduce the Senator, claiming that a Jedi's life is harsh, which is why he likes her, because she's soft and moist. Or something like that. She finally gives in and kisses him, but Anakin can't handle it and starts feeling cheap when Padme doesn't call him the next day. He feels even worse when he hears that she later showed up in gym class and started passing his thong around with her friends.

At this point we get the full force of Lucas's screenwriting prowess, and to call the dialogue purple is to damn it with understatement. It's like a vivid, three-day old bruise: purple, sure, but already starting to turn that greenish yellow around the edges. Anakin looks deep into her eyes and says, "I'm haunted by the kiss you should never have given me," in the same way he might inform a Home Depot salesclerk, "I'm having second thoughts about that Weed Eater you should never have sold me."

And it doesn't end there. "My heart is beating," he informs her. "You are in my very soul." Then he blurts something that sounds like "Hormel!" But given his mush-mouthed delivery, it's possible he was mentioning an entirely different brand of canned pork products.

Our own hearts begin beating when he says, "I will do anything you ask," hoping she'll ask him to shut up. Alas, there is only more pouting, and Anakin storms off to bed, where he has a nightmare about his mother being savaged by Sand People (paging Dr. Freud...). Afraid that his dreams are real, Anakin and Padme fly home to Tattoine, for one of those awkward meet-the-parents things.

They arrive at the subterranean Little House on the Wasteland where we first met (or will later meet?) Luke in *Star Wars*. Apparently, Pa Ingalls bought Anakin's mom as a slave, but later married her, giving their story a sort of Marla Maples/Donald Trump quality. Threepio is still there, doing chores and chirping away in his twee accent, cementing his place as the Galaxy's most effeminate farm implement. Yes, Lucas is still trying to insist that Anakin really did build C3PO, which begs the question why his mother the slave and her husband the poor dirt farmer didn't dismantle the protocol droid and use it for tractor parts years ago.

Anakin has an uncomfortable meeting with his new stepfather and step-brother. Finding your place in these blended families is always challenging, especially for a sensitive adolescent, and the whole scene has the feeling of a *Brady Bunch* episode. ("It's the story/Of a slave named Shmi...") But a *first* season episode, when the tone was a trifle bittersweet, and the children still had some difficulty adapting—especially in that episode where Carol was sexually abused by Tuskan Raiders.

Meanwhile, Obi-Wan finds Count Dooku (Christopher Lee) meeting with the Viceroy of the Trade Federation in a secret matte painting. Seems Chris is behind the assassination attempts, and is building a new droid army so Lucas can repeat the climax of the last movie and try to get it right this time.

Anakin tracks the Sand People who kidnapped his mother to their camp, where he finds Mom in bondage. She's bleeding, badly injured, and for some reason has begun talking in the voice of "Mrs. Olsen," from those old Folgers Coffee commercials. Shmi takes one look at her long lost son and promptly croaks. It's sad (well, it's supposed to be, anyway), but she was already in pain, so it seems cruel to subject her to the rest of the movie. Unfortunately, her death sends Anakin into a grand mal freakout of Holden Caulfield-style angst; he swings his light saber around wildly, decapitating Sand People right and left and yelling, "You guys are so *phony!*"

Later, Anakin brings Mom's body back to the farm wrapped in some Sand Person's drapes, then goes to throw a fit in the garage. He screams that he slaughtered them all, men women and children, then crumples to the floor and sobs. Padme's response is to bring him snacks.

The Saving Private Shmi thing didn't work out too well, so Ani and Padme decide to pick up the spare and go save Obi-Wan. They blunder into the droid factory, where they get caught in a gigantic assembly line, in a scene that powerfully evokes of the climax of *Chicken Run*. Eventually, they are captured, chained to stone pillars in a massive coliseum, and set upon by wild computer generated beasts, etc., etc. But first, we have another Harlequin Romance for Teens scene between Ani and Padme. She whispers, "I truly...deeply...love you," in a way that sounds chillingly like a song cue. You half expect her to break into the 1974 Olivia Newton John smash, "I Love You, I Honestly Love You." Hey, when are those Clones going to Attack? I don't mean to be petty, but even the title of *Waiting for Godot* is *technically* correct. Come on!

Instead, the Jedi attack; and do a fairly piss-poor job of it. Still, we get to see the different Jedi head hoses. Most of the Knights appear to be standard humanoids, but they do have an astonishing variety of crap dangling off their skulls. Alas, this isn't enough to help them overcome the New and Improved Droid Army, and they're about to be wiped out, when...THE CLONES ATTACK!

It doesn't really help much. But it does inspire Count Dooku to flee with the plans for the Death Star. And it also leads to the single funniest shot in the film: Christopher Lee flying through the air on a speeder. Considering that he's over 80, it looks like Count Dooku is doing a commercial for one of those battery-operated scooters that elderly folk routinely use to spread terror in the grocery store ("I'm a little rascal in my Little Rascal.") I expected to see a couple of bumper stickers on the back of his speeder: "Try Electric Mobility!" and "Ask Me About My Grandchildren."

Our heroes try to stop him, but Dooku opens a can of mystical whoop-ass on Obi-Wan, and cuts off Anakin's arm. Fortunately, Yoda arrives, but the resulting light saber duel between the 6'5"-tall Lee, and the two-foot-tall puppet looks less like a titanic battle between good and evil, and more like a slightly panicky Yao Ming trying to club an rabid groundhog.

Dooku (whose Hip-Hop name is Darth Tyrannus) manages to escape with the blueprints for the Death Star, which destiny foretells us will be constructed in the next movie by Darth Halliburton after he receives a no-bid contract.

So, it looks like our heroes screwed the computer-generated pooch. And just to add deceit to incompetence, Anakin and Padme break Jedi law by marrying in secret. Their doomed love is foreshadowed by the final image of Anakin holding Padme's hand with the cold, fleshless, skeletal fingers of his new prosthesis. Although really, what's the point of that? Granted, the skinless robot hand is lower in fat and calories, but it looks kind of grisly.

How do you solve a problem like Anakin? Grounding him didn't work. Neither did withholding his allowance. Even love (as represented by a slo-mo romp in a field of flowers with the dewy young senator who used to be a queen twice his age) failed to keep him on the right track. I guess we just have to admit that some teens are bad seeds, and despite our best efforts, will end up enslaving civilizations, destroying planets, and stealing James Earl Jones' voice. Our only hope comes from the fact that someday these Jedi gone wild will have kids of their own, and those kids will end up almost committing incest before defeating their father and making lots of money by selling Ewok pelts on Ebay, thus restoring balance to the universe.

Now, armed with our close study of these films, let's revisit the "Youth Abatement" plans proposed by each and determine which one offers the best hope of wiping out annoying teens in our lifetime.

The drug solution, as shown in *Teenage Devil Dolls*, while effective, is too expensive to be practical, since it requires issuing each teen his or her own narcotics cop to follow them around and narrate their life.

Being open-minded, caring, and perfect, like in *Because They're Young*, does tend to keep kids out of jail, but it puts them in drama school instead—and leads to an ecologically unsustainable oversupply of "Dawson's Creek" actors.

"The Force" plan seems to be the worst idea of all, since not only does it fail to keep teens from becoming super villains, it gives them the tools to lash out against the entire galaxy instead of just moping in their rooms and playing their music really loud.

So, it looks like the scientific brain reprogramming presented in *Disturbing Behavior* is our best bet. Even though Dr. Bruce Greenwood was defeated by the *Dawsonkinder*, we believe this can be prevented in the future by keeping kids out of school basements and not allowing them to socialize with janitors. We hope that the current MTV mind control tests prove successful, and we look forward to a nation full of polite, well-behaved young ladies and gentlemen who only kill people when shown the queen of spades.

Live Fast, Die Young, and Leave a Bad-Looking Movie

Southern California was the birthplace of two uniquely American institutions—the motion picture industry and the hotrod culture—so it's no surprise that the two have enjoyed a long and incestuous romance. In fact, many of our celluloid heroes only reach their peak of raw sexuality when behind the wheel: James Dean's sensitive, alienated teen in *Rebel Without a Cause*, Barry Newman's melancholic speed-freak in *Vanishing Point*, and Dick Van Dyke's brooding, existential loner in *Chitty Chitty Bang Bang*.

As Hollywood has repeatedly demonstrated, looks, fame and money are all well and good; but if you want love, you need a love machine. No matter how stupid and unappealing a character may be, if he's got a hot car, then he's legally entitled to a hot chick (as established in the landmark "Knight Rider" case *Hasselhof v. Landers Sisters, et al*). The hero's auto-erotic auto doesn't even have to be a sports car; because let's face it, we all know that Freddy and Daphne were periodically steaming up the windows of the Mystery Machine. Hell, we bet even Shaggy and Thelma had at least one awkward and embarrassing fumble in the back of the van. True, Shaggy's relationship with Scooby was less "a boy and his dog" and more "a man's best friend with benefits," while Thelma was Saturday Morning's most prominent Lesbian Separatist, but there had to have been one magic night, when they were both wasted on weed and Annie Greensprings Country Cherry Wine after exposing Old Man McCauley, the 73rd in a long line of abandoned amusement park owners who found it necessary to gad about in a sheet. And he would've gotten away with it too, if it hadn't been for those diddling kids!

Anyway, if you can believe that a bad Maynard G. Krebs caricature could make a poorly animated lesbian claw his back and rend the night air with full-throated cries of "Jinkies!" then you're the perfect target audience for our first film. Buckle up.

Gone in 60 Seconds (2000)
Directed by Dominic Sena
Written by Scott Rosenberg

Unkempt ragamuffin Giovanni Ribisi steals a brand new Porsche by driving it through the plate glass window of the dealership. Not content with property damage and grand theft auto, he pops the clutch and tells the World to Eat My Dust. The World responds that they've already eaten, thank you, and now they're flaked out in front of the TV watching a crappy action movie. So it's up to the police to dine on Giovanni's dust, and they react with an influx of cruisers and helicopters, which follow him back to the headquarters of kindly, avuncular auto theft mentor Will Patton.

Cut to the desert, where Giovanni's brother, Nicolas Cage is giving a motivational speech to a bunch of eleven-year-olds at a Go-Kart track. Will arrives, and tells Nick that Giovanni was working for a criminal mastermind so evil that his underworld confederates call him "The Carpenter," because the name "The Texture-Coater" was already taken.

The Carpenter is so angry over Giovanni's stunt with the Porsche, that he puts the kid inside an auto-press and turns it on. Then he delivers an ultimatum to Nicolas: he must steal 50 cars in four days, or Giovanni will be squeezed into a cube and displayed along with the cross-sectioned cow in the Brooklyn Museum.

Nick mulls it over as his brother screams, giving the auto-crusher just enough time to squeeze a quart of oil out of Giovanni's hair before agreeing. Oh, by the way, Nick's character is the World's Greatest Car Thief (one of the less popular theme mugs at Spencer's Gifts) and his name is "Memphis Rains." No, we don't believe it either, but felt we ought to mention it, since the screenwriter obviously spent a lot of time coming up with the name, first considering and rejecting such possibilities as April Showers, or London Fogg.

Robert Duvall, co-star of *Days of Thunder* shows up to lend dignity to yet another stupid car-crash movie. Hopefully, he's lending at a high rate of interest, and sending people out to break the director's thumbs when he can't pay the vig.

This time out, Robert is a kindly old former chop shop owner who helps Nick reassemble his crew, which includes Sphinx, a Lurch-sized mute who is employed by the county morgue to leave half-eaten sandwiches on all the cadavers as part of their turn-down service, and Angelina Jolie, who leads a sort of *Flashdance* Meets *Coyote Ugly* life, working as a car mechanic by day, and a bartender by night. She also sports a huge head of bleached blonde dreadlocks that make her look like a cross between Edgar Winter and Bob Marley.

With time ticking toward the deadline, the crew goes to work trying to pinpoint the 50 exotic and expensive cars on their list. Nick himself visits an exclusive Mercedes dealership and inquires about the contents of their warehouse. But he allays suspicion by going incognito, dressing in a suit and speaking in an English accent. Specifically, Kevin Costner's English accent from *Robin Hood: Prince of Thieves*; so apparently he's gone disguised as a bad actor.

Unfortunately, police detective Delroy Lindo figures out the entire scheme after receiving an anonymous tip from the screenwriter, and begins to stake out the crew. But stakeouts are boring, so the filmmakers throw in a subplot about a rival ring of super car thieves trying to kill Nick and Giovanni, which leads to a big chase scene. *On foot*. How's *that* for irony?

Huh? Car thieves? Chasing each other *on foot*?

What do you think about *that*?

Okay, we agree, it's pretty stupid. The filmmakers seem to agree too, so they cut to a scene where the crew breaks into a Ferrari warehouse, and we get a bunch of soft-core porn shots of saucy quarterpanels and perky pop-up highbeams.

Various automobiles are stolen by various people, and delivered to the port. Nick himself shows up to steal one of the staked-out cars, but he senses a Great Disturbance in the Force, and realizes that all the Mercedes for which they obtained laser-encoded keys are under surveillance. They have other keys, but *those* cars are in the police impound lot. Oh, and Robert's dog just *ate* the other keys. (It's a good thing they're not being graded on this theft, because I seriously doubt the teacher would accept that excuse.) Nick snaps into action, ordering Robert to administer Ex-Lax to the dog, and wait for it to pass the keys. This leads to a light-hearted scene in which two of the crew are walking the dog, when suddenly they're jumped by a gang of homeboys who threaten them with knives. Fortunately, the dog chooses that moment to evacuate its bowels, and the two crew members eagerly retrieve the keys from the steaming excreta. This hilariously triggers the gangbangers gag reflexes, and they withdraw in high dudgeon, refusing to sully themselves by eviscerating fecalphiliacs.

Enjoyed that? Well, there's plenty more whimsy where that came from, as our heroes now use the foul-smelling keys to boost three late model Mercedes from the impound lot. Meanwhile, one of their number distracts the police clerk by putting on a pimp costume and a shoulder-length black wig with bangs, and showing us how the world would look if "Superfly" had been played by Bettie Page.

Eventually, Nick meets up with the 1967 Shelby CT 500 that will be his love interest for the remainder of the film. He steals the car just as Delroy arrives, and finally, the big car chase is on! There's action! Crashes! Near death experiences!

But enough of that. Let's grind to a dead stop, shall we, so that Will Patton and Giovanni can have a slow, Bergmanesque colloquy about the past. A lugubrious, dimly-lit disquisition that reeks of Fate, Calvinist determinism, and greasy hair.

Now back to the chase. It's not a bad chase as these things go, but there aren't quite as many custom '67 Mustangs around as there were when the original film was made in 1974, so Nick has to drive *very* defensively, and can't afford to bump into anything, or get too crazy. As a result, they have to cut the big chase scene short, and the movie ends as most of these movies do—with a foot pursuit through a steam plant.

Eventually, Nick pushes The Carpenter off a catwalk, and he falls 60 feet and lands in his own hand-carved coffin. Which is either a clever *homage* to Truman Capote, or a sign that scripter Scott Rosenberg, who also wrote *Disturbing Behavior*, believes that every movie has to end with somebody plunging to their death from a great height. I admit that he's got a pretty firm argument with movies like *North by Northwest* and *Die Hard*, but feel that he's on somewhat weaker ground when citing films like *A Dog of Flanders*, or *Camille*. Although in future remakes of *Camille*, sudden impact trauma would be one good way to cut short the traditional lingering death scene.

Some film enthusiasts object to Hollywood remaking classic movies, insisting that this sort of cinematic recycling is best reserved for missed opportunities—stories that *almost* worked the first time, but could benefit from better acting, higher production values, or improved special effects.

Gone in 60 Seconds, a shoestring budgeted cult classic, may seem tailor-made for the Summer Movie Makeover treatment. The problem is that the filmmakers took a charming, unpretentious little programmer full of hot cars, fun chase scenes, and porn-style mustaches, and cluttered it up with dull motivations, petroleum-based hair products, and a bunch of characters cut from Syd Field's Colorform Dolls Screenplay Workbook.

As consumers, we have no objection to cheesy movies. Unfortunately, the remake of *Gone in 60 Seconds* is Cheez-Wiz in a jewelry box, while the original is an honest block of tangy, wholesome Wisconsin cheddar.

It's far better, instead, to write and direct an entirely original treatment of that almost mystical symbiosis between man and machine. Oh wait. No it's not...

Days of Thunder (1990)
Directed by: Tony Scott
Screenplay by: Robert Towne (believe it or not!)
Story by: Robert Towne and Tom Cruise (ahhh, *now* it all makes sense…)

Well, we're in for 107 minutes of NASCAR, so let's get into the spirit of the thing, shall we? Put on that mesh trucker cap with the Confederate flag patch on the front, Polident your partial upper, and chug down a 64-ounce waxed paper cup full of flat, body temperature Budweiser. There.

Gentlemen…Start your movie!

We're at Daytona, where Henry: Portrait of a Serial Killer is whizzing around in his little car, laughing as other drivers crash. Cut to a farm in North Carolina, where Randy Quaid tries to convince Robert Duvall to build him a racecar, while Robert attempts to run Randy over with a tractor and spray his crushed skull with liquid fertilizer. Neither one is succeeding.

Randy and Robert show up at the track, to meet and evaluate Randy's new driver, Tom Cruise. Tom has no experience driving stock cars, and will have to prove himself to a skeptical NASCAR establishment by demonstrating how handsome he is. Tom is aided in this task by the director, who casts a lot of weird-faced hillbilly types in the supporting roles.

Robert agrees to build a car for Tom, and quickly leaves to go have a *Flashdance*-like welding montage with his crew of greasy, unattractive crackers.

Thirty seconds later, the car is finished, and we're in Phoenix, Arizona, where a large and loyal following has come out to the track to get heat-stroke.

Henry: Portrait of a Bumper Car Operator proceeds to ram repeatedly into Tom's rear end, expressing some deep-seated urge that only Freud could figure out. Robert tells Tom that Henry's only "rubbing" him, and adds, "*Rubbing* is *racing*." So apparently, every weekday the Tokyo subway system is packed with NASCAR drivers.

Tom wins his first race and gets drunk, so we can find out what off-screen tragedy made him obsessed with his dead father *this* time. It turns out his dad was a fighter pilot who was killed in Vietnam, and…No. Wait. Wrong one. Oh! Right. His father was U.S. Attorney General, and Tom's afraid his own legal prowess can't measure…No. No. That's a different—Ah! Got it. Tom's dad was a con man who disgraced the family name, and Tom's trying to redeem himself and find a new father figure, which makes Duvall shift uncomfortably in his seat, and furtively eye the exit.

Realizing this is the key to a successful career as a leading man, crew member John C. Reilly (*Magnolia*) suddenly has an outbreak of Dead Dad, and confesses that his famous race car-drivin' pappy croaked at Daytona. But Tom's not about to be out-Dead Dadded in his own movie, and quickly establishes how much deeper and more profound his own grief is, by having sex with a hooker while the drunken pit crew looks on.

In our next race, Tom and Henry crash, and are airlifted to Supermodel Memorial Hospital, where Tom is placed in the car of Dr. Nicole Kidman. Nicole is a distinguished neurosurgeon, even though she hasn't had her first period yet, and manages to make the Candy Stripers look wizened.

Now the movie becomes a delightful romp, as Tom mistakes Nicole for a prostitute. During the examination of his brain, he puts her hand on his stick-shift, but she's repulsed and leaves (Nicole was absent from anatomy class the day they covered the stickshift). Tom, feeling unloved, splays on the bed in his reveal-ing hospital gown, with his legs spread to the camera. Out in the lobby, the con-cession stand reports a sudden drop in hot dog sales.

Tom is released, and asks Nicole for a date as she's getting into her car. She declines, while discreetly attempting to slam his penis in the door. Instead, Tom winds up going out on a date with Henry: Portrait of a Rebound Relationship.

Eventually, Nicole realizes that if she wants any additional screen time, she's going to have to date Tom. So she cuts cheerleader practice and flies down South, where she flings the little fellow into a wall and sexes him up.

Cut to an IKEA commercial, where Tom and Nicole are lounging on 300-count percale sheets on a Scandinavian lacquered pine bedstead, while Tom attempts to sneak packets of NutraSweet inside Nicole's vagina.

This is getting weird, so they go visit Henry, and watch him pass out. It's now obvious that Henry isn't handsome enough to provide Tom with sufficient com-petition on the racetrack, so they replace him with Cary Elwes, while Nicole must break the sad news that he is now Henry: Portrait of a Subdural Hematoma.

Meanwhile, Tom has lost his nerve, while Nicole has lost her fake American accent. She gives Tom a Big Speech about Courage, Denial, and Thine Own Self Be True, and ends by saying, "Go to hell, you (unintelligible) son-of-a-bitch! You made me sound like a *doctor!*" Well, to be fair, he actually made her sound like an out-of-her-depth actress playing Polonius as a hot Australian teenager.

Meanwhile, Randy fires Tom and hires Cary, when he realizes that blondes have more fun. Henry asks Tom to drive his car at Daytona. Cary is sponsored by Hardees. Tom is sponsored by MelloYello. If they crash, they're going to produce a fairly disgusting Meal Deal.

As the cars roar around the track, Tom's face becomes caked with oil and grease, until he looks like Al Jolson in *Mammy's Boy*, although his teeth remain startlingly white. In the stands, meanwhile, exhaust fumes mix with the smell of off-brand cigarettes and gardenia-scented toilet water.

When you sit back and absorb the grand and glorious pageant that is NASCAR, it makes you proud to be an American. Oh sure, we have to import oil from the Mid-East, musicals from Great Britain, and ingénues from Australia; but when it comes to Circus Maximus-style spectacles designed to stupefy the tobacco-chewing proletariat, the United States is entirely self-sufficient.

It should be noted that Tom Cruise's character in *Days of Thunder* is named "Cole Trickle," and undoubtedly contributed to his Golden Globe win for "Best Actor in a Lead Role That Sounds Like a Venereal Disease."

This visionary 1990 film played a major role in the ascendance of NASCAR from obscure, regional sport to national pastime, by highlighting many unknown elements of the stock car racing culture. For instance, if you tell long, rambling, lachrymose stories about your dead and/or felonious dad, your co-workers will buy you a gorgeous hooker, instead of just reminding you to put a cover sheet on your TPS report, and then going out of their way to avoid you in the break room. Also, NASCAR offers many opportunities to stimulate the labia minora of female Doogie Howsers with packets of artificial sweetener (little known trivia—the film's original title was, *Splenda in the Grass*). And if condiment-assisted coitus isn't your thing, there's always the chance to have your rear bumper rubbed by a hillbilly.

But the most vivid lesson imparted by *Days of Thunder* is also its most poignant. Like the gladiatorial games of old, the thrill of the race derives from the ever-present threat of death, and in the heat of competition, even your best friend can send you to the hospital, or the graveyard. But eventually, his brain will begin to leak, and he'll give you the keys to his car, so it all evens out.

But today's typical NASCAR event is like the Autopia ride at Disneyland compared to the Old School stock car circuit, back when drivers set themselves ablaze with such frequency that Vietnamese Buddhists considered them show-offs. As we see in our next film, back in the free-wheeling, free-loving, anything goes Sixties, men were men, women were mistaken for men, and the sexy, Vegas-style nightclub shows involved a motel waitstaff performing a medley of traditional Appalachian folk songs.

Red Line 7000 (1965)
Directed and produced by Howard Hawks. Screenplay by George Kirgo, based on a story by Howard Hawks. Music by Nelson Riddle.

Champion racecar driver Jim Loomis confides in colleague Sonny Corleone that he's met the girl of his dreams and intends to live with her happily ever after. Then he dies in a fiery car crash.

After the funeral, team owner Pat and Sonny return to the local Holiday Inn, which is apparently NASCAR World Headquarters. The hotel manager tells them that Loomis's fiancée showed up, claimed that the Dead Guy's death was all her fault, and asked for booze. The fiancee, Budget Suzanne Pleshette, tells Sonny that Dead Guy died because she's a jinx. When Sonny seems unconvinced, she exclaims, "Twice before the same thing happened. And each time I ended up going to a funeral and not a wedding!" When we learn that Budget Suzanne will receive Jim's $10,000 insurance benefits, it all starts to make sense!

The next day, hulking hick Ned watches an attractive blonde girl ride up on a motorbike. He suavely confesses, "I thought you were a boy." She replies, "Don't you think a girl can ride of these things?" He answers, "Not unless they're a lot like a boy." Yes, it's just like *The Philadelphia Story*, only not very good. Anyway, it turns out the blonde is Julie, Team Owner Pat's sister, and that Ned is there to apply for Dead Guy's job. After Ned finishes his test drive, he demands of Pat, "You trying to make me look like a squirrel?" Pat doesn't have any more idea what this means than we do, but he hires Ned anyway.

Ned takes Julie out to dinner to celebrate. She asks him about his hopes and dreams. He says, "You talk an awful lot—still trying to prove you're a girl?" Julie murmurs, "Ned, I don't want you to go on thinking I'm a boy"…and we cut to a scene of them in bed together. It seems that insulting a woman's femininity is a surefire seduction technique!

The next day it's the big race (I think it's the Indianapolis 401k). We cut from footage of real racing (and real crashes) to close-ups of the actors pretending to drive. There are also a few shots of Richard Petty to make things look authentic. Sonny wins this race (thanks, no doubt, to his mob connections), but Ned comes in third and gets extra points for pouting.

That night at the lounge, all the men are wowed by new girl Gabby (she eese so very how-you-say "fake French"). It seems that champion driver Almost Doug McClure brought her back from Paris instead of the dirty postcards everyone was hoping for. As a live band plays a happenin' version of "The Old Gray Mare" (apparently, due to budgetary constraints, Nelson Riddle was confined to public domain tunes), Gabby throws off her elegant fur hat, unbuttons her Channel jacket, and shakes her booty. It's a proud moment for French culture.

The next day Budget Suzanne sees Almost Doug's car in a ditch and offers him a ride. She finds his predicament a bit ironic for a champion racecar driver. He explains that he swerved to avoid a cat, which "must have been female, since she couldn't make up her mind which way to go." Um, I think I'm beginning to detect some sexism in this screenplay.

That night at the lounge, the waitresses do their big musical number, "Wild Cat Jones." This is the highlight of the movie, and is possibly the best song ever performed in a Holiday Inn lounge by a group of waitresses about a racecar driver with an idiotic name. Even though you've seen it countless times on *That's Entertainment*, you really should watch it in context.

Gabby spies meal ticket Almost Doug gazing with adoration at Budget Suzanne and realizes it's All Over. Unfortunately, Budget Suzanne is reluctant to date Almost Doug because her love has killed so many men that the police are starting to suspect. But French Tart Gabby doesn't let any grass grow under her feet before trying to hit on Sonny, commenting, "The music is good, isn't it?" However, as the music is a cover of "She'll be Comin' Around the Mountain," this isn't the best come-on line ever invented and Sonny prudently snubs her.

Later, Team Owner Pat encourages Sonny to give Gabby a call. Sonny refuses because Gabby used to date Almost Doug, explaining that he has a new shirt, new pants, new underwear, etc. In fact, "Everything I got is new! Secondhand just don't appeal to me." Pat reminds Sonny that new girls start depreciating as soon as you drive them off the lot, and so used girls really are a better value.

That night, Sonny and Gabby discover a mutual love of Pepsi, and fall madly in lust. Meanwhile, Almost Doug convinces Budget Suzanne that he is willing to risk his life to be her new love. She confesses that she loves him too, and has him sign the insurance papers quickly. Almost Doug returns to his hotel room to find Gabby there. She tells him that Sonny hates him now because Almost Doug didn't leave her factory fresh.

Sonny watches from the shadows as Gabby leaves Almost Doug's. He mocks her French accent when she tries to explain that she was just telling Almost Doug about Sonny's homicidal tendencies. He yells, "You said it was over! You're a liar! A LIAR! A slut! A SLUT!" Well, he should have bought American.

During the next day's race (I think it was the Windows 98), Sonny forces Almost Doug's car off the track and over the wall. A fiery explosion ensues, but Almost Doug survives. Gabby stops by Almost Doug's room to say she can't find Sonny, and she's afraid of what he might do (possibly Godfather III). Then

Sonny shows up to say he's giving up racing because the attempted murder will raise his insurance rates. Gabby goes after him, they kiss, and then he agrees to forget about her reconditioned hymen if she will forget about him trying to kill people.

Then there is another race (either the Daytona 1040 or the Hawaii 5-0). When Ned promptly crashes, the announcer is delirious with joy. "This is the most spectacular crash I've ever seen!" Ned is taken to the hospital, and Julie rushes to see him. He pulls away the sheets to reveal…no, not that! His arm has been amputated. Julie doesn't care, and tells Ned she'll stay with him if he asks. He asks, but indicates that since he has only one hand, his career options are pretty much limited to killing David Janssen's wife. She enthuses, "You can drive, I know you can!"

So, we jump to a scene where Ned is driving with the aid of a metal hook. And at night he goes out and terrorizes Lovers' Lanes, and an urban legend is born. We conclude our educational glimpse into the world of NASCAR with the three women sitting in the stands, rooting for their respectively doomed, murderous, and maimed men. There are some more crashes, fires, and explosions. Budget Suzanne says pluckily, "It's a hell of a way to make a living!" A.J. Foyt dies. The end.

As we have seen, fast cars have long been a signifier of The Rebel in society, from world renowned car thieves to pouty stock car racers who live so far on the edge of bourgeois conformity that they think nothing of attempting murder, or committing statutory rape with brain surgeons. On the bright side, they're environmentally conscious enough to recycle French women.

But what about other forms of renegade transportation? Motorcycles, for instance, which have historically delivered many of Hollywood's most memorable rebels to their respective grim fates. Alas, Hollywood hasn't really made a successful motorcycle movie since *Easy Rider*. Back then, hog-straddling heroes were poetic loners drawn to the mythic wellspring of the American soul. Nowadays, if a motorcyclist does figure prominently in a film, he's more likely to be an alien parasite that uses inconceivably advanced technology to mildly inconvenience some effeminate National Guardsmen in Griffith Park. At least, he is in the kind of movies we watch.

Murdercycle (1999)
Directed by: Tom Calloway
Written by: Daniel Elliot

(Note: All the characters in this film are named after comic-book artists of the '60s and '70s: Kirby, Lee, Ditko, etc. This conceit is not germane to the plot; we mention it only because knowing this fact makes the movie considerably more irritating.)

A meteorite falls to earth, and a passing motorcyclist pauses to investigate. The extraterrestrial rock bursts open, and badly animated tentacles reach out and grab the rider, hideously transforming him from a human being into a human being with model airplane parts stuck to his clothes. His vehicle, meanwhile, has metamorphosed from a typical Yamaha into a fearsome alien killing machine with tarpaper roofing shingles and latex enema hoses glued to it.

A CIA agent assigned to a nearby top-secret facility is attacked by the Murdercycle—apparently in the midst of posing for the J. Crew fall catalogue. The Murdercycle shoots the CIA man with a laser, which causes him to talk like William Shatner.

The next day, a Marine Corps sergeant who resembles a slightly tougher-looking Gomer Pyle is sitting half-naked in a mobile home with a 9mm automatic. He starts to re-enact Mel Gibson's suicide attempt from *Lethal Weapon* when there's a knock at the door, and he's summoned to a meeting with the big brass at Camp Abraham Lincoln Junior High School.

One of the CIA's top J. Crew models is missing, and Lethal Gomer has been picked to lead a crack squad consisting of two other guys to investigate. They are accompanied by Dr. Lee, a government psychic who was apparently recruited from the "Ringlets Can Spice Up a Dowdy 'Do" pictorial in *YM*. Commanding the mission is another CIA agent, Mr. Wood, who is presently undercover on the cover of *GQ*.

Psychic Friend Dr. Lee is concerned about their chances for success. She realizes that Lethal Gomer is unstable, because he wears the dog tags of his Longtime Companion, a Marine who was killed in a Gulf War operation that went tragically wrong when it was accidentally conducted in Griffith Park.

Meanwhile, the team approaches the top-secret facility. Suddenly, MC Yamaha is in the house! He roars toward the squad, shoots one of them with his amazingly ineffective laser, and putters off.

Lethal Gomer demands to know what's going on. Reluctantly, Agent GQ confesses that the facility is actually a high-tech listening post. "And certain foreign powers," he intones ominously, "Would *kill* to get their hands on this equipment." (Which appears to consist of a graphic equalizer, an 8-track tape player, and a See-and-Spell.)

The Murdercycle returns and rides around while they all shoot at him, but their bullets have absolutely no effect. So they do it again. And again. Then, for a change of pace, the director cuts to some pastoral scenes of the Murdercycle cruising down country lanes while the theme to *Shaka Zulu* plays.

Then it's back to our movie, as Lethal Gomer's squad shoots their ineffective bullets at the Murdercycle, while he shoots his ineffective lasers at them. Finally, Lethal Gomer demands to know exactly what GQ is hiding, and orders Dr. Lee to read the CIA agent's mind. But he thwarts her psychic probe by singing the "Sobbin' Women" number from *Seven Brides for Seven Brothers*.

Eventually, GQ breaks down and reveals a secret underground bunker housing an extraterrestrial softball locked in a high-security microwave oven. The softball holds the sum of all human knowledge, except for the information contained in Syd Field's book, *Screenplay*.

Another, less photogenic CIA agent breaks into the microwave and surreptitiously removes the softball so he can heat up his breakfast burrito. There's some minor treachery, and a lot more shooting. Finally, the day is saved when Dr. Lee beans the Murdercyclist with the alien softball, and instead of advancing to first base, he explodes. The end.

Well, it's not exactly *The Motorcycle Diaries*, but we still think this film offers several important lessons. For instance, if you're cruising the rustic byways bestride your Kawasaki, searching for America, don't stop to investigate meteors. First of all, what business is it of yours? Who appointed *you* the Meteor Police? In the whole history of film, from *War of the Worlds* to *Die, Monster, Die!*, nothing good has ever come from this kind of thing. Loitering around freshly fallen space rocks will just get you incinerated, mentally possessed, or turned into an incredibly wimpy killing machine who can't even take a little chin music from a girl.

And while we're on the subject, we'd like to take this opportunity to address our alien readers. As you've seen, your average Yamaha rider makes a piss-poor weapons platform. Take a tip from the evil meteor in *Killdozer*, and possess something a little more substantial, like a forklift or a Ditch Witch. After all, it seems a shame to cross billions of miles of space, plunge through the atmosphere in a flaming hollow rock and then crash into the Earth at enormous velocity, only to have your carefully wrought plan for conquest and genocide fall apart because it relied a little too heavily on the combined military might of Earth surrendering to Chad and his pimped-out Vespa.

The Space-Crap Continuum

When it comes to film, we all have closeted skeletons; lousy but unforgettable movies that lodged in our subconscious and inflamed our adolescent shame and desire—your *Roller Boogies*, your *Xanadus*, your *Blue Lagoons* and *Porky's*. But while these films may have shaped our budding sexuality or nascent sense of camp, most of us eventually outgrow them, and they live on—if at all—as guilty secrets; videotapes stuffed into the back of the sock drawer, or DVDs concealed beneath an innocent stack of *Hustler* magazines.

But there is a certain kind of picture whose primal badness is so powerful that even when the genre that spawned it has become a forgotten footnote, it survives to inspire new generations of gullible lunkheads. A film whose unique meta-mediocrity has allowed it to transcend its own era, and become part of the time-less continuum of crap. Such a film is 1984's *Red Dawn*.

Hollywood cranked out a number of these two-fisted anti-Commie screeds in the 1980's—*Red Scorpion, White Nights, Invasion USA, Rambo II* and *III*—but none of them packed the same visceral wallop, because *Red Dawn* showed the ultimate nightmare: the Red Horde *right here in America!* Trampling our flag! Burning our Constitution! Brazenly eating our Otter Pops!

Even twenty years later this unflinching masturbatory aid remains a lodestone for right wing pundits. In early 2006, the Washington Post hired a home-schooled prodigy named Ben Domenech to write a conservative blog on the newspaper's website, and in his very first column he named-checked *Red Dawn*: "You must know it—the greatest pro-gun movie ever? I mean, they actually show the jackbooted communist thugs prying the guns from cold dead hands."

Powerful words. Unfortunately, Ben was fired less than a week later for plagia-rizing everything that had ever had his name attached to it, including college newspaper stories, online editorials, movie reviews, and his underpants from camp.

But let's give Ben the benefit of the doubt and assume he conceived this par-ticular encomium on his own. How could a twenty year-old relic of Cold War paranoia and priapism still exert such a hold on the imaginations of young conservatives? Could it be that this brawny, one-fisted tale of Yankee indomitability holds the key to bridging the acrimonious divide between Red and Blue America?

Probably not. But Netflix delivered it anyway, so let's plunge in:

Red Dawn (1984)
Directed by John Milius
Written by John Milius (the semen stains on the screenplay confirm this) and Kevin Reynolds. Story by Kevin Reynolds

The story of *Red Dawn* is familiar to anyone who had a C. Thomas Howell-induced wet dream during the late 1980's: Russians and Cubans invade the United States after the Soviet Union suffers its "worst wheat harvest in 55 years," which somehow allows them to conquer the world. I found this perplexing, but inspiring, since I was recently fined for putting a Rubbermaid storage tub on my balcony. Taking a leaf from the Commie playbook, I poured a bottle of Round-Up into the planter in the courtyard and killed the hydrangeas, which should permit me to conquer the Condo Board and rule the Homeowners Association with an iron hand.

Anyway, this lurid peek into John Milius' porn collection clocks in at a surprisingly epic 1 hour and 54 minutes, which admittedly sounds long until you actually watch it, at which point you'll swear that sometime prior to the closing credits the Sun collapsed into a neutron star and humanity evolved into a species of pure energy.

Our film opens in South Park, Colorado. It's a typical all-American community, except apparently they don't have cable TV, which means that 1) nobody has been able to tune in CNN and learn that the Red Army has invaded America, and 2) they won't be able to enjoy this movie when it eventually enters heavy rotation on HBO with *Ice Castles* and *The Beastmaster*.

Patrick Swayze drops his brother Charlie Sheen and Some Other Guy off at South Park High, whose football team is named...the Wolverines. (Pay attention! Later in the movie this seemingly trivial detail will become an extremely important source of irritation.) It finally dawns on the oblivious townsfolk that something is amiss when Soviet *spetsnaz* troops parachute onto the campus and blow up the cafeteria. (Apparently their battle plan read: 1) Secure major access roads. 2) Detain local authorities. 3) Destroy all stockpiles of Sloppy Joes and Sporks.)

In the midst of the invasion, Patrick roars back into the parking lot to pick up Charlie and Some Other Guy. Bullets and rocket propelled grenades are flying around the school, teachers are being cut down by machineguns, busses are exploding and burning, but none of the kids seems all that upset, since this basically gives them the equivalent of a Snow Day.

Cut to: a bumpersticker that reads, You'll Get My Gun When You Pry It From My Cold Dead Hands. Pan down to the vehicle's owner, who is lying dead in the street with a gun in his cold hand. A kindly Russian soldier pauses to make the corpse's dream come true.

Patrick collects a motley assortment of future direct-to-video stars and prostitution trial witnesses and drives them to a service station/armory run by C. Thomas Howell's dad. Suddenly, there's an explosion in a distant vacant lot, and Patrick realizes the special effects crew is closing in on them. Under Dad's expert guidance, they quickly gather up survival gear (soup, toilet paper, footballs) and weapons (shotguns, Playskool My First Archery kits, Jarts) and pile into Patrick's pickup.

They get about ten feet before the truck breaks down. The only way to fix it? Urinate into the radiator. (Although the truck bed is overloaded with supplies, no one thought to bring a bottle of water. They do have several crates of New Coke, however). It should also be noted that co-scenarist Kevin Reynolds returned to celebrate the salutary effects of man piss in *Waterworld*, where the Kevin Costner character is introduced gulping down his own pee like a Jello shot. Anyway, having voided their bladders for the cause of freedom, the daring neo-Minute Men of *Red Dawn* resume their panicky flight.

Meanwhile back in South Park, the Russkies are randomly firing RPGs into plywood false fronts. Suddenly, from out of the billowing fog of war strides Cuban revolutionary Ron O'Neil as Commandante Super Fly! A breathless subordinate tells the Commandante that U.S. Army tanks are approaching the town! Yeah, fine, but what really worries him is the local cadre of doughy, middle aged men, for Super Fly knows that their predatory instincts have been honed by many a half-drunken Saturday afternoon spent firing randomly into clumps of sagebrush in an effort to wing a pen-raised quail. The Commandante orders a couple of loitering soldiers to go stop the Third Armored Division, while he routs the *real* enemy by pawing through a filing cabinet in the sporting goods store.

How did it come to this? U.S. soil, invaded and occupied by the Red Army and the Buena Vista Social Club! Well the movie was made in 1984, which means the invasion took place during the end of Ronald Reagan's first term of office, a time when the President was admittedly having trouble focusing on details. (He later delivered a stirring mea culpa: "A few months ago I told the American people I did not let Russians and Cubans invade the United States. My heart and my best intentions still tell me that's true, but the facts and the evidence tell me it is not." Good enough for me, Dutch!

Still, you have to wonder why we didn't annihilate the invading Soviets with any of those tens of thousands of thermonuclear weapons on our ICBMs, B-1 bombers, and submarines. Well, the answer to that is two little words: Good sportsmanship. Yes, we could have obliterated the approaching land and naval forces with strategic and tactical nukes, but that would have been like playing *Grand Theft Auto: San Andreas* and using the SQUARE, L2, R1, TRIANGLE, UP, SQUARE, L2, UP, X cheat code. Sure, we'd be certain of winning the war and escaping a life of wretched servitude beneath the iron heel of Communist oppression, but would it really be as much fun?

Meanwhile, the Band of Brothers and Other Guys have reached the mountains, and are camping beside their piss-powered 4x4. Almost immediately there is dissension in the ranks, as half of our sniveling heroes suggest that the only rational course is surrender. Patrick Swayze, however, is visibly a'swell with the spirit of patriotic defiance, and will brook no whisper of capitulation. He delivers a spine-tingling oration that puts Henry V's St. Crispin's Day speech to shame, with lines like "Here, haul ass, take your shit!" and "This is your chance—git walkin'!" Patrick and Charlie Sheen spontaneously hug. Patrick shakes hands and makes up with Richard Beymer from *West Side Story*. They all snuggle in close and Patrick explains that he and Charlie have been coming up here to Brokeback Mountain for a lot of years, and they can hunt and fish and avoid the invading Soviets and their increasingly suspicious wives for a long time.

It's now October. Patrick, Charlie, and C. Thomas are all heavily accessorized with pine boughs and fern-bedecked headbands (apparently they took time out from the insurrection to appear in the second season of *Project Runway*). The greenery suggests that these nascent guerrillas will use their command of wood lore to approach their enemies unseen, although the effect is somewhere between that Japanese soldier on *Gilligan's Island*, and an 6-year old going to a Halloween party dressed as an Ent.

C. Thomas shoots a stag, and Patrick and Charlie haze C. by making him drink its blood. "You gotta do it," Patrick says, handing him a cup full of steaming gore. C. gazes queasily into his beverage as Charlie solemnly nods and murmurs, "Then you'll be a *real* hunter." Well, then you'll be an easily browbeaten moron with a mouthful of bloodborne ruminant parasites, but let's not quibble.

C. obligingly chugs it down and then grins at them through his blood mustache, and they all exchange manly, plasma-soaked handshakes. Charlie leans in close and confides to C., "My dad said, once you do that, there's gonna be something different about you." Yeah. It's called Lyme disease. Enjoy.

As the group opens its last can of Campbell's Chunky Smoked Chicken with Roasted Corn Chowder, they figure, hey, it's been a month; they really ought to head to town and find out what happened with their families and that whole invasion thing.

As they approach South Park, Patrick, Charlie and Other Guy are shocked to see that people are walking around the streets, the stores are open, and unlike, say, Iraq, the town apparently has running water and more than 3 hours of electricity a day. So here's a shout-out to our peeps in the Red Army. Props, Commie dudes.

Nevertheless, it's clear the townsfolk groan beneath the yoke of totalitarianism. Tanks rumble down Main Street. *Alexander Nevsky* is showing at the movie house. Russian soldiers stand round a bonfire, burning copies of "Catcher in the Rye" and "The Handmaid's Tale," assisted by volunteers from the Kansas State Board of Education.

Our heroes are shocked to learn that the Soviets have rounded up local men in violation of the Geneva Convention, and thrown them into a makeshift camp where they rot away without due process, or even access to an attorney. Fortunately the camp is at the drive-in, so the boys can visit their imprisoned families and still catch that double feature of *Krush Groove* and *Police Academy 2: Their First Assignment*.

But when they surreptitiously approach the camp, the boys are aghast at the conditions. Prisoners are beaten mercilessly during interrogations, and continually exposed to the elements, living outdoors in a chain link enclosure while a voice drones over the loudspeaker "America is a whorehouse" and propaganda images flash on the screen, interrupted periodically by that "Let's All Go to the Snack Bar" commercial.

Patrick and Charlie find their father, Harry Dean Stanton, who looks like he's gotten a bit piggy with the elk blood. Harry Dean stoically observes that his sons are alive and rather smugly says, "See? I was tough on you—did things that made you hate me at times." But apparently his unique brand of discipline—the verbal abuse, the floggings with extension cords, the forced chugging of doe blood—it built character. So I guess the joke's on them.

Dad sternly orders Patrick and Charlie to never to cry again for the rest of their lives, before he's dragged away, shrieking, "Avenge me! AVENGE ME!" The boys saunter off, their body language seeming to say, "Yeah. Sure. We'll get right on that, Pop."

After the motivational death of their dad, Patrick, Charlie and C. head on over to Old Man Exposition's farm, where they learn that South Park is in Occupied Territory, while the far side of Brokeback Mountain is "F.A." (Free America. Doesn't that sound like a nice place? I'd like to go there right now. Who's with me? Anyone want to kick in for gas and tolls, we could carpool…)

Old Man Exposition tries to cheer up C. by revealing that the Russians shot his Dad on account of all the guns and Fresca they took from his Gas Station/ Soup Plantation/National Guard Armory. C. tries to feign a convincing breakdown by screaming into his hands, but it doesn't really work, so he turns to the farmer's wife and buries his face in her wizened décolletage (which is as close as we get to sex in this movie).

As a consolation prize, Old Man Exposition gives the boys his granddaughters (Lea Thompson and Jennifer Grey) as a free gift. He also gives them horses; Jennifer gets her own stallion, but Lea has to ride behind C., and she mounts up with a look that seems to say, "As soon as they yell 'cut!' I'm calling my agent and accepting that *Howard the Duck* offer!"

Our heroes finally start the revolution by murdering three Russian tourists (apparently for the war crime of comically mistranslating a Forestry Service dedication plaque). But they do a crappy job of it, and one of Soviets manages to radio for help—from God! *Where's your Lenin NOW, Mr. Commie?* Anyway, Patrick corners the helpless, wounded man, and summoning the courage of his frontier forefathers and our current vice president, shoots him in the face. (And then presumably drinks his blood. Rules are rules.)

Jennifer and Lea also prove their mettle by shooting another grievously injured man in the back with a submachinegun. Apparently, this baptism of fire turns them into radical lesbian feminists, because later they shrilly refuse Charlie Sheen's suggestion that they do the dishes. Charlie can't understand what he did wrong, but for the sake of their survival as an effective fighting unit, he grudgingly tries to make up by offering to pay them for sex.

The Russians execute two dozen townspeople, either in reprisal, or because all the townsfolk are singing a rendition of "America the Beautiful" that's really off-key and grating. (Here's a tip for future victims of Russo-Cuban atrocities: When you get to the "above the fruited plain" part, never go up half an octave on "fruited" if you just don't have the range for it.) Commandante Super Fly grimly orders all the civilians gunned down before they undermine the solemnity of the moment by belting out that "O beautiful for Pilgrim feet" line.

Charlie observes the massacre while dressed like a sheave (with the coming of fall, our heroes have naturally switched from ferns to wheat and wild grasses to preserve that Fashion Forward look). When he later returns to Brokeback and reports the mass murder, Charlie breaks down and weeps bitterly until Patrick grabs him and screams, "Don't cry! Don't you ever cry again as long as you live! Don't do it!" He tells Charlie, who just saw their father murdered, to let his grief "turn into something else." Perhaps a butterfly, or a Pop-Tart—he doesn't specify.

Back to the uprising. Jennifer Grey destroys a Soviet tank by giving the crew a booby-trapped picnic basket (as seen in *Yogi Bear: The Final Conflict*). Then, "the greatest pro-gun movie ever" proves that your deer rifle really ain't gonna cut it come the Conquering Commie Horde, because suddenly our heroes have rockets and grenade launchers, Kalashnikovs and .50 machine guns. They proceed to slaughter the highly trained Soviet paratroopers, pausing only occasionally to bellow, "Wolverines!" (Originally the insurgents called themselves "The Magilla Guerrillas," but the brand performed poorly in focus-testing.)

Just when you thought things couldn't get any more tedious, the Russkies shoot down Top Gun Colonel Powers Boothe (callsign "Backstory"), who informs the kids that America was conquered by illegal aliens. Apparently, itinerant farm workers opened the door and "the whole Cuban and Nicaraguan armies just waltzed right in" and took over the whole country. I don't know about you, but my support for that UFA grape boycott is *over*!

The seasons pass. In real time. The snows come, and Patrick takes to wearing a white burnoose like Lawrence of Arabia. Some tanks suddenly appear and things get confusing: Ralph Macchio dies, and he wasn't even in this movie. Someone lights a Smokey Joe. Powers Boothe gets blown up real good, putting the kibosh on Lea's blossoming sexuality.

A Russian colonel with a John Stossel porn 'stache arrives and gives a long speech about fur-bearing quadrupeds, but it doesn't boost the Russkies' morale like he'd hoped.

Then some people walk around the forest while some other people shoot at them, but since they're all wearing snowsuits and hoods it's kind of hard to tell who. Richard Beymer goes to town, and in an astonishing twist, he's betrayed *by his own father*, captured by the Russians and tortured until he swallows a tracking device that will lead the invaders right to the Wolverines! Finally! Something exciting happens—too bad it all happens off screen and we just get to hear about it later. Oh well.

Patrick decides to shoot Richard in the face, but Charlies cries "What's the difference between us and them?" Patrick retorts, "We *LIVE here!*" and fires. So apparently I *can* summarily execute my condo board, since a lot of them actually rent out their units.

Everyone leaves, but Patrick sits on a horse and looks at the body for a long time, so apparently he's feeling some sort of emotion. Fortunately for us, he has the good taste to keep it to himself.

Day Four of our ascent up *Red Dawn*. We have established base camp at the timberline, and despite gusty winds and the loss of two sherpas from hypothermia and boredom, we are preparing to make our final assault upon the north face of the third act...

Anyway, Patrick sits alone and sobs, the little hypocrite, while mooning over a picture of two 8-year old boys in Little League uniforms. This is never explained, for which I, for one, am grateful.

The snows melt. The Wolverines prepare to attack a convoy, but the Russians decide to insult their intelligence by pushing crates of food off the trucks to lure them into a trap, and they decide to fall for it. Our heroes collect and devour the provisions—nothing more exciting in an action film than the sight of people eating cornflakes—and the director takes this belated opportunity to give the characters a shred of personality by having Jennifer Grey squeeze orange juice onto Patrick's head.

Suddenly, a Soviet attack helicopter appears and shoots Jennifer in the gut, which is tragic, because only moments ago she was so *alive*, dribbling citrus juice on a mediocre actor's do-rag. Patrick shouts, "Nobody shoots Baby in the gut!" and throws her onto his horse and rides away. But she almost instantly falls off.

Then more assault choppers fly in and for the next five minutes it's an aimless barrage of running, screaming, and squibs a'plenty.

C. thrusts his rifle in the air and bellows, "Wolverines!" which the Russians take as a request to shoot him with a variety of projectiles until he is primarily a stain. Meanwhile Jennifer, despite taking a small rocket through the sternum and falling off a galloping horse is still alive, which seems kind of cruel (what the hell do you have to do to get *out* of this movie?) and she quite reasonably asks Patrick to shoot her. Alas, he's too much of a whimpering little pussy to pull the trigger.

"Give me a grenade," she whispers. "I don't want to be too cold." Yeah. That'll warm you right up. She explodes, taking one of the Russkies with her, then the colonel with the Stossel 'stache shows up to have an ironic (okay, boring) discussion about body counts.

Meanwhile, Patrick and Charlie rob corpses and profess their love for each other. In an achingly poignant exchange, Patrick observes, "It's hard being brothers." Charlie thinks about this for a really, really long time, then says, "Yeah."

Back at Red Army HQ, tender, haunting music plays as we hear in voice over a letter Commandante Super Fly is writing to his wife, complaining about the weather. (According to Video Watchdog, the producers brought in award-winning documentarian Ken Burns to direct this scene.)

Then a bunch of crap blows up. A guard-tower falls over ala the opening credits of "F-Troop." Finally, Colonel Porn Stache and Patrick face off in a Wild West style shootout. "You lose," Patrick sneers, just before he gets shot a bunch of times.

Even though his lungs now contain a lavish assortment of bullets, Patrick carries the wounded Charlie to a playground, while Commandante Super Fly watches them stagger off, and whispers, "Vaya con Dios." They die together, embracing by a swingset.

Meanwhile, Lea and Some Other Guy re-enact the end of *The Sound of Music* and walk over the mountains to Free America. Then she turns into John-Boy Walton and sums up the Third World War with a pithy and listless voice over. Apparently, even though everybody's dead, we won.

WOLVERINES!!

So now that our blade-like manhoods have been tempered in the crucible of War, it's time to bury our dead and review the hard and bitter lessons we have learned.

Having slogged our way through the film, we can now finally tell who the Real Americans are. They're the cold, dead ones with the guns. And they're plentiful: look for Real Americans decomposing in the downtown shopping district, or posthumously re-enacting the Pieta on an elementary school playground.

We've also learned that according to the Colorado State Penal Code, you are legally required to drink the blood of anything you kill, under penalty of being a pussy. According to FBI statistics, this is a law honored more in the breech, since it's hard to siphon enough blood out of that spider you smooshed with a paper towel, especially if you used one with "thirst-pockets" or some other high-absorbent technology. But hunters follow the law scrupulously, which explains why Vice President Dick Cheney waited 24 hours before reporting that he'd shot an elderly lawyer in the face.

Some suspicious minds claimed Mr. Cheney must have been drunk, but it's hard to imagine that a man of such gravitas, who is 40 pounds overweight and suffers from chronic gout, could ever be guilty of overindulgence. Alcoholism, however, is a prerequisite for admission to the Bar (I'm pretty sure I read that somewhere) and older members of the profession would perforce be the most extensively pickled. Clearly what happened was that Cheney shot the septuage-narian attorney, mistaking him for a Bobwhite quail, and then dutifully drank his blood, not realizing that the dead bird was actually a live man. Naturally, imbibing the plasma of a soused senior citizen raised the Vice President's own blood alcohol level above the legal limit, and he was forced to lie down for awhile until this wholly unfamiliar sense of drunkeness passed. (Similar hunting mishaps are undoubtedly the cause of Cheney's two DUI convictions as well).

The Cheney affair can also be read as a cautionary tale for vampires, who should be careful about operating a motor vehicle after biting Tara Reid or Lindsay Lohan.

Thirdly, and perhaps most importantly, we've learned that while infantry divisions, main battle tanks, and air superiority are all well and good, our enemies are most vulnerable to attack by high school football teams. Therefore, we urge the president to immediately draft the cast of *Friday Night Lights* and ship them to Iraq.

978-0-595-40023-2
0-595-40023-X